MW01114911

Double Accounting for Goodwill

Goodwill, sometimes purchased but often more significantly internally gener-ated, is the major constituent of the value of many listed companies. Accounting aims to provide users of financial statements with useful infor-mation, and more than fifty current International Financial Reporting Standards prescribe accounting disclosure requirements in minute detail. However, these Standards dismiss internally generated goodwill with a single brief provision that it is not to be brought to account at all. The impairment regime now laid down for dealing with purchased goodwill contains severe flaws, while previous methods have also been found to be unsatisfactory.

This book traces the history of the goodwill accounting controversy in detail and demonstrates that it has been a prime example of an issue 'con-ceived in a way that it is in principle unsolvable'. It explores the problem of recognizing the importance of goodwill as a whole and finding a way of pre-senting meaningful information regarding it in the context of the financial statements. The author's proposed solution builds upon research under-taken and uses a Market Capitalization Statement, based on a modification of nineteenth century 'double accounting' in a modern context. Examples show that the proposed Market Capitalization Statement has the potential to provide significant information not currently available from conventional financial statements, which in turn are freed to present clearer information.

This book is essential reading for all those who seek an understanding of the issues involved. It is useful to students of, and researchers in, theoretical accounting, including commerce, professional accounting and business courses.

Martin Bloom is a Chartered Accountant who has been in public practice for over forty years and is currently a Director in the Sydney office of Deloitte, a global network of accounting, consulting and business advisory firms.

Routledge New Works in Accounting History

Edited by Garry Carnegie (Melbourne University Private, Australia), John Richard Edwards (Cardiff University, UK), Salvador Carmona (Instituto de Empresa, Spain) and Dick Fleischman (John Carroll University, USA).

Double Accounting for Goodwill
A problem redefined

Martin Bloom

Routledge
Taylor & Francis Group

LONDON AND NEW YORK

First published 2008
by Routledge
2 Park Square, Milton Park, Abingdon, Oxon OX14 4RN

Simultaneously published in the USA and Canada
by Routledge
270 Madison Ave, New York, NY 10016

Routledge is an imprint of the Taylor & Francis Group, an informa business

© 2008 Martin Bloom

Typeset in Times New Roman by
Taylor & Francis Books
Printed and bound in Great Britain by
TJ International Ltd, Padstow, Cornwall

British Library Cataloguing in Publication Data
A catalogue record for this book is available from the British Library

Library of Congress Cataloging in Publication Data
A catalog record for this book has been requested

ISBN13: 978-0-415-43748-6 (hbk)
ISBN13: 978-0-203-01459-2 (ebk)

Contents

Tables

Preface and acknowledgments

This book is based on my doctoral thesis completed at The University of Sydney. I was driven to the research following some forty years as a professional accountant and auditor. During this time, I became convinced that the conventional accounting treatment of goodwill was unsound in theory and of little use in practice.

This was more than confirmed by my research, which showed that goodwill is a major component of the value of many listed companies. By far the greatest proportion of goodwill is, in turn, made up of internally generated goodwill, which Accounting Standards expressly prevent being brought to account. At the same time, those Standards seek to ensure that readers of annual financial statements are provided with meaningful information.

I have attempted to trace the history and reasons for this paradox, and ultimately to suggest a possible solution based on an adaptation of the 'Double Account' – a concept having its genesis in the nineteenth century. I do not pretend that the solution advocated is the final word; indeed, the need for further research is emphasized. However, the issue of properly accounting for goodwill (and identifiable intangible assets) is so important that its successful resolution will be critical in the development of twenty-first century accounting.

My thesis supervisor, Professor Graeme Dean, has supplied invaluable advice and direction on every aspect of this publication, as well as constant moral support. Professor Frank Clarke also made many useful suggestions.

Without my secretary, Margarida Reis, it would not have been possible to complete this book. Her attention to detail and patience in coping with its endless revisions entitle her to be regarded as a full partner in its production.

The University of Sydney provided me with exceptional working facilities and access to the R. J. Chambers Collection, a unique store of research material. I was also fortunate to have access to The Institute of Chartered Accountants in Australia's Library in Sydney and its cheerful and helpful staff.

My partners have been endlessly supportive in arranging for me to have the time to work on both my PhD and this book and providing me with access to office facilities. I would also like to express my appreciation to my ex-senior partner, Julius Feinstein, for providing me with a role model in every aspect of accounting as a profession.

Abbreviations

AARF	Australian Accounting Research Foundation
AASB	Australian Accounting Standards Board
AIA	American Institute of Accountants
AICPA	American Institute of Certified Public Accountants
AIFRS	Australian version of International Financial Reporting Standards (virtually identical to IFRS)
APB	Accounting Principles Board
ARB	Accounting Research Bulletin
ARS	Accounting Research Study
ASC	Australian Securities Commission
ASIC	Australian Securities and Investments Commission
ASX	Australian Stock Exchange (name changed to Australian Securities Exchange in December 2006)
ATT	Accounting Trends and Techniques
CICA	Canadian Institute of Chartered Accountants
CoCoA	Continuously Contemporary Accounting
FASB	Financial Accounting Standards Board (US)
FIAC	Financial Institutions Accounting Committee (US)
FRS	Financial Reporting Standard
IAS	International Accounting Standard
IASB	International Accounting Standards Board
IASC	International Accounting Standards Committee
ICAEW	Institute of Chartered Accountants in England and Wales
IFRS	International Financial Reporting Standards
IIA	Identifiable Intangible Asset
MCS	Market Capitalization Statement
NCSC	National Companies and Securities Commission (Australia)
NRV	Net Realizable Value
SAC	Statement of Accounting Concepts (Australian)
UK	United Kingdom
US	United States

1   An overview

We accountants do not resolve issues, we abandon them, . . . We debate them loud
and long . . . until another issue comes along that is more current and more controversial, and then we forget the former issue. . . . The explanation for our inability
to resolve issues is to be found in the way we conceive issues. We conceive of the
issues in such a way that they are in principle unresolvable. . . . We phrase the
questions in a way that prohibits answers. We define our problems so that the very
definition precludes the possibility of a solution.

(R. R. Sterling, 1975)

1.1 Introduction

The most comprehensive review of the long and complex history of accounting for goodwill examined in the research process was compiled by Hughes
(1982). It is salutary to read the foreword to his book, which commences:

When I first began this project in 1969, I believed that I would come up
with the intrinsic nature of goodwill – maybe even define the asset for
all time. Perhaps all of those writers were arguing and struggling toward
some unforeseen Truth, and it was for me to chart the direction, extract
the essence of their works, and obtain the ultimate answer that maybe
all were moving unconsciously toward. My own personal exuberant and
intellectual Charge of the Light Brigade was rewarded with frustration,
disappointment, and – finally – relief. I at last came to accept fully that
all of those unfortunate souls who struggled with goodwill's nature and
treatment did so, not in some possibly great movement toward Truth,
but because there was no one Truth and never will be. The origin of
goodwill can be revealed through history, but its nature is a matter of
personal interpretation.

Keeping the scope of the 'struggle toward some unforeseen Truth' within
reasonable bounds, the proposal in this book will be limited to the more
prosaic problem of accounting for goodwill in the context of publicly listed

entities, in particular those corporate entities included in the All-Ordinaries Index on the Australian Stock Exchange (ASX). It follows that it will exclude those companies involved predominantly in the mining and extractive industries, as the concept of 'goodwill', as normally understood and as defined herein, is not relevant to that category. There are no particularly 'Australian' issues that would limit the applicability of the proposals and the discussion to this country, and the implications of the matters dealt with extend, to a large extent, beyond Australia. Nevertheless, it will be necessary to review the particular framework of Accounting Standards and legislation applicable in Australia. The general history and philosophical background to the controversy which has for so many years surrounded both goodwill as a subject and how to account for it properly are also explored.

1.2 The objectives of financial reporting in relation to intangible assets

A shareholder in a listed company is typically remote from direct contact with the management of that company, and is reliant on information provided in the company's Annual Report and the information furnished to the ASX, including six-monthly interim financial reports. It is intrinsic to such reports that they are prepared with the requirement of Statement of Accounting Concepts (SAC) 2 'Objective of General Purpose Financial Reporting' in mind, that 'The objective of general purpose financial reporting is to provide information to users that is useful for making and evaluating decisions about the allocation of scarce resources' (para. 26).

Allowing for the organizational complexity that has developed since the point was made, this requirement was put equally well in 1788 by Hamilton:

> Bookkeeping is the art of recording mercantile transactions in a regular and systematic manner. A merchant's books should contain every particular which relates to the affairs of the owner. They should exhibit the state of all the branches of his business; the connection of the different parts; the amount and success of the whole. They should be so full and so well arranged as to afford a ready information in every point for which they may be consulted.
>
> As cited in Chambers (1995: 338)

Two hundred years later, the International Accounting Standards Committee (IASC) put the same point succinctly: 'To be reliable, the information in financial statements must be complete within the limits of materiality and cost' (IASC 1989: 38). 'Cost', in this context, refers to the expense incurred in producing the financial statements, not the limitations imposed by the historical cost principle of accounting.

Investors in a listed company constantly evaluate how best to use scarce resources with regard to that particular investment: whether to hold, sell or increase their shareholding. The general body of investors face a similar problem. They attempt to maximize the economic benefits of portfolios, limited by their resources, by allocating those resources among alternative listed investments. The market price of a share at any one point in time is given for virtually all investors. Their judgment as to the allocation of scarce resources depends upon whether they consider that the present value of continuing to hold a particular share, receiving dividends for a further period (if applicable) and realizing their investment at a later date exceeds the amount obtainable by realizing that share immediately. Each investor will bring differing utility functions, experiences and current constraints to bear on those judgments.

Intangible assets have become increasingly important in the modern economy, and Lev has developed forceful arguments that this development requires to be more fully recognized in financial statements.

> We are using a 500 year old system to make decisions in a complex business environment in which the essential assets that create value have fundamentally changed.
>
> What's the evidence for this transformation?
>
> Look at the Standard & Poor's 500 – 500 of the largest companies in the United States, many of which are not in high tech industries. The market-to-book ratio of these companies – that is, the ratio between the market value of these companies and the net-asset value of the company (the number that appears on the balance sheet) is now greater than six. What this means is that the balance sheet number – which is what traditional accounting measures – represents only 10% to 15% of the value of these companies. Even if the stock market is inflated, even if you chop 50% off the market capitalization, you're still talking about a huge difference in value as perceived by those who pay for it day-to-day and value as the company accounts for it.
>
> As cited in Webber (2000)

Although stock market indices have both risen and fallen considerably since the publication of this article, Lev's fundamental argument that traditional accounting measures ignore a large percentage of corporate value remains true. Contrast this with a comment by Walker, who wrote an incisive article on goodwill in 1953: 'Probably because of the fact that goodwill is of relatively minor importance, the accounting treatment of goodwill has barely been touched by attempts to broaden the consistent application of accounting principles' (Walker 1964: 241).

Tobin's Q is the ratio between the market value of a company and the replacement costs of the productive, physical assets of that company. This formulation was confirmed by Tobin in an interview in December 1996. He pointed out that 'people think of it as book value of a company' rather than replacement cost. A 'Tobin's Q' analysis of the ASX showed that, whereas intangible assets represented only 10 per cent of the total value of the shares listed in the All-Ordinaries Index of the ASX in June 1984, that proportion had risen to approximately 58 per cent in June 1999 (Lonergan, Stokes and Wells 2000). The 'tech wreck' occurring since that date may have reduced this figure, but intangible assets still represent a material proportion of market capitalization. A comparative United States graph clearly shows the increase in the Tobin's Q index over the past fifty years and lends support to the comments by Walker and Lev quoted previously (see Table 1.1).

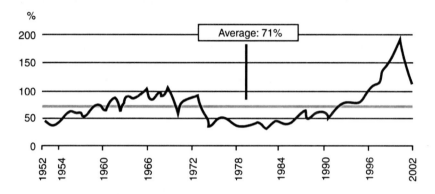

* Market value of equities as a % of tangible asset replacement cost

Table 1.1 Tobins Q ratio for US equities 1952–2002.

Goodwill, by definition, does not represent the total amount of the intangible assets incorporated in the market value of a company, merely the amount of the unidentifiable portion thereof. Notwithstanding this, accounting that does not properly take account of goodwill is becoming increasingly irrelevant to many users.

1.3 The problem and its redefinition

An extensive review of the literature on accounting for goodwill over the last 100 years confirmed that it is impossible to account for goodwill logically and completely within the context of the historical cost system. This is clearly demonstrated by the asymmetry of mandated methods of accounting for internally generated goodwill, on the one hand, and for purchased goodwill, on the other. This asymmetry occurs despite the universal acknowledgment, confirmed by an Australian Accounting Standard issued in 1996, that there is *no* qualitative difference between the two forms of goodwill: 'This Standard specifies that the concept of goodwill as an asset is the same regardless of whether it has been purchased in an exchange transaction or generated internally' (AASB 1013: 5.1.3).

SAC 3 'Qualitative Characteristics of Financial Information' notes:

This Statement identifies relevance and reliability as the primary qualitative characteristics which financial information should possess in order to be the subject of general purpose financial reporting. These characteristics may need to be balanced against each other; however, this Statement does not rank either characteristic above the other.

SAC 3 (para. 7)

There is currently agreement (as there has been for many years) between standard setters in all countries that internally generated goodwill should not be brought to account because it cannot be measured reliably, despite its relevance to readers of financial statements. A complementary reason for the non-recognition of internally generated goodwill is that it does not usually have an identifiable, reliably measurable cost, which is particularly important within a historical cost system.

On the other hand, purchased goodwill does have an identifiable, reliably measurable cost; the debate has centred around the treatment of that cost. Over the years, many methods have been advocated such as recognition at nominal value, immediate write-off against reserves, amortization against income over various arbitrary periods and continuous revaluation to measure and record impairment. The arguments have been heated over the years, but have become largely sterile. As the Sterling chapter header noted:

We accountants do not resolve issues, we abandon them, ... We debate them loud and long. ... until another issue comes along that is more current and more controversial, and then we forget the former issue. ... The explanation for our inability to resolve issues is to be found in the way we conceive issues. We conceive of the issues in such a way that they are in principle unresolvable. ... We phrase the questions in a way that prohibits answers. We define our problems so that the very definition precludes the possibility of a solution.

Sterling (1975) as cited in Chambers (1995: 907)

Traditionally, the debate has been concerned with how best to present goodwill within the context of the conventional accounting framework, which has been taken as a given. However, the problem can be redefined as follows:

Recognizing that information regarding the goodwill attributable to a listed entity is useful to a person making and evaluating decisions relating to that entity, how can the current level of information relating to goodwill in the financial statements contained in the Annual Report of that entity be improved?

The aim of this book is to identify a logically defensible method of accounting for goodwill that addresses the redefined problem. Initial experience indicated that it would not be costly to implement. Whether it is cost effective is a matter for further research.

1.4 Research method and development of conclusions

In general terms, the research approach adopted herein is in the genre of that described by Chambers (1966: 6–8) as the 'method of construction'. In brief, it entailed establishing how accounting for goodwill would best be incorporated within the general objectives of financial reporting. Initial archival research established that the accounting treatments employed previously and those currently proposed within the historical cost framework failed to meet those objectives. Deductive reasoning has been employed to propose an accounting treatment, adapted from a resilient nineteenth century concept (the double account), that would avoid, or at least mitigate, the defects observed in the current system. This was supported by research in which a number of practical examples were examined in order to determine whether implementation of the suggested accounting treatment was practical and whether it had the potential to improve on the treatments examined in the course of the historical analysis in meeting financial reporting objectives.

Specifically, an extensive literature review revealed general agreement that goodwill could be conveniently divided into two classes: that which had been internally generated and that which had been purchased. There was also general agreement that the former category should not be brought to account because it was impossible to do so within the accepted rules of double entry bookkeeping and historical cost based accounting – in other words, the inherent limitations of the system prevented the recognition of one of the two elements of goodwill. On the other hand, there was no difficulty in bringing purchased goodwill to account, but controversy raged as to how to treat the amount, once recognized. Various methods were tried and abandoned, only to resurface later when the defects of the current paradigm became apparent. There was generally recognition that, in practice, the two classes of goodwill were indistinguishable in terms of their ability to generate streams of revenue, but accounting theorists nonetheless strove to maintain a distinction to serve the limitations of the accounting system.

During the course of the research, the 'double account', which was originally employed by nineteenth century railway and other utility companies, was reviewed. This effectively divided the Balance Sheet into two sections, the former dealing with funds raised and expended on fixed assets, while the latter dealt with current assets and liabilities. The two sections were linked by the unspent amount on capital account, carried down as a balancing item into the 'floating account' section.

A modification of the double account concept, termed the Market Capitalization Statement (MCS), will furnish useful and integrated information that caters for both purchased and internally generated goodwill. The link between the conventional Balance Sheet and the MCS (or modified double account) is provided by purchased goodwill, which is thereby removed from the conventional Balance Sheet. An illustrative MCS is set out in Section 1.5 below, where its operation is more fully explained. Although there have been previous suggestions that market capitalization data should be furnished in Annual Reports, the historical research carried out did not reveal any instances in which such data were both linked to the Balance Sheet and used in a broad sense to account for goodwill.

In order to illustrate the feasibility and simplicity of preparing the MCS in practice, two groups of case illustrations were developed using actual data relating to companies listed on the ASX. The first consisted of fourteen 'dot.com' companies, a class of companies whose share price was extremely volatile over the illustrative period of three years from 30 June 1999 to 30 June 2002. The second, covering the same time period, comprised six companies drawn from a list of the top thirty companies by market capitalization, as they were likely to have been less affected by exaggerated market speculation than those companies in the former group.

The examples were limited in number to twenty, and were not selected in a controlled manner that would permit generalized conclusions to be drawn. However, they illustrated that it was feasible, simple and not costly to produce the MCS for all of the companies chosen, and that the MCS yielded useful information that would not otherwise have been available to readers of the Annual Report to analyse directly. Furthermore, while the focus of the MCS itself is on goodwill, there were a number of instances in which information available from the conventional Balance Sheet and Profit and Loss Account was clarified by the device of removing purchased goodwill to the MCS. The examples successfully demonstrated the potential of the MCS to improve on traditional methods of accounting for goodwill.

1.5 An illustrative MCS

The MCS takes, as its starting point, the concept that the value of a company, at its financial year-end, is easily and objectively ascertained by reference to its market capitalization. This is by no means a new idea. For example, in the Anglo-American literature as long ago as 1939, MacNeal wrote:

> The total value of a business as a whole is best expressed by the price of its equities in the market place. The difference between this value and the value of the net assets without goodwill constitutes the present market value of theoretical goodwill.
>
> MacNeal (1939: 232)

The MCS is to be created as an additional financial statement. Conceptually, it does not form part of the conventional Balance Sheet, or Statement of Financial

Position (these terms are synonymous and are used interchangeably), but is rather an additional document included in the Annual Report, similar to the Statement of Cash Flows, which was introduced relatively recently.

Virtually every listed entity examined during this study, as well as during the writer's forty years' experience, has operated as a 'group' of companies, with a holding company and one or more subsidiary companies. The Annual Report has therefore included both the accounts of the holding company and consolidated accounts, in accordance with Corporate Law requirements throughout that period. In practice, the MCS would almost always relate to the consolidated, or group, financial statements, rather than to those of the holding company itself. The current requirement to prepare consolidated accounts as a single, integrated document covering all entities in the group will simplify this presentation. Previously, group accounts could take several forms, involving varying combinations of the entities to be consolidated or even presentation of all the individual accounts of the relevant entities in accordance with the Companies (NSW) Code definition of 'group accounts' in Section 266(I). This was effectively superseded by the Corporations Law 1989; Section 295(A) of that Law required a single Consolidated Profit and Loss Account and Consolidated Balance Sheet to be prepared.

For simplicity, the following illustrative example will refer to 'the company' rather than 'the group'. In the first instance, assume that financial statements are prepared on a historical cost basis in accordance with currently generally accepted accounting principles. Assume also that:

i.   the company decides to recognize goodwill for the first time (comparative figures are ascertainable for the previous year);
ii. during the year, the company has purchased an enterprise, resulting in purchased goodwill, determined in accordance with traditional methods, of $1 million;
iii. the book value of net identifiable assets at the year-end is $9 million;
iv. the market capitalization of the company is $12.5 million at the year-end;
v.   all other figures used are illustrative.

This would be reflected in the Annual Report as shown in Table 1.2.

1.6 Constituents of MCS goodwill

Goodwill is noted and calculated, in the MCS, as the difference between the market capitalization of the company and the 'comparison value', being the net carrying value of the other constituents of the Statement of Financial Position. For the purposes of this overview, it is recognized that MCS goodwill is a residual that is affected by a number of significant factors (summarized in Chapter 2.2 and generally examined in greater detail in Chapter 2) in addition to pure goodwill, including:

Table 1.2 Initial illustration – simplified MCS

EXTRACT FROM STATEMENT OF FINANCIAL POSITION
(all figures are $'000, except as noted)

	Current year	Previous year
Shareholders' equity	10,000	7,000
Less: Cost of purchased goodwill*	(1,000)	–
Book value of net identifiable assets	9,000	7,000

*This amount would be specifically disclosed, as above

NEW 'Market Capitalization Statement'	Current Year	Previous Year
Number of issued shares ('000)	50,000	50,000
Market price per share ($)	0.25	0.15
Market capitalization	12,500	7,500
Comprising:		
Purchased goodwill, at cost**	1,000	–
Internally generated goodwill	2,500	500
MCS goodwill	**3,500**	**500**
Net identifiable assets**	9,000	7,000
Market capitalization	12,500	7,500
Ratio of MCS goodwill to market capitalization (%)	28%	7%

**Per Statement of Financial Position

For the purpose of this statement, 'MCS goodwill' is defined and calculated as the difference between market capitalization and the book value of the company's net identifiable assets (including identifiable intangible assets).

i. the market's net evaluation of the 'real' value of assets owned by the company, compared with their carrying value; and
ii. the valuation of assets, such as identifiable intangible assets (IIAs), not normally classified as goodwill precisely because they are identifiable, but which are excluded by accounting convention from the Statement of Financial Position (see Chapter 1.9 below).

The MCS, as formulated, makes no specific allowance for the contention that purchased goodwill, of itself, reduces in value over time. Furthermore, internally generated goodwill may relate, wholly or partially, to portions of the company's operations in respect of which goodwill was also purchased or to those in respect of which goodwill is entirely internally generated.

Finally, market capitalization, as computed, is not a 'fair value' of the company; specifically, it excludes any control premium that would normally be included in such a valuation.

These matters are all more fully explored in Chapter 2 and other chapters in this book. They are noted here to emphasize that they should not be ignored in evaluating the usefulness and other advantages of the MCS.

1.7 The advantages of the simplified MCS

With the important qualifications noted above, the MCS, as illustrated:

i. maintains the Statement of Financial Position in its traditional form, apart from the elimination of goodwill, for those analysts who consider it useful;

ii. provides, for the first time, information in the Annual Report as to the stock market capitalization of the company at the year-end which can be directly compared with Balance Sheet carrying values at that date;

iii. focuses attention on goodwill, even in cases where no goodwill has been purchased;

iv. continues to reflect the purchase of goodwill. If MCS goodwill is higher than purchased goodwill, there is a reasonable *prima facie* case that the value of purchased goodwill has been maintained, using an objective measure, viz. market capitalization. If MCS goodwill is less than purchased goodwill, there is a very strong indication that purchased goodwill has been impaired;

v. reflects both purchased and internally generated goodwill within the MCS, and thus recognizes that, in practice, they are usually both difficult to separate and complementary;

vi. enables the Statement of Financial Position to reflect, unambiguously, the book value of net identifiable assets (that 'book value' itself would initially be determined, for both tangible and IIAs, in accordance with the accounting principles generally accepted at the time of preparing the financial statements in question);

vii. removes the necessity to amortize goodwill over a period that, in practice, is usually arbitrary, thus relieving the Statement of Financial Performance from arbitrary and incorrigible amortization charges, and from abnormal one-time charges resulting from large goodwill write-offs (the term 'incorrigible' is discussed in Chapter 5.2);

viii. removes the necessity to calculate impairment of goodwill, using arbitrary assumptions and subjective forecasts;

ix. treats corporate goodwill as a single item, without the needless complexity imposed by allocating it across segments or units of the enterprise; and

ix. indicates the relative importance of goodwill as a constituent of market capitalization.

Furthermore, the MCS is easy to understand, even by a relatively unso-phisticated reader. It would entail minimal cost to implement, in terms of time, effort or development of new accounting techniques. It uses readily available data to provide additional information that clearly assists readers of an Annual Report to improve their understanding of the state of a com-pany's affairs.

1.8 Integration of the MCS with net realizable value accounting

Canning (1929: 42) observed that, if goodwill were merely a master valuation account, it could not be regarded as an asset. Transfer of goodwill from the conventional Statement of Financial Position to the MCS does much to answer this criticism. Nevertheless, it would be considerably more satisfying were goodwill to be transformed from a 'master valuation' account to a mean-ingful residual. In order to achieve this, logical consistency calls for all assets and liabilities in the Statement of Financial Position (including, of course, IIAs) to be recognized at their net realizable value following the recommendation of Chambers (1996/1974), in particular, and others such as Sterling (1970, 1979). Using exit values for those items, the MCS would still be prepared in the format illustrated above. This would have the following further advantages:

i.   both the Statement of Financial Position and the MCS would be pre-pared on logically consistent and meaningful bases;
ii.   the value of assets that do not have a realizable or exit value but do generate future income, either by themselves or in combination with other assets of the enterprise, would effectively be recognized via the MCS;
iii. the largely sterile debate as to whether goodwill is an asset would be avoided via the recognition of goodwill in a separate statement that does not require goodwill to be classified in that way;
iv.   additional and useful information would be made available via the Annual Report (as in the illustrative example in Section 1.5 above, but to a far greater degree).

1.9 A variation of the MCS to take account of IIAs

Recently, International Financial Reporting Standard (IFRS) 3: 'Business Combinations' has been adopted dealing, in particular, with the allocation of the purchase price of an acquired business or subsidiary company. This Standard and its Australian equivalent, AASB 3, have led to valuations of the IIAs of the acquired business being undertaken on a regular basis. Expertise in this area is growing, and methods and procedures of IIA valuation are becoming more standardized. Given this, there is no reason why the same valuation techniques should not be expanded to include internally generated IIAs.

In its simplified form, as presented above, the MCS does not allow for any allocation of goodwill to IIAs. It could easily be modified to take this aspect into account. Detailed discussion of the implications of this expanded treatment is contained in Chapter 6.7. Table 1.3 shows the MCS expanded to take account of IIAs.

1.10 The advantages of the modified MCS

Compared with the simplified version, the modified MCS

i.   still maintains the Statement of Financial Position in its traditional form, but eliminates all intangible assets, rather than just goodwill;
ii.   provides the same information regarding market capitalization;
iii.   focuses attention on all intangible assets, instead of merely goodwill. In particular, readers would gain knowledge (previously almost totally absent) on which specific intangible assets were deemed to contribute towards the value of the enterprise and the extent of any unallocable residual (i.e. 'pure' goodwill);
iv.   continues to reflect the amounts expended on the purchase of goodwill, but adds information regarding expenditures on IIAs;
v.   does away with the distinction between purchased and internally generated goodwill. It will be strongly argued that, in practice, this distinction is, in any event, meaningless;
vi.   ensures that the Statement of Financial Position continues to reflect an unambiguous book value, viz. net tangible assets (albeit determined in accordance with current accounting principles);
vii.   removes the necessity for arbitrary goodwill and intangible asset amortization;
viii.   indicates the relative importance of both goodwill and specified IIAs as constituents of market capitalization.

The advantages do come at a cost in terms of the extra preparation of financial statements, as it would be necessary to carry out valuations of key IIAs at balance dates. Whether that cost would be justified by the usefulness of the information provided to readers is a subject for academic research and discussion among standard setters.

1.11 Structure of the argument

Chapter 2 explores fundamental concepts relating to goodwill. These include the concept of goodwill as a residual and what that residual includes and excludes. The chapter examines the relationship between goodwill and super-profits and the debate as to whether goodwill should be treated as an asset.

Chapter 3 examines the 'Alice-in-Wonderland' world of accounting (or non-accounting) for internally generated goodwill. It clarifies the inherent

Table 1.3 MCS expanded to account for IIAs

The current Equity portion of the Balance Sheet would read as follows: (using illustrative figures)

	Current Year	Previous Year
Contributed equity	40,000	38,000
Reserves	10,000	10,000
Retained profits	20,000	15,000
	70,000	63,000
Less: Cost of goodwill and other intangible assets purchased	20,000	18,000
Net tangible assets	50,000	45,000

The accompanying MCS would be structured as follows:
Market Capitalization Statement

	Current Year	Previous Year
Number of issued shares	150,000	140,000
Market price per share ($)	50¢	60¢
Market capitalization	75,000	84,000

	$'000	$'000
Comprising:		
IIAs, at valuation		
Patents	3,000	4,000
Contracts with suppliers	5,000	5,000
Licences	2,000	1,500
Technology	4,000	6,000
Total IIAs	14,000	16,000
MCS goodwill	11,000	23,000
Total intangible assets	25,000	39,000
Net tangible assets	50,000	45,000
Market capitalization	75,000	84,000

	Current Year	Previous Year
Ratio of MCS goodwill to market capitalization	15%	27%
Ratio of total intangible assets to market capitalization	33%	46%

Details of cost of goodwill and other intangible assets purchased:

	Current Year	Previous Year
Patents	2,000	3,000
Contracts with suppliers	4,000	4,000
Technology	4,000	6,000
Total IIAs purchased	10,000	13,000
Goodwill	10,000	5,000
	20,000	18,000

contradictions and difficulties of the stance taken by the standard setters. In addition to reviewing the historical developments and current standards, it points out that, in certain cases, a transaction involving the purchase of goodwill may also provide satisfactory evidence regarding the existence and value of internally generated goodwill. It concludes by drawing on the work of Ma and Hopkins (1988), which demonstrates how difficult it is to identify a stream of benefits arising from the purchase of goodwill independently from that arising from goodwill which is internally generated.

Chapter 4 examines accounting for purchased goodwill. Most acquisitions of businesses or corporate entities result in an amount being established as the cost of the goodwill component of the acquisition. The result has been that the accounting debate has focused on how to treat this amount once it has been recognized. The argument has been heated and repetitive; the numerous changes in the fashionable treatment have confirmed that a generally acceptable solution is yet to be found. It is an outstanding example of the 'unresolvable issues' identified by Sterling (1975). The heat and repetitive nature of the controversy accompanying the transition to IFRS from January 2005 is the latest illustration.

The current developments (as at January 2007), which are examined in detail in Chapter 5, provide further evidence of the inability of traditional accounting methods to cope with purchased goodwill, let alone internally generated goodwill. For many years, the amortization paradigm has ruled, and the debate has centred on the period and method of amortization. The defects of this approach have now become apparent, and the standard setters are turning to an 'impairment' regime to solve them. Chapter 5 argues that this paradigm also has inherent defects that will lead to its eventual abandonment.

The Australian Accounting Standards Board (AASB) indicated, on 17 March 2004, that it aimed to ensure that 'for-profit entities applying AASB Standards for reporting periods beginning on or after 1 January 2005 will also be complying with IASB Standards' (http://www.aasb.com.au/work-prog/aasb_index.htm). With the release of the set of relevant IFRS on 31 March 2004, and the adoption of virtually identical Standards by the AASB in April 2004 (AIFRS), the impairment regime has now become accepted practice in Australia. This renewed focus on accounting for goodwill emphasizes the need to do so in a way that helps, rather than hinders, proper interpretation of accounting data.

Chapter 6 explains the MCS in greater detail than this chapter's illustrative examples. It provides further detail as to the growing importance of goodwill and intangible assets as a component of market capitalization of listed companies, and clarifies the structure of the MCS and some matters of definition. It explains how it caters for the various views as to whether goodwill is an asset, examines the constituents of 'MCS goodwill' in greater detail and sets out the limitations of the MCS.

Finally, the MCS has been noted as still being subject to certain problems and distortions in the context of the historical cost basis of the remaining financial statements. Chapter 7 demonstrates that, if used in the context of an exit price based system, Chambers' CoCoA, many of these distortions are removed.

Appendix 1 illustrates the practical application of the MCS by reference to a number of examples, which have been drawn from data relating to companies listed on the ASX. The companies examined in Appendix 1A were drawn from the 'dot.com' companies, which were the major contributors to the Stock Exchange boom that commenced in late 1999 and concluded by 30 June 2002. The market capitalization of most of these fourteen companies consisted mainly of intangible asset values, including both technology and goodwill. The fluctuation in stock market prices over a comparatively short period provided ideal conditions to demonstrate the operation of the MCS and enable a preliminary assessment of the potential value of the information produced by its incorporation in an Annual Report.

Appendix 1B provides a similar analysis, over a similar period, of six of Australia's leading public companies. The need for the type of information provided by the MCS was demonstrated by the finding that, over a period of three years encompassing wide fluctuations in the stock market as a whole, the MCS goodwill content of these companies' market capitalization averaged some 67 per cent; of this 67 per cent, only some 5 per cent could be ascribed to the cost of purchased goodwill. This analysis indicated that the MCS was potentially relevant in the case of 'blue-chip' companies as well as speculative companies.

Disclosure via the MCS regarding the amount of goodwill (both purchased and internally generated) contained in a company's market capitalization is likely to intensify demand by readers of the Annual Report for information to enable them to assess the factors that contribute to the generation of goodwill. Appendix 2 examines some of the most significant current developments in this area.

In summary, the evidence, the argument and reasoning presented in the following chapters and appendices:

Chapter

Historical review of the 'goodwill problem'

2   What is goodwill?
3   Internally generated goodwill – 'Alice-in-Wonderland accounting'
4   Purchased goodwill – historical treatment
5   Impairment – the current conventional wisdom

The MCS – how it contributes towards a solution of the problem

6   The MCS

2   What is goodwill?

Goodwill, when it appears in the Balance Sheet at all, is but a master valuation account – a catch-all into which is thrown both an unenumerated series of items that have the *economic*, though not necessarily the *legal*, properties of assets, and an undistributed list of undervaluations of those items listed as assets. It is the valuation account par excellence. It cannot under any circumstances be called an 'asset' unless that term is confessedly meant to include at least two kinds of things which have no common attribute peculiar to them.

(J. B. Canning, 1929)

2.1 Introduction

The first accounting article on goodwill cited in the literature examined here was published in 1884 (Harris 1884: 9–12, as cited by Hughes 1982: 24), although the term itself has a much older usage. Leake (1948: 1), for example, cites a reference in 1571: 'I gyue to John Stephen. ... My whole interest and good will of my Quarelle' (i.e. quarry). He also claims (1948: 2) that the earliest reported legal decision on goodwill seems to be Crutwell v Lye (1810, 17 Ves. 335), in the course of which Lord Eldon commented: 'The goodwill which has been the subject of sale is nothing more than the probability that the old customers will resort to the old place'.

Since that time, innumerable articles and books have been written with reference to the subject of 'accounting for goodwill'. Similarly, generations of legislators and setters of accounting standards have grappled with the problem. Pet theories have been promoted, solutions articulated and various practices have been tried, rejected and then tried again.

Perhaps the one constant in all definitions and discussions of goodwill is that it is classified as intangible, rather than tangible. It is common, in accounting parlance, to distinguish between tangible assets and intangibles, although the distinction is not as clear as conventional wisdom would suggest. A right is intangible, and many assets, in fact, depend for their existence on rights. It is probable that all accountants would classify amounts owing by debtors, for example, as tangible assets under a heading such as 'debtors' or 'accounts receivable' but, in fact, the asset that an entity possesses is not the debtor as an individual, but only the right to collect a sum of money from that debtor. Similarly, land itself is clearly tangible, but an entity enjoys many intangible rights attached to it, such as the right to occupy it or use it in other ways, such as renting it to a tenant or using it as collateral to borrow.

For the purpose of accounting for goodwill, however, the distinction between the right and the asset itself is not material. It is sufficient to note that tangibility, in this context, is relevant only because it enables very precise definition. A receivable recognized in the accounts of a company is a claim against a particular, identifiable debtor; land recognized as an asset is a right to own, occupy and use (including sell) a particular, well defined portion of terrain.

A major attribute of goodwill that sets it apart from those assets is the difficulty faced in identifying it precisely. Intangible assets such as patents, copyrights and mastheads are excluded from the definition of goodwill precisely because they can be identified with similar precision to tangible assets. Traditionally, then, goodwill is 'the unidentifiable intangible asset', although its status as an asset is still hotly debated (see Section 2.5 below).

2.2 Goodwill as a residual

The notion of goodwill as a residual amount is well established. For example, IFRS 3, para. 51 defines goodwill, in the context of an acquisition, as 'any excess of the cost of the acquisition over the acquirer's interest in the net fair value of the identifiable assets, liabilities and contingent liabilities acquired as at the date of the exchange transaction'. Thus, goodwill is defined, not in terms of its attributes, but in terms of the calculation by which its supposed 'worth' is established.

The UK definition contained in Financial Reporting Standard (FRS) 10 'Goodwill and Intangible Assets' is similar. Purchased goodwill is 'the difference between the cost of an acquired entity and the aggregate of the fair values of that entity's identifiable assets and liabilities'. In these definitions, it is almost implied that the calculation brings goodwill into existence.

In Australia, the previous Accounting Standards (also designated AASB, but numbered from 1001 to 1047), were superseded with effect from financial periods beginning on or after 1 January 2005, in conformity with Australia's harmonization programme with International Standards. Australia's AASB 1013 'Accounting for Goodwill', which was in force from July 1996, makes the same point, but more precisely. At para. 5.7, it states: 'Goodwill which is purchased by the entity must be measured as the excess of the cost of acquisition incurred by the entity over the fair value of the identifiable net assets acquired'. This definition is preferable to the others cited, because it does indicate that goodwill has an identity and existence independent of the determination of its accounting magnitude. The Standard makes it quite clear that the residual concept of goodwill is a measurement concept. AASB 1013 (5.7.4) confirms that costs relating directly to the acquisition, such as legal fees, stamp duty and other government charges and applicable professional fees, should, in the first instance, be capitalized as part of the cost of the acquisition. These costs can be substantial, and the Standard provides (5.8) that 'to the extent that the cost of acquisition incurred by the entity exceeds the fair value of the identifiable net assets acquired but the difference does not constitute goodwill, such difference must be recognized immediately as an expense in the profit and loss account'.

A small extension of the above concept is required to cover non-acquisition situations, such as those in which a company is valued at a point in time, rather than being acquired. Here, goodwill is measured as the difference between the total value of the company and the fair value of its identifiable net assets on that date. This is logical, because a valuation of an entire company usually assumes a sale of the entire share capital of that company as a going concern at fair value.

The phrase 'fair value' occurs in all the above definitions. Both AASB 1013 and IAS 16 'Accounting for Property, Plant and Equipment' (1982 version) define 'fair value' as 'the amount for which an asset could be exchanged between a knowledgeable, willing buyer and a knowledgeable, willing seller in an arm's length transaction'.

The definition does not explicitly deal with liabilities, but it is expanded in AASB 1012 'Foreign Currency Translation' (10), which defines 'fair value' as 'the amount for which an asset could be exchanged, or a liability settled between knowledgeable, willing parties in an arm's length transaction'.

Fair value

The development of the concept of fair value is discussed at length by Clarke in two articles (Clarke 1980, 1998). In an early case (Smyth v. Ames 1989 – 169 US 466), it was held that, in order to ascertain fair value (in the context of pricing of utility company assets), a number of factors had to be taken into account, such as the original cost of construction and improvements, the present construction cost, probable earning capacity, the amount and value of the utility's lands and stock, and current operating expenses. Paton (1918: 53, cited in Clarke 1998) extended this concept well beyond its original context by recommending its use in ordinary commercial accounting. Bonbright (1937, cited in Clarke 1998) endorsed a deprival value or 'value to the owner' concept (in cases where the owner had actually been deprived of his property), but this concept was extended by other writers as a surrogate for fair value in cases in which no such deprival occurred. The voluntary exchange definition of fair value appears in the US in 1970, in Accounting Principles Board (APB) 54 'Basic Concepts and Accounting Principles Underlying Financial Statements of Business Enterprises' (as cited in Chambers 1995: 521) and internationally in 1982 in International Accounting Standard (IAS) 16, as noted above.

In September 2006, the Financial Accounting Standards Board (FASB) issued Statement Financial Accounting Standards (SFAS) 157 'Fair Value Measurements', which clarified the concept of 'fair value' by defining it (para. 5) as 'the price that would be received to sell an asset or paid to transfer a liability in an orderly transaction between market participants at the measure date'. Paragraph 6 of SFAS 157 clarified that the definition applied not only to an individual asset or liability, but to groups of assets and/or liabilities such as a business.

The measurement of fair value assumes a transaction in the principal (or most advantageous market); the market participants in such a market are required (para. 10) to be:

i.   independent of the reporting entity; that is, they are not related parties;
ii. knowledgeable, having a reasonable understanding about the asset or liability and the transaction based on all available information, including information that might be obtained through due diligence efforts that are usual and customary;
iii. able to transact for the asset or liability;
iv. willing to transact for the asset or liability; that is, they are motivated but not forced or otherwise compelled to do so.

Making allowances for some clarifications and minor emphasis changes, the definition itself is not, for practical purposes, significantly different from previous definitions in other SFASs. These were not constant, as SFAS 157 points out, but, for example, FASB 115 'Accounting for Certain Investments in Debt and Equity Securities' typically defined 'fair value' at para. 137 as 'the amount at which an asset could be bought or sold in a current transaction between willing parties, that is, other than in a forced or liquidation sale'. Indeed, at para. 50 of Appendix C, the Board notes that it 'agreed that the measurement objective encompassed in the definition of fair value is generally consistent with similar definitions of fair market value used for valuation purposes'.

Where SFAS 157 has established new ground is its statement (para. 7) that 'the objective of a fair value measurement is to determine the price that would be received to sell the asset or paid to transfer the liability at the measurement date (an exit price)'.

In a striking departure from the traditional deference paid to cost in a historical cost based system, SFAS 157 emphasizes (para. 16) that 'conceptually, entry prices and exit prices are different. Entities do not necessarily sell assets at the prices paid to acquire them'. Indeed, the statement goes much further in the following paragraph, pointing out that while, 'in many cases, the transaction price will equal the exit price and therefore represent the fair value of the asset or liability at initial recognition', this is not necessarily so. Cost (or entry price) may not represent fair value if it arises in a related party transaction, if the seller operates under duress, if there are other elements affecting the transaction or if the transaction did not occur in the most advantageous market.

At the time of writing, the IASB has responded to SFAS 157 by issuing a discussion paper on fair value measurements, comments on which were due by 2 April 2007. The definition of 'fair value' used in the IASs is very similar to that quoted above in AASB 1012 'Foreign Currency Translation', viz. 'the amount for which an asset could be exchanged, or a liability settled, between knowledgeable, willing parties in an arm's length transaction'.

The discussion paper highlights (para. 10) that the SFAS 157 definition differs from that used in the IFRSs in three important ways:

i.   The definition in SFAS 157 is explicitly an exit (selling) price. The definition in IFRSs is neither explicitly an exit price nor an entry (buying) price.
ii. The definition in SFAS 157 explicitly refers to market participants. The definition in IFRSs refers to knowledgeable, willing parties in an arm's length transaction.
iii. For liabilities, the definition of fair value in SFAS 157 rests on the notion that the liability is transferred (the liability to the counterparty continues; it is not settled with the counterparty). The definition in IFRSs refers to the amount at which a liability could be settled between knowledgeable, willing parties in an arm's length transaction.

Although these issues are interesting, they are not directly relevant to the goodwill issue explored herein. The IASB emphasizes (para. 7) that 'the fair value of the discussion paper measurements project is not a means of expanding the use of fair value in financial reporting'.

Measurement of goodwill

Given an accepted definition of fair value, goodwill is theoretically measured, for accounting purposes, as a residual, or differential, between:

i. the 'aggregate value' of the enterprise, being its actual or theoretically computed fair value in total, remembering that, if actual cost is used as a measure of the 'aggregate value' of the enterprise, costs of acquisition must be excluded if these, by being capitalized, would result in the actual cost exceeding the 'aggregate value' as defined; and
ii. the 'comparison value', being the fair value of its net identifiable assets.

Prior to the current requirements of the Accounting Standards, which emphasize the use of fair values, the comparison value was often determined more loosely, by reference to book value in a conventionally prepared

Balance Sheet. This could represent pure, unadjusted historical cost but, in today's accounting world, it is more likely to represent historical cost adjusted in accordance with the prevailing accounting principles. Such adjustments to historical cost are made in a large number of ways, including depreciation or amortization over a period (often arbitrary), revaluation (permitted in Australia for certain assets in defined conditions that have now been further reduced by the newly adopted Standards), reduction to net realizable value, actual market value, capitalization of certain costs which in other circumstances would be expensed and pure computation (e.g. future income tax benefits).

Goodwill has a logically consistent value, given its residual nature, if the comparison value were to be determined on a fair value basis, as defined above, because all items in the equation would be determined on a similar basis. Some theorists seek to utilize replacement value rather than realizable value as a basis for Balance Sheet recognition of assets and liabilities. While recognizing that there is an argument to be put for that view, it is worth noting only that, in this context, the definition of 'fair value' chosen here, with its emphasis on an exchange transaction, is more consistent with the use of realizable value. It is also in agreement with the exit value concept inherent in the fair value definition in SFAS 157.

If all other Balance Sheet items were kept at pure, unadjusted historical cost, goodwill would also have an intellectually consistent meaning, although it would not be the meaning usually assigned to goodwill. In the context envisaged by Leake (see Section 2.4 below), the appropriate risk adjusted rate of interest applied to capital invested would be applied to the historical cost of that capital. All increases in value above that figure, whether due to variations in the earning power of any asset or liability, or to the development of other assets that combine to constitute goodwill, would be subsumed in the valuation of goodwill. Goodwill would then represent a pure valuation surplus over the historical cost of the net assets. It is emphasized that, for this to be true, even common adjustments to historical cost such as depreciation would not be made.

On the other hand, if the comparison value represents historical cost adjusted in several ways in accordance with the prevailing accounting standards, goodwill calculated and brought to account as a residual is a 'master valuation account', as defined by Canning (1929, see Chapter 1.8). It is worth setting out a more detailed quotation here because nobody has articulated the issue better, notwithstanding the passage of nearly eighty years:

> It is no matter for surprise that where many of the component elements of future income have been omitted from the asset valuations and where those component elements which have been included were predominantly undervalued, the concern should exhibit, year after year, a ratio of operating profit to book value of assets much above that which is found in other concerns in the same industry. Such a concern is said

to have a valuable goodwill. If it changes hands, it will do so at a total consideration in excess of the difference between its book totals of assets and of liabilities. To the extent to which this goodwill is reliably appraised, all that can be said of it is that it results from, and amounts to, the sum of values of items of future incomes omitted from its asset schedule plus the sum of undervaluations of those future items (and series of items) of future income that are shown in its asset schedule, less the sum of corresponding overvaluations (if any) of those asset items that appear in the schedule.

Goodwill, when it appears in the Balance Sheet at all, is but a master valuation account – a catch-all into which is thrown both an unenumerated series of items that have the *economic*, though not necessarily the *legal*, properties of assets, and an undistributed list of undervaluations of those items listed as assets. It is the valuation account par excellence. It cannot under any circumstances be called an 'asset', unless that term is confessedly meant to include at least two kinds of things which have no common attribute peculiar to them.

Canning (1929: 42)

If self-generated goodwill (as distinct from purchased goodwill) is to be brought within the ambit of accounting, Canning's point is still important.

A modern exposition of the point made by Canning is found in Upton (2001: 2). He accounts for the difference between accounting book value (i.e. the comparison value according to modern generally accepted accounting principles) and market capitalization as shown in Table 2.1.

Table 2.1 The difference between accounting book value and market capitalization

	$
Accounting book value	XXX
±Market assessments of differences between accounting measurement and underlying value of recognized assets and liabilities	XXX
±Market assessments of the underlying value of items that meet the definition of assets and liabilities but are not recognized in financial statements (e.g. patents developed through internal research and development)	XXX
±Market assessments of intangible value drivers or value impairers that do not meet the definition of assets and liabilities (e.g. employee morale)	XXX
±Market assessments of the entity's future plans, opportunities and business risks	XXX
±Other factors, including puffery, pessimism and market psychology	XXX
Market capitalization	XXX

In order to account for goodwill fully, it is necessary to find a technique that accounts not only for goodwill arising in the context of an acquisition, or purchased goodwill, but also internally generated goodwill. As will be seen in Chapter 3, much of the debate in this latter area has focused on the difficulty of establishing an accurate cost and/or an accurate valuation of internally generated goodwill. This leads to a critical premise in this book. Bearing in mind the measurement of goodwill as a residual, it is essential that the comparison value be determined in a logically consistent and useful manner if a logically consistent and useful method of accounting for goodwill is to be developed.

It might appear as though the requirement to determine fair values, at the time of an acquisition, to determine the comparison value of the acquired entity goes some way to meet this criticism. In fact, it does not, for the following reasons:

i. 'Fair value', in this context, is merely a way of allocating costs to specific assets and liabilities at the time of the acquisition. The effluxion of time will ensure that these costs, like all other costs utilized in the Statement of Financial Position, become of lesser use as a measure of current value. The consequence is that the value of goodwill obtained using dated fair values becomes, in turn, dated and, in Australia's SAC 3 terms, less reliable and less relevant.
ii. Costs determined on this basis become subject to the adjustments inherent in currently accepted prevailing accounting principles, in the same way as costs recorded for assets acquired prior to and after the acquisition.
iii. The aggregate fair value changes, both for the acquirer and, to the extent that it remains possible to calculate it separately, for the acquired entity.

2.3 The constituents of goodwill

The measurement of goodwill as a residual is consistent with the 'top-down' perspective of goodwill explained by commentators such as Johnson and Petrose (1988: 294 *et seq.*) in that goodwill is viewed as a subset of a larger asset, i.e. the company in total: 'That larger asset is broken down into its constituent parts and after the various identifiable net assets acquired are recorded, the remainder is assigned to goodwill. As such, goodwill is what is "left over" ... '.

In contrast, the 'bottom-up' perspective is that, if the acquisition price exceeds the fair value of the acquired entity's net assets, presumably some other resources were acquired that were of value to the acquirer. That view focuses attention on the constituents of goodwill, rather than its measurement.

In an Exposure Draft issued in September 1999, 'Business Combinations and Intangible Assets', the US FASB used the following definition of goodwill:

The amount recognized as goodwill may consist of one or more unidentifiable intangible assets and identifiable intangible assets that are not reliably measurable. The elements of goodwill include new channels of distribution, synergies of combining sales forces, and a superior management team. Because those and similar elements cannot be reliably measured separately from each other, they are accounted for separately as goodwill.

The distinction between measurable IIAs (to be accounted for separately) and those that cannot be reliably distinguished from goodwill has been carried through into the new Australian Standards.

A more extensive list has been slightly adapted from one provided by Lonergan (1995: 7):

i.   synergy benefits; although these are often identified as a benefit that arises on acquisition of another entity, there are synergistic benefits arising out of relationships between people, systems and/or divisions in an enterprise which may be very material in generating profits;
ii.   the quality of the marketing team and general market expertise;
iii.   consumer loyalty;
iv.   economies of scale within the organization itself or resulting from acquisition;
v.   a well developed distribution network;
vi.   benefits arising from location in a particular area;
vii.   possession of a monopoly in one or more areas of operation;
viii. know-how (as distinct from patents) and technical skills vested in individual executives or teams within the organization;
ix.   innovative use of technology.

Although the author was writing in the context of purchased goodwill, the constituents of goodwill do not change significantly whether goodwill is purchased or self-generated. Lonergan (1995) does not suggest that the list is exhaustive; in particular industries or businesses, there may well be other factors that could validly be included in goodwill. What is made clear, however, is that goodwill needs to be defined and considered in terms of intangible items existing within an entity, and that it is not sufficient to attempt to understand or account for goodwill in the context of the residual or 'top-down' view alone.

It has been generally accepted that it is difficult, if not impossible, to attach values to these individual constituents of goodwill, although this view was not universal. Tearney (1981: 527) argued, in a prescient article, that:

Current accounting practices for goodwill as well as for other valuable assets not appearing on an acquired company's balance sheet are not in conformity with available valuation techniques. By substituting the catchall account 'goodwill' for many assets purchased in business combinations, such as personnel skills and marketing channels, accountants are not only ignoring the existence of expert appraisers but perpetuating a disservice to clients and the general public as well. It is high time that we accountants recognized our social responsibility in this area.

Valuation techniques have been developed to a point where goodwill no longer need appear on financial statements. All assets acquired in business combinations, regardless how intangible they may be and whether or not they appear on the acquired entity's balance sheet, should be identified, valued and disclosed, thereby removing one of the thorns in the accountant's side.

Tearney (1981: 527)

He cites an instance reported in 1964 (Heath 1964: 557–58) in which the residual amount normally attributable to goodwill was allocated on the basis of specific values assigned to patents, trademarks and licensing agreements, designs for new and existing product lines, new product model rights and the company's unique engineering staff.

Until comparatively recently, it has been the practice in accounting for an acquisition to include in goodwill the value attributable to all intangible assets but patents, trademarks and other clearly identifiable assets that are comparatively easy to value. However, with the introduction of IAS 38 'Intangible Assets', the Australian version of which (AASB 138) took effect on 1 January 2005, the practice has fundamentally changed. References herein are to paragraphs of AASB 138, which is virtually identical to IAS 38.

For an asset to be 'identifiable' (para. 12), it:

i. is separable, that is, is capable of being separated or divided from the entity and sold, transferred, licensed, rented or exchanged, either individually or together with a related contract, asset or liability; or
ii. arises from contractual or other legal rights, regardless of whether those rights are transferable or separable from the entity or from other rights and obligations.

Where such an asset is acquired separately, it will normally be brought to account at cost. The more interesting question arises in the case of a business acquisition, which may well include a number of intangible assets fitting the above definition. The Standard states (para. 35):

The fair value of intangible assets acquired in business combinations can normally be measured with sufficient reliability to be recognised separately from goodwill. When, for the estimates used to measure an intangible asset's fair value, there is a range of possible outcomes with different probabilities, that uncertainty enters into the measure of the asset's fair value, rather than demonstrates an inability to measure fair value reliably. If an intangible asset acquired in a business combination has a finite useful life, there is a rebuttable presumption that its fair value can be measured reliably.

The various techniques of valuation lie outside the scope of this publication. As the Standard notes (para. 39), 'quoted market prices in an active market provide the most reliable estimate of the fair value of an intangible asset'. There are comparatively few cases where such prices are available; however, since the introduction of the Standard, techniques have been developed and are in current use for intangible assets such as key contracts with suppliers held by the acquiree, as well as items such as customer lists and databases. Valuations of assets such as patents, trademarks and copyrighted items have had a longer history, and the techniques of valuation are well established.

In 2001, the FASB issued a list of 'Intangible Assets that meet the Criteria for Recognition apart from Goodwill' (as cited in Mard et al. 2002: 20). The list includes items that either have a contractual–legal basis or are severable from the enterprise. Trademarks, non-competitive agreements and customer contracts fall into the former category, while customer lists, databases and unpatented technology qualified via severability. Mard et al. (2002: 21) also refers to a list of over ninety items that could qualify as IIAs for accounting purposes, issued by the American Institute of Certified Public Accountants (AICPA) in 1999. Some of the more interesting items in that list are credit information files, easements, prizes and awards, retail shelf space and trading manuals. The key point, for present purposes, is that, to the extent that such identifiable intangible items can be identified and valued, they do not form part of goodwill.

Modern writers, such as Lev (2001), have developed innovative techniques for the measurement of intangible assets. An alternative development has been the 'Intellectual Capital Supplements' developed by the Swedish insurance company, Skandia, discussed at length by Upton (2001: 32 *et seq.*), or similar non-financial metrics used by other companies and writers. The use of non-financial metrics is a useful supplement to the MCS and is more fully canvassed in Appendix 2.

Skandia, for example, includes a lengthy supplement to its annual financial statements, covering a number of 'soft' issues such as female potential, new opportunities and health and human capital. However, it also furnishes quantified details under headings such as 'customer focus' (e.g. a customer satisfaction index), 'human focus' (e.g. details of employee training and turnover), 'process focus' (e.g. number of contracts per employee, ratio of IT expense to administrative expense) and 'renewal and development focus' (e.g. number of ideas filed with the Ideas Group, share of gross premiums written from new launches). Quantified data include ratios, pure numbers and dollar values.

2.4 Goodwill value and super-profits

Most entities possess at least some of the items listed above as intangible assets but, in accounting terms, not all entities possess goodwill. The reason for this is given by the excess profit, or 'super-profit', theory of goodwill. Yang (1927: 88) defined goodwill as 'the present worth or capitalized value of the estimated future earnings of an established enterprise in excess of the normal results that it might be reasonably assumed would be realized by a similar undertaking established new'.

Paton (1962: 317) had made a similar point in his *Accounting Theory*, originally published in 1922: 'Goodwill, as has been indicated, expresses the value of an excess earning power. It represents the capitalization of the peculiar rights and advantages enjoyed by the supramarginal enterprise'; and the same author, together with A. C. Littleton (Littleton and Paton 1940: 92, as cited by Gynther 1974: 220), clarified the point further in defining goodwill as 'the discounted value of the estimated excess earning power – the amount of the net income anticipated in excess of income sufficient to clothe the tangible resources involved with the normal rate of return'.

Leake (1948: 2) further refined this concept. He defined commercial goodwill as 'the right which grows out of all kinds of past effort in seeking profit, increase of value, or other advantage', and formulated the exchangeable value of that right as depending upon 'the probability of earning future super-profit, the term super-profit meaning the amount by which the revenue, increase of value, or other advantage received exceeds any and all economic expenditure incidental to its production'. Such economic expenditure included 'a rate of interest on capital invested which will attract and retain any necessary capital having regard to the degree of risk incidental to the character of the undertaking'.

This articulation of the concept of 'super-profit', being the power of an entity to earn more than a 'normal' rate of return on capital invested, represented a significant development of the elementary definition which had been given by Lord Eldon in 1810 (see Section 2.1 above). Put simply, the value of the goodwill of an entity is the present value of expected earnings (or increase in value or other advantage) in excess of the risk adjusted return on its investment in net identifiable assets. It follows that, despite the possession of any or all of the constituents of goodwill described above, if an entity is not viewed as being capable of generating such excess earnings, or super-profit, it is not able to bring goodwill to account.

Boswell (1783/1967, as cited in Chambers 1995) quotes Johnson at the sale of a brewery. Asked what he really considered to be the value of the property to be disposed of, Johnson replied 'We are not here to sell a parcel of boilers and vats, but the potentiality of growing rich beyond the dreams of avarice' (Boswell 1783/1967: 432) – a 1783 definition of anticipated super-profits.

The super-profit exposition of goodwill accords precisely with the residual method of measuring goodwill described in Section 2.2 above. If the fair value of the net identifiable assets corresponds with the total value of the enterprise by virtue of the fact that the enterprise only earns its expected, risk adjusted rate of return on those net identifiable assets, there is no residual and, hence, no goodwill. Such a limiting case enterprise would have a Tobin's Q of exactly 1. If the total value of the enterprise is less than the fair value of its net identifiable assets, the lack of goodwill is even more evident. The graph in Table 1.1 above shows that, with reference to US equities in the last fifty years, the average Tobin's Q ratio exceeded 1 only briefly until the late 1960s but has done so consistently since 1996; prior to 1996, the ratio was below 0.7 for over twenty years.

It is sometimes salutary to realize that goodwill is not only an accounting concept; it is also a legal concept. The legal concept of goodwill was reviewed at length in the Murry case (FC of T v Murry 98 ATC 4585; 1998 39 ATR 129). One of the points highlighted was that, in Australia at least, the attraction of custom (as distinct from the earning of super-profits or, indeed, any profits at all) was central to the legal concept of goodwill. The judgment noted (ibid. para. 31) that the understanding of accountants and businessmen as to the meaning of the word 'goodwill' differed from that of lawyers. This is emphasized by another meaning ascribed to goodwill in the case: 'the legal right or privilege to conduct a business in substantially the same manner and by substantially the same means which in the past have attracted custom to the business'. It does not seem that the legal principles have departed much from those established by Lord Eldon in 1810.

Economic definitions of profit also underlie the 'super-profit' concept, although not unambiguously. The concept of imperfect, or monopolistic, competition has long been an economic staple (see, for example, the exposition by Boulding 1955: 630; the first edition of his book was published in 1941). Whereas, under perfect competition, each supplier faces a perfectly elastic demand curve, a monopolistic competitor enjoys a group of customers who prefer its product to that of its competitors and will be prepared to pay a premium price. The economic analysis implies some differentiation of product (which may be due to factors such as location, as well as a trademark or patent).

The economic analysis in this area has concentrated more upon the relative inelasticity of the demand curve facing a monopolistic competitor and, hence, upon the revenue effect, rather than profits. Accountants have recognized that super-profits may be due to unusually effective cost containment techniques as well as an element of monopoly pricing. Most accountants and economists agree that the competitive advantage attaching to any particular enterprise is unlikely to be perpetual in nature, given the natural forces of competition and the rapid development of techniques aimed at cost reduction.

Knight (1921: 48 *et seq.*) pointed out that profit (including, by inference, super-profit) was due not so much to the enjoyment of a monopoly, but to the entrepreneurial ability to forecast and deal with uncertainty (which he distinguished from risk, or actuarially calculable unknown futures). In Knight's model, as long as an entity is able to predict and deal with uncertainty more effectively than its rivals, it will continue to make super-profits. Theoretically, there is less reason why such an ability should have a limited life, providing the factors that created it are maintained.

2.5 Is goodwill an asset?

If goodwill is to be reflected at all in a conventionally prepared Statement of Financial Position, there would seem at first instance to be little alternative to showing it 'on the assets side'. However, much of the controversy surrounding accounting for goodwill has revolved around whether it is properly regarded as an asset. Some analysts routinely remove it in financial statement analysis, while in most debenture trust deeds, solvency ratios are computed without having regard to any goodwill figure in the Balance Sheet. By removing goodwill to a new, separate section of the financial statements which does not require it to be classified as an asset, the MCS defuses the controversy as to whether goodwill qualifies for inclusion on the assets side of the Balance Sheet. In the MCS, goodwill is a residual that does not require classification or description as an asset.

The most extensive Australian Statement of Accounting Concepts, SAC 4, defines (in the 'Summary of Concepts') 'assets' as 'future economic benefits controlled by the entity as a result of past transactions or other events'. AASB 1013 (5.1.1) specifies that goodwill is an asset and that this is consistent with SAC 4. The definition has an economic, rather than a legal, basis and focuses on future cash flows rather than current cash equivalents.

Sir David Tweedie, the Chairman of the IASB, in a speech delivered in Australia on 15 August 2002 on the subject of harmonization of accounting systems, referred to the Statement of Principles supporting the International Accounting Standards, and commented that it 'is underlying the whole thrust where I think accounting and financial reporting is heading'. Under that statement, an asset is defined as 'a right to a stream of benefits in the future' – a definition very similar to that used in Australia. (Given the definition of 'asset' as quoted, it is perhaps surprising that the IASB maintains a rigid stance against revaluing IIAs even when the projected stream of income generated by such assets is manifestly increasing. Notwithstanding this, the IASB insists on impairment write-downs of such assets when the projected income stream is falling.) This economics based definition is similar to that propounded by leading economist Irving Fisher in 1906:

> ... the accounting ordinarily employed in business. ... is, in fact nothing but a method of recording the items of income and their

capitalization at different points of time. A merchant's balance sheet is a statement of the prospects of his business. Each item in it represents the discounted value of items he may expect later to enter in his income account. Rightly interpreted, the capital account merely represents as a whole the capitalization of expected items in the income account.

Fisher (1906/1965: 264)

Chambers (1979) reviewed the ideas of Fisher in his review of Canning's 1929 *Economics of Accounting*. He was particularly concerned with the implication that Fisher's definition was the product of observing 'merchants' balance sheets'. Of course, Chambers' view on assets was markedly different. He defined an asset as 'any severable means in the possession of an entity' (1966/ 1974: 103). This would logically include a non-transferable right that could be leased or licensed to a third party without transferring the right itself. The stress on severability in his definition is not found in any of the definitions discussed above; indeed, the word 'severable' is hardly mentioned in the various definitions until the emphasis on the concept in IAS 38 (at para. 12(a), as quoted above). Defining an asset in this way focuses on ownership and emphasizes legal rather than economic principles.

Schuetze (2001a: 4–5) quotes the US FASB current definition of asset, which is similar to that in SAC 4 (viz. 'probable future benefits obtained or controlled by a particular entity as a result of past transactions or events'). He points out that this is 'followed by six pages of about six hundred words explaining the definition' and claims that a very large majority of the 330,000 members of the AICPA would not understand the definition. Schuetze's somewhat simpler asset definition, in turn, is 'Cash, claims to cash, for example, accounts and notes receivable, and things that can be sold for cash, for example, a truck'. Thus, definitions of asset fall into two opposing categories. One emphasizes the actual object possessed (e.g. Schuetze's truck), and the other the actual or potential benefits flowing from the use of the object.

Returning to goodwill, Chambers does not regard it as an asset, primarily because it is not severable (although he also claimed that it was not measurable and that it should properly be regarded as accruing to the constituents, or owners, rather than the firm itself). Goodwill is also excluded because it is conditional on the future, rather than being part of the present facts to be accounted for. To Schuetze, purchased goodwill is 'a quintessential "gain contingency" that should not be recognized as an asset until it materializes in the form of cash' (2001a: 21). On the other hand, the 'stream of future benefits' definition of an asset meshes well with the super-profit concept; with this mindset, goodwill does qualify for recognition as an asset, because it is aligned with a specific (though residual) flow of benefits.

The UK Accounting Standards Board has produced a compromise view on this issue. In its FRS 10 (1997: para. (b) of Summary), it concludes:

Goodwill arising on acquisition is neither an asset like other assets nor an immediate loss on value. Rather, it forms the bridge between the cost of an investment shown as an asset in the acquirer's own financial statements and the values attributed to the acquired assets and liabilities in the consolidated financial statements. Although *purchased goodwill is not in itself an asset* (emphasis added), its inclusion amongst the assets of the reporting entity, rather than as a deduction from shareholders' equity, recognizes that goodwill is part of a larger asset, the investment, for which management remains accountable.

For ease of exposition, and because it conforms with prevailing accounting practice, goodwill will be referred to herein as an asset. It is especially useful to be able to distinguish goodwill by referring to it as 'the unidentifiable intangible asset' in order to distinguish it clearly from the other intangible assets such as patents, trademarks or management rights. On this point, the definition of 'identifiable' given by Leo, Radford and Hogget (1995: 44) is also useful: 'Identifiable assets ... are those assets ... which ... can be measured without measuring the total net assets of a business entity'.

One point on which Tweedie, Chambers, Schuetze and the professional conceptual frameworks all agree is that a key objective of accounting, and hence the annual financial statements, is the provision of information relevant for decision making. As is explained in Chapter 6, the MCS recognizes the special nature of goodwill and takes much of the heat out of the debate about its classification as an asset. Moreover, it enables additional information to be furnished to readers of the Annual Report which will assist in ascertaining the financial position of the company.

2.6 Negative goodwill

It will occasionally occur that, in an acquisition, the cost of the acquisition is less than the fair value of the identifiable net assets acquired. Such a bargain purchase usually occurs when the seller is at a disadvantage compared with the buyer in negotiating the terms of purchase, and generates a discount on acquisition, or 'negative goodwill' (i.e. a credit balance rather than a debit balance) in the books of the acquirer if the acquired assets are expressed at fair value. AASB 1013 (para. 8.1) provided:

> Where the fair values of the identifiable net assets acquired by the entity exceed the cost of acquisition, the difference represents a discount on acquisition and must be accounted for by reducing proportionately the fair values of the non-monetary assets until the discount is eliminated. Where, after reducing to zero the recorded amounts of the non-monetary assets acquired, a discount balance remains it must be recognized as a revenue (*sic*) in the profit and loss account.

The treatment is consistent with the general principle which requires assets to be recorded initially at cost. It is an interesting example of the primacy of the historical cost principle in that it explicitly requires assets to be brought to account at 'deemed cost', despite the fact that cost is lower than fair value. AASB 3 'Business Combinations' now requires that negative goodwill be recognized immediately as a profit (para. 55). This book does not deal in detail with historical trends in accounting for negative goodwill, although it does explain how it can be dealt with in the context of the MCS; the principles set out in AASB 1013 were generally accepted prior to the adoption of the Australian International Financial Reporting Standards (AIFRS).

2.7 Goodwill in the context of the historical cost system

It is critical to stress that the 'exchangeable value' (Leake) or the 'discounted value' (Paton and Littleton) is not the goodwill of an enterprise. It is merely how that goodwill is measured. This point was well made by Gynther (1974: 230): 'the widespread "present value of excess profits" idea of goodwill confuses the nature of goodwill with a popular method of measuring it. The measurement method has been rationalized into a concept, but into a concept that is incorrect and misleading', and by Leo, Radford and Hoggett: 'For any entity, the earning power of the entity is a function of its assets. The existence of goodwill. ... does not give rise to "superior" earning capacity, unless this is interpreted as extra earning capacity that would not exist if the group of assets did not exist, which is true of all assets by definition' (1995: 37).

From a practical point of view, the fair value of an enterprise is best established when it changes hands; at that point, the price at which it is sold becomes a *prima facie* indicator of value. It is for this reason that virtually all accounting standards permit the recognition of goodwill established at this point – and equally significant that they require a valuation of identifiable assets and liabilities at that point in order to establish the comparison value and, hence, the quantum of purchased goodwill.

The concept of goodwill is inextricably linked with the concept of valuation, which sits uneasily within the context of historical cost accounting. So deeply was the historical cost principle entrenched in currently generally accepted accounting principles that AASB 1001: 'Accounting Policies' did not even find it necessary to specify that an entity must use it in preparing financial statements; the only policies mandated are the going concern basis (unless inappropriate) and the accrual basis. These are also the only two 'underlying assumptions' specified in the 'Framework for the Preparation and Presentation of Financial Statements' issued by the AASB in July 2004, although the Framework acknowledged (para. 100) that, in addition to historical cost, measurement bases employed did include current cost (or replacement cost), realizable or settlement value and present value.

Owing to their recurring nature and importance in the 'goodwill debates', the next two chapters of this book will examine, in turn, the historical treatments of internally generated goodwill and purchased goodwill, respectively, and how accounting theorists and standard setters have attempted to deal with the inherent conflicts and difficulties. Then follows a chapter which examines the currently favoured treatment of purchased goodwill – the impairment model.

3 Internally generated goodwill

'Alice-in-Wonderland accounting'

The manifest danger is the practice of Alice-in-Wonderland accounting, which will lead inescapably to a loss of professional credibility in the business community ... the search for a correct method of recording and amortizing goodwill within the historical cost framework is unlikely to succeed.

(R. Ma and R. Hopkins, 1988)

3.1 Goodwill categories and why internally generated goodwill has not been recognized

Goodwill may conveniently be divided into two categories for the purpose of the following chapters:

i. 'internally generated goodwill', which is developed by processes and non-specific expenditures within the entity itself. Non-specific expenditures would include items such as advertising, product development and staff recruitment and training, but are not limited to these items; nor does all such expenditure create goodwill;
ii. 'purchased goodwill', which is much easier to define and isolate. It arises whenever the entity makes a purchase of another entity for a consideration in excess of that justified only by the fair value of the identifiable assets acquired.

This chapter will examine the accounting treatment of the former, while Chapter 4 deals with the latter.

AASB 1013 maintains the traditional approach to internally generated goodwill, viz. 'Goodwill which is internally generated by the entity must not be recognized by the entity'. The Standard (para. 4.1.1.) identifies the two major reasons for this as:

i. Principally because of the difficulty, or impossibility, of identifying the events or transactions which contribute to the overall goodwill of the entity.

ii. The extent to which they (i.e. the past events or transactions) generate future benefits and the value of such benefits are not usually capable of being measured reliably.

AASB 138, the now current Statement, confirms at para. 48 that 'internally generated goodwill shall not be recognized as an asset' because (para. 49) '... it is not an identifiable resource (i.e. it is not separable nor does it arise from contractual or other legal rights) controlled by the entity that can be measured reliably at cost'.

The reasons have changed perceptibly, but the conclusion remains the same.

Skinner captures the traditional approach and its identification with the historical cost framework:

> ... goodwill cannot be fully accounted for within the historical cost model because it is largely not the result of a cost outlay. It is not surprising that generally accepted accounting principles do not permit attempts to cost or value general goodwill as it grows or diminishes during the conduct of the business. Even if accounting were to adopt a valuation approach in place of the historical cost model, accounting for the value of goodwill would be very difficult ... valuation of goodwill would be almost completely subjective.
>
> As a practical matter, therefore, under almost any system of accounting one can think of, it would be preferable to ignore goodwill ...
>
> Skinner (1987: 192)

In a historical cost based system, it is difficult if not impossible to identify the specific costs attaching to specific transactions that generate or contribute to the goodwill of an enterprise (other than a defined goodwill purchase). This means that the precision and objectivity that many have agreed are the main foundations of the historical cost system of accounting are not available in the case of internally generated goodwill. (This is not the place to debate whether historical cost accounting as applied in practice is in fact precise and objective.) As noted above, in Chapter 1.4, SAC 3 'identifies relevance and reliability as the primary qualitative characteristics which financial information should possess'. The Statement 'does not rank either characteristic above the other'.

It is clear from data furnished elsewhere in this book (Chapters 1.2 and 6.1) that information regarding internally generated goodwill is relevant to readers of an Annual Report. Nevertheless, the difficulties of making reported information on internally generated goodwill reliable enough to be useful, within the constraints imposed by historical cost reporting, have been formidable. The views espoused by the quoted extracts from Accounting Standards and Skinner, cited above, continue to have virtually complete dominance among Australian and international standard setters. This consensus is discussed further in the rest of this Chapter.

3.2 Early views in Australia and the UK

One UK legal view of the need to bring internally generated goodwill to account, in a limited context, is found as early as 1900. A judgment in a case (Barrow Haematite Steel Co. 1900, 2CH. 846, quoted in Dicksee and Tillyard 1920: 72) which dealt with an application to the court to reduce capital on the grounds that part of the capital had been lost or was no longer represented by available assets concluded:

> As to the accounts of companies ... any special account of the nature of a complete account of the assets should contain a fair estimate of the value of the Goodwill. As to Goodwill, it is no doubt true that the company has never entered Goodwill as an asset. For the purpose of the company as a going concern there was no necessity for doing this: but, nevertheless, any Goodwill must be regarded as an available asset for the purpose of a reduction petition. ...

This comment implied that goodwill could be valued reliably in that it required that it should be recognized for the purpose of a capital reduction petition. It should be noted that reduction of capital is not inconsistent with continuing to operate as a going concern; it is a process employed by companies to reorganize a historical capital structure which is inappropriate in the light of the company's present circumstances, and may involve either repayment of capital excess to a company's needs or formal recognition of capital previously invested but lost.

Barton was the author of an early Australian accounting text book that advocated non-recognition of internally generated goodwill, although there was no attempt to justify why recognition should not take place:

> It may be taken as a general rule that goodwill should not be brought into account until it becomes necessary owing to the fact that some monetary or other consideration has been given or received therefor. Such being the case it will be seen that the question of the book entries required to bring goodwill to account will only arise on the sale or purchase of a business or on the admission or retirement of a partner, and it is only necessary therefore to deal with this portion of the subject from these standpoints.
>
> Barton (1919: 92)

Dicksee and Tillyard expressed a UK text book view at approximately the same time, although it is clear that this opinion is based heavily on the accounting treatment that would be appropriate for a sole trader.

> Supposing, however, the business is of such a nature that the Goodwill thereof is worth two years' purchase, is it to be seriously contended

that. ... it is to be stated on the face of the accounts that his wealth has increased not merely £1,000 in respect of unspent profits, but also a further £1,000, as being two years' purchase of the increase representing enhanced Goodwill? From one point of view, perhaps, this question may be answered in the affirmative, for it may be stated that the man's Capital Account should represent the worth of that which he has invested in the business – but there is an overpowering argument in favour of the other view, namely, that the object of accounts is not merely to keep a record of profits earned in the business and of these profits alone, but also that everything in connection with such accounts is based upon the assumption that the undertaking is a going concern, and that, as a going concern, the value of the Goodwill, whether it go upwards or downwards, has no bearing upon the matter. In other words, the value of Goodwill (or of a share thereof) does not crystallise until a sale takes place, and all attempts at an intermediate valuation are idle.

> Dicksee and Tillyard (1920: 91–92)

At the time the writers quoted were published, sole traders and partnerships would have been relatively more important than today, although by 1913 Esquerre had pointed out:

The nature of the goodwill of corporations appears to be quite different from that of the goodwill of sole proprietorships and of copartnerships. When corporations sell their assets, it often happens that the identity of the vendor is lost in that of the vendee. In this case the purchaser does not expect that the customers of the vendor will resort to the old place. He acquires the earning power of an established business whose products will sell, no matter who offers them for sale. He may also, perhaps, figure that with more up-to-date methods of conducting the business through the application of scientific economy and the union of forces which, up to now, had been antagonistic, larger profits will be obtained than could be had before the consolidation of interests took place. For this he is willing to pay a sum of money which may be far in excess of the value of the tangible properties acquired.

> Esquerre (1913/1965: 481)

Financial statements of sole traders and partnerships play a very different role from those furnished to shareholders of listed companies. For the latter, the separation between ownership and management is very clear, and the information required consequently differs greatly from that required by proprietors. The crystallizing of value by way of sale, to which Dicksee and Tillyard refer, is a rare event for an individual proprietor, whereas for a shareholder in a listed company, a sale of shares is a daily possibility. Moreover, at no time has there existed a readily accessible market that enables independent and verifiable determination of the market value of sole traders or partnerships.

In Australia, this dichotomy has been recognized in SAC 1 'Definition of the Reporting Entity', which specifically exempts certain entities from the preparation of general purpose financial reports, defined in para. 6 as being those 'intended to meet the information needs common to users who are unable to command the preparation of reports tailored so as to satisfy, specifically, all of their information needs'. Further, para. 20 notes:

> The greater the spread of ownership/membership and the greater the extent of the separation between management and owners/members or others with an economic interest in the entity, the more likely it is that there will exist users dependent on general purpose financial reports as a basis for making and evaluating resource allocation decisions.

The counterpart provision is found in para. 37:

> In most instances the following private sector entities are unlikely to be required ... to prepare general purpose financial reports: sole traders, partnerships, privately-owned companies and trusts other than those where funds are subscribed by the public.

Walker (2007) has argued that wider disclosure requirements should be made mandatory for a more extensive list of corporations as well as entities with a wide public responsibility, such as charities.

3.3 A US anomaly – goodwill write-up temporarily condoned

The practice of writing up internally generated goodwill based on its estimated value did have some adherents at this time, particularly in the US. Hughes (1982: 48–9) indicates that the practice was utilized, at least briefly, in the period around 1920. This is the only reference located that breaks the nexus between recognition and the need to demonstrate a historical cost:

> ... another problem arose that brought about a good deal of controversy. In the previous discussion, where some item was capitalized under the caption of goodwill (whether the caption was appropriate or not), some consideration had been given, and the amount capitalized as goodwill, rightly or wrongly, had been limited to the fair value of the consideration given. The practice of writing up goodwill departed from this one common thread. It might be thought of as the opposite of the cost principle, with other items (such as the capitalization of certain advertising expenditures) falling in varying degrees between these two extremes. Justification for the practice seems to have relied on an attempt to record the value of goodwill in the accounts. A firm might

be experiencing extraordinary returns, and its management might feel that this good fortune was due to the goodwill built up from advertising. Instead of possibly capitalizing the advertising costs in the goodwill account, a practice itself that was open to controversy, the firm might appraise the goodwill. Goodwill would be debited for this amount, and some surplus account would be credited.

Part of the impetus for this practice stems from the fact that the cost principle was not nearly so accepted at this time as it later came to be. An article in Printers' Ink noted that 'many financiers ... believe that the value of goodwill should be capitalized and that it is readily ascertainable'. The value of goodwill would be appraised so that return on investment would be normal for the year. As an instance of the practice, one writer mentioned that: 'Just the other day a great corporation added $2,000,000 to its statement under the head of good will, and most conservative bankers and investors agreed that the new asset was fully worth that figure' (Basset 1918: 558). Carrying the practice one step further, a goodwill account and a special surplus account might be opened, and a stock dividend would be issued for the same amount. Although feeling that the cost principle should be followed generally, Bell and Powelson (1929: 42) felt that little harm resulted from the foregoing practice.

Hughes (1982: 48–9)

Hughes does note that, at the time, the practice of writing up goodwill 'met criticism from all quarters' even during this period, and that 'virtually no phase of the process from appraisal to presentation was left unscathed'. His use of the term 'fair value' is interesting, particularly as the term was not as rigidly defined then as it is today (see Chapter 2.2 above). It is also noteworthy that 'the cost principle was not nearly so accepted (in the 1920s) as it later came to be'.

By the 1930s, probably reflecting the aftershock of the Great Depression, things had changed. Hughes (1982: 84) refers to a statistic that illustrates why the enthusiasm for revaluing goodwill had probably abated. 'During the eleven-year period 1929–1939, ninety-eight industrial concerns in the United States decreased the values of intangible assets on their books by approximately $786,000,000' (Avery 1942: 354). Hughes also notes:

The old rule, which permitted and in some cases encouraged the recording of unrealized appreciation on the books of corporations, fell into disrepute because of the abuses that were committed in its name, and because of a change in the general concept of the major objective of accounting from the determination of net worth to the measurement of income and earning capacity. Emphasis shifted from the balance sheet to the income statement – a fact duly noted and considered in official publications of the accounting profession.

Hughes (1982: 84)

Fabricant (1936/1976) analysed the accounting practices of 208 corporations listed on the New York Stock Exchange over the period 1925–34. Of these corporations, only sixty valued their intangible assets at more than US $1 by 1934. However, it is apparent from Fabricant's analysis that the writing up of intangibles was practised over this period; such write-ups aggregated more than US$53 million over the period, although write-downs were far greater, exceeding US$308 million. The aggregate figure is misleading, in that the intangible write-ups were carried out by only two companies in 1928 and one in each of the other years from 1927 to 1932 (there were no goodwill write-ups in the other years covered by the sample). In contrast, an average of some ten companies contributed to the intangible write-downs between 1925 and 1934. Fabricant's figures relate to intangibles as a whole, rather than merely to goodwill; it is likely that patents and trademarks were also included in this heading.

In 1938, Walker (1938: 253–9) published an article which contained a detailed case against the recognition of 'Non-purchased Goodwill', which opens with the claim that: 'Accountants, almost without exception, agree that goodwill should not be recognized in accounts until a bona fide purchase has been made'. He lists several major reasons in support of the view that it was 'unnecessary, inexpedient and confusing to recognize non-purchased goodwill in accounts':

i. 'watered stock' frauds of early days, in the perpetuation of which the term 'goodwill' was freely used (apparently to support inflated values of stock issued to the public);
ii. it is inconsistent with the generally accepted function of accounting to recognize an asset represented by the present estimated value of the earning power of a business;
iii. quoting Henry Hatfield, a leading US academic of the early twentieth century, it is correct not to recognize non-purchased goodwill 'because of its vague nature and the difficulty of verifying its appraisal';
iv. the value of the owner's or manager's services should not be brought to account because to do so would represent a conflict between the position of the proprietor as an owner and a purchaser of his own services – a point also made by Yang (1927: 151);
v. capitalization of goodwill would, in practice, be ignored by prospective purchasers, who would place their own value on the business;
vi. goodwill created by above average earnings is better ascertained from the income statement than the Balance Sheet.

Although, by 1936, the American Institute of Accountants (AIA) (cited by Hughes 1982: 77–8) had reaffirmed that 'intangibles are usually stated at cost or some other historical basis without regard to present realizable or replacement value', it still had not expressed any specific prohibition against writing up goodwill values. (At that time, its power was still only prescriptive.)

Hughes (1982: 80) also cites Sanders, Hatfield and Moore (1938: 56–67), writing in the late 1930s: 'It is generally accepted that a value should be placed on goodwill in the books only when goodwill has been purchased. The corollary is that goodwill should not be entered in the books of the business which builds it up'. He qualifies this by adding 'This quote, taken by itself, appears to be a departure from the practice of the time', although the general tenor implies that, even as late as 1938, the practice of writing up goodwill to valuation was only used in a limited number of cases, which supports Fabricant's data.

Walker (1938: 257) also referred to some other instances in which items were recognized under the heading of goodwill.

i. Initial deficits capitalized as goodwill. The capitalization of developmental expenses (or even outright losses) was noted by Montgomery (1934: 312) and condemned. 'To capitalize net losses arbitrarily as goodwill, even during the initial stages of an enterprise, is misleading'.

ii. Discount on stock charged to goodwill. Even harder to support was a practice of capitalizing discount on stock issued (clearly below par) as goodwill. Walker (1938) makes the obvious point that the issue of stock below its par value is *prima facie* evidence that no goodwill exists. The practice was clearly not that unusual; Walker quotes Finney (1946: 315, as cited in Walker 1938: 258) as claiming 'The goodwill account has been chiefly misused by charging it with discount on stock ... (for which) there is no justification whatever ...'.

iii. Organization expenses charged to goodwill. This practice was also roundly condemned by Walker (1938: 258), who pointed out that, by its very nature, a new enterprise could not have goodwill, so that capitalizing organization (or, in modern parlance, preliminary) expenses is conceptually incorrect. This argument should be distinguished from the case in which a new entity is formed to acquire an existing enterprise, which does have goodwill. This is not an uncommon occurrence for a newly listed company, especially when it is easier to structure the share capital of a new holding company to accommodate listing requirements than to restructure the share capital of the existing entity.

iv. Direct write-up of goodwill. This was deemed inappropriate because of the violation of the cost principle and because it would be likely to be overestimated.

Walker's article gives an indication of a number of abuses practised under the heading of bringing non-purchased goodwill to account and which no doubt contributed to the prevailing orthodoxy. While a few of his criticisms are less applicable in a publicly listed corporate context, this does not apply to all of them. Indeed, unwarranted capitalization of expenditure (although not, today, included under the heading of goodwill) is an accounting technique still employed to mask the parlous situation of some modern corporations.

Most notably recently, the giant corporation WorldCom masked increasing losses by the capitalization of some of its operating expenses.

3.4 Non-recognition of internally generated goodwill established in the US

Hughes (1982: 75–80) reviews the history of US accounting pronounce-ments on goodwill in the 1930s and early 1940s. ARB 1 'Introduction and Rules Adopted', which was issued in 1939, mentioned the shift in emphasis from the Balance Sheet to the Income Statement, which carried with it a change in the major objective of accounting from the determination of net worth to the accurate determination of income. With this change of emphasis, any attempt to see the Balance Sheet as a statement of value was discouraged in favour of a rigid adherence to cost principles and, as ARB 1 noted, conservatism in the determination of income.

The AIA (1936: 118, as cited in Hughes 1982: 77) claimed that account-ing was not concerned with valuation but with 'the allocation of historical costs and revenues to current and succeeding fiscal periods', and noted that the procedure of revaluing assets up or down had proved unsatisfactory. This philosophy was very clearly put some years later, in 1960, by Kollar-itsch (1960: 488, as cited in Chambers 1995: 12), who claimed that: 'A new definition for the general balance sheet. ... is long overdue. It would make clear that [its function] is not to review the financial position, but rather it is to show the deferred charges and the unconsumed or inappropriate values for future operations and their financing'. This approach to the Balance Sheet left little room for recognizing internally generated goodwill.

The issue of ARB 24 'Accounting for Intangible Assets', in December 1944, finally established historical cost as the basis for recognition of intangibles, including goodwill. Hendriksen commented that the US view was apposite:

> Costs incurred by a firm to improve its future earning power are gen-erally charged immediately to expense unless they can be directly asso-ciated with specific tangible or intangible assets. Since goodwill represents advantages not specifically identifiable when acquired in the normal course of business, it is not recorded as an asset even though future periods will be benefited. The main reasons supporting this practice are the inability to identify and measure the goodwill created each period and the absence of any logical method of associating these costs with any specific revenue in future periods. This is in accord with APB Opinion No. 17 ('Intangible Assets' – AICPA: 1970) which states that expenditures for 'nonpurchased' goodwill should be deducted from income when incurred. The author agrees with this practice, because no apparent advantage would be obtained by attempting to capitalize goodwill acquired in this fashion.
>
> Hendriksen (1977: 436)

One unusual feature of this comment is that it highlights a concern with matching cost and revenue that is often expressed when considering the amortization of purchased goodwill, but is less common when considering whether to record internally generated goodwill in the first place.

The provisions of ARB 24 with regard to purchased goodwill were extensive, and will be discussed in the next chapter. The requirement therein to account for goodwill initially at cost effectively eliminated the possibility of bringing internally generated goodwill to account.

As mentioned in Chapter 3.1, Skinner (1987: 192–3) had pointed out that the value of 'general goodwill ... grows or diminishes during the conduct of the business'. Goodwill valuations are not constant over time. Even if the forecast cash flows of a business remain constant over time (which is inherently unlikely), the valuation placed upon those cash flows, and hence goodwill values, will vary with changes in both the basic risk free interest rate and the 'risk premium' element of the discount rate applied to those cash flows.

While most justifications for the non-recognition of internally generated goodwill relied on either the difficulty of valuing goodwill or the difficulty of ascertaining its cost, Paton (1941: 405, as cited in Hughes 1982: 82–3) criticized recognition on two other grounds. First, if goodwill were revalued, a credit would have to be made to an account such as 'Reappraisal Surplus', which formed part of Owners' Equity. The ultimate effect of such a credit would be to increase net worth twice: once at the time of the write-up of goodwill and again as excess profits were earned. Therefore, Paton claimed the same thing would be represented twice, both in Owners' Equity and in the asset section of the Balance Sheet.

Secondly, Paton claimed that recognizing goodwill at its true value (and, in making this point, he does not distinguish between purchased and internally generated goodwill) would cause an important distinction between companies to become blurred.

> The adoption of an accounting policy which necessitated the adjustment of asset values in such a way that no enterprise in a particular field earned a rate of above 10 per cent, for example, would destroy an important basis for comparison.
>
> Goodwill, as has been indicated, expresses the value of an excess earning power. It represents the capitalization of the peculiar rights and advantages enjoyed by the supramarginal enterprise. Evidently, then, if goodwill were completely recognized as an asset in the accounts of all businesses in a given industry all unusual rates of return would be thereby annihilated. The most successful company would earn no more than the ordinary competitive rate, the percentage realized by the representative concern. As far as net income rates were concerned all particularly successful businesses would be reduced essentially to the normal or representative level.
>
> Paton (1962: 317–18)

Chambers (1966/1974: 211) makes a similar point. If the present value of super-profits is recognized and capitalized as goodwill, 'all opportunities would seem to be alike and the potential constituents (i.e. potential buyers) could not choose between them. The process is circular and self defeating'.

Similarly, Walker (1938: 254) claimed that 'an accounting policy which necessitated the adjustment of the goodwill account in such a way that no enterprise in a particular field earned a rate above the normal rate would hide an important basis for comparison'.

Of course, the point made by these writers is tautologous. If the amount included among a company's assets for goodwill is defined to be such that the rate of return on those assets, including goodwill, is the 'normal' rate, it follows that the rate of return on the assets in question will be normal for all companies that have followed this accounting procedure.

In practice, different members of an industry are likely to have different risk profiles, given that the existence of a perfectly competitive industry is a theoretical economic limiting case. This means that, even if goodwill computations were based on a normal, or average, rate for a given industry, some firms within it would still earn returns on assets that are higher or lower than the industry norm.

3.5 International Standard IAS 38 (1998)

The extract from AASB 1013 which prescribed the treatment of internally generated goodwill prior to the adoption of AIFRS was quoted in Section 3.1 above. Internationally, IAS 38 'Intangible Assets' is currently definitive on internally generated goodwill, and it follows the principles established in the 1994 IASC Draft Statement of Principles on Intangible Assets:

> 36. Internally generated goodwill should not be recognized as an asset.
>
> 37. In some cases, expenditure is incurred to generate future economic benefits, but it does not result in the creation of an intangible asset that meets the recognition criteria in this Standard. Such expenditure is often described as contributing to internally generated goodwill. Internally generated goodwill is not recognized as an asset because it is not an identifiable resource controlled by the enterprise that can be measured reliably at cost.
>
> 38. Differences between the market value of an enterprise and the carrying amount of its identifiable net assets at any point in time may capture a range of factors that affect the value of the enterprise. However, such differences cannot be considered to represent the cost of intangible assets controlled by the enterprise.

The revised IAS 38, issued in March 2004, contains identical provisions (now paras 48–50) in respect of internally generated goodwill, other than for the fact that it explains that it is not regarded as being an identifiable resource because 'it is not separable nor does it arise from contractual or other legal rights'. (As noted in Section 2.5 above, Chambers also was of the opinion that goodwill should not be regarded as an asset because it is not severable, although he did not distinguish, in this context, between internally generated and purchased goodwill.)

This must be read in conjunction with the provisions of IAS 38, which define an 'intangible asset' and specify the criteria for recognizing it:

> An intangible asset is an identifiable non-monetary asset without physical substance held for use in the production or supply of goods or services, for rental to others, or for administrative purposes. An asset is a resource:
>
> (a) controlled by an enterprise as a result of prior events; and
> (b) from which future economic benefits are expected to flow to the enterprise.
>
> IAS 38 (para. 7)

IAS 38 (para. 19) requires an enterprise to recognize an intangible asset, at cost, if and only if:

> (a) it is probable that the future economic benefits that are attributable to the asset will flow to the enterprise; and
> (b) the cost of the asset can be measured reliably.

In view of the harmonization between Australian and International Accounting Standards, it is interesting to note the differences between IAS 38 and AASB 1013, although both explicitly refuse to permit the recognition of internally generated goodwill:

i. IAS 38, like SAC 4, stresses the need for control by the enterprise if an asset is to be recognized; this is not mentioned explicitly in AASB 1013 as a requirement for asset recognition, although it is probably implied;
ii. IAS 38 is far more emphatic about the need to recognize an asset at cost; AASB 1013 (para. 4.1.1.) cites only the 'difficulty, or impossibility, of identifying the events or transactions which contribute to the overall goodwill of the entity';
iii. AASB 1013, on the other hand, stresses that the extent to which internally generated goodwill is able to generate future benefits and the value of such benefits would not usually be capable of being measured reliably. IAS 38 (para. 38) acknowledges that, to some extent, goodwill may be measured as a residual, but points out that this residual value could not be viewed as a surrogate for cost, even though it 'may capture a range of factors that affect the value of the enterprise'.

Having noted these historical differences, from 1 January 2005, the Australian Standard AASB 138 is identical to IAS 38 following Australia's decision to adopt the International Standards. IAS 38 prohibits the recognition of internally generated IIAs, such as mastheads, brands, customer lists and similar items. The relevant Australian Standards previously permitted both recognition and subsequent revaluation of such assets.

3.6 Some other countries

a. US

At present, the costs of internally developing, maintaining or restoring unidentifiable intangible assets should not be recognized as assets but should be expensed. This was established in APB Opinion 17, issued in 1970, and remains the position in the US. SFAS 142 'Goodwill and Other Intangible Assets', which substantially changed the method of accounting for purchased goodwill, specifically noted that the provisions of APB Opinion 17 relating to internally developed intangible assets were carried forward without reconsideration.

b. UK

The UK position is that internally generated goodwill should not be capitalized. This simple and blanket prohibition is restated in FRS 10 (para. 8), issued in December 1997.

c. Canada

Canadian Institute of Chartered Accountants (CICA) Accounting Recommendation 32 (para. 05(b)), issued in December 2002, specifies that the costs of internally developing, maintaining or restoring unidentifiable intangible assets are recognized as an expense when incurred. Goodwill is defined only in the context of purchased goodwill: 'the excess of the cost of an acquired enterprise over the net value of the amounts assigned to assets acquired and liabilities assumed'.

d. South Africa

The applicable South African Standard, AC 129 'Intangible Assets' (paras 37–38), issued in June 1999, also lays down that internally generated goodwill should not be recognized as an asset. The South African Standard notes that such goodwill is not an identifiable resource controlled by the enterprise, nor can it be measured reliably at cost, thus reiterating two of the major reasons historically furnished for non-recognition.

e. Hong Kong

The Hong Kong Standard on the question of recognition of internally generated control is found in SSAP 29 'Intangible Assets'. It is identical to the South African Standard and quotes the identical reason for non-recognition.

It is evident from the above that there is currently widespread agreement between the international authorities, Australian standard setters and those of other countries that internally generated goodwill is not to be recognized in financial accounts. This principle will continue to be reinforced as countries adopt the IFRS.

3.7 Summary of arguments for non-recognition

Apart from the relatively infrequent and much criticized exceptions that occurred in the US in the period 1910–40, there appear to have been few, if any, instances in which the value of internally generated goodwill has been recognized. The major reasons for this have been deemed largely self-evident, and have attracted little debate in the literature. In summary:

i. In the context of an accounting system based on historical cost, it is difficult, if not impossible, to isolate the cost of internally generated goodwill, as explained in Section 3.1 above.
ii. Even if accounting principles were to move away from a dependence on historical cost, it is difficult to produce a reliable and accurate value for internally generated goodwill. In the limiting case, where there is no purchased goodwill, it would still be necessary, in valuing goodwill, to have recourse to estimates of future cash flows, which are themselves inherently unreliable. Evidence for the latter assertion is provided in Chapter 5.6.

As noted earlier, Paton (1962) provided further reasons why non-recognition is appropriate:

i. He claimed that recognition of internally generated goodwill (usually accompanied by way of credit to Revaluation Reserve) would duplicate the credit to Owners' Equity when the profits generated by that goodwill are subsequently brought to account. However, proponents of amortization of purchased goodwill would similarly argue that failing to amortize has a similar effect in that profits are brought to account by the acquiring company without an offset of the matching cost, while opponents of amortization argue that, given that the value of goodwill is being maintained, the expenses of doing so are being charged against profits as well as goodwill amortization.
ii. Bringing internally generated goodwill to account as an asset would, by definition, mean that all comparable companies would show a similar

rate of return on Owners' Equity, so that the company that does earn an exceptional rate of return would no longer be distinguished. (See Chapter 3.4 above for comments on this contention.)

3.8 Internally generated 'negative goodwill'

The literature search undertaken in preparing this book did not unearth any reference to internally generated negative goodwill. 'Negative goodwill' is a concept defined only in the context of an acquisition. The definitions of negative goodwill quoted in an Agenda Paper (AASB December 2001), while using slight variations in terminology, show a broad consensus, e.g.

i. Australia – 'the excess of fair values of identifiable net assets acquired over the cost of acquisition'.
ii. IASC – 'the excess of the acquiror's interest in the fair value of the identifiable assets and liabilities acquired over the cost of the acquisition as at the date of the exchange transaction'.
iii. US – 'the excess of total market or appraisal values of identifiable net assets acquired over cost of acquisition'.

Similar definitions are furnished in the Accounting Standards quoted in respect of Canada, the UK and New Zealand.

This brief account has shown that Accounting Standards unanimously prohibit the recognition of internally generated goodwill. However, they do not deal with the situation that arises when, independent of any acquisition, the fair value of the company as a whole is less than the fair value of its assets and liabilities. The reason for this, of course, is that the current, conventionally prepared Statement of Position does not purport to reveal the fair values of those individual assets and liabilities, either treated severally or in context as assets and liabilities of a total enterprise.

The influence of market values is not entirely ignored, although it is treated asymmetrically. Current assets are normally stated at the lower of cost or market value, so that declines in value are brought to account while appreciation is ignored. This rule is also rigorously applied, so that a decline in the value of one asset in a class is not permitted to be offset against an increase in the value of another asset in that class. Similarly, impairment provisions relating to fixed assets (including IIAs) ensure that the carrying value is not above recoverable value, although appreciation in value is normally not recognized.

The previously noted recommendation by writers such as Chambers and Sterling that severable assets be valued at net realizable value does address this matter to some extent. Chambers (1961/1986: 88) is quite specific: 'Accounting is concerned with value in only one sense – the values of individual assets and claims. It is not concerned with the value of a going concern *in toto*'.

All financial statements prepared by ASX listed companies use the historical cost framework as modified by Australian Accounting Standards and are produced under the 'going concern assumption', which assumes that assets will be realized and liabilities paid in the normal course of business, unless this is expressly rejected.

AAS 6 'Accounting Policies' (para. 7.1) states: 'The financial report must be prepared on a going concern basis unless it is intended to either liquidate the entity or to otherwise wind up its operations, or there is no realistic alternative but to liquidate the entity or to otherwise wind up its operations'.

Prior to the adoption of an impairment regime, even though an entity was performing poorly and its aggregate value was below the net aggregate carrying value of those assets as revealed by its Statement of Position, the loss of value was not recognized in the financial statements unless and until the deterioration reached a point where the going concern assumption was imperilled. Now the recorded book value of assets may be reduced if their value is regarded as being impaired. This applies to purchased goodwill, but not, of course, to internally generated goodwill, as this would normally never have been brought to account. Impairment could therefore be applied to tangible assets even though the assets themselves may not have suffered a reduction in value (e.g. on a net realizable basis).

3.9 A note on an objective and reliable basis for recognition of internally generated goodwill

In common with these counterparts, and as shown in Section 3.1 above, the old AASB 1013 and the new AASB 138 both state that internally generated goodwill should not be recognized, the former because the value of the future benefits is not capable of being measured reliably and the latter because it is not an 'identifiable resource' and its cost cannot be measured reliably. SAC 4 specifies that '... an asset should be recognized in the statement of financial position when and only when it is probable that future benefits embodied in the asset will eventuate and the asset possesses a cost *or other value* that can be measured *reliably*' (emphases added).

SAC 3 (para. 5) defines reliability as 'that quality of financial information which exists when that information can be depended upon to represent faithfully, and without bias or undue error, the transactions or events that either it purports to represent or could reasonably be expected to represent'. Traditionally, cost data meet the reliability requirement, in the absence of exceptional circumstances.

AAS 18 'Accounting for Goodwill' (para. 5.1.1.) explicitly states that: 'When goodwill is purchased in a business acquisition, the exchange transaction enables the value of goodwill (i.e. the purchased goodwill) to be measured reliably', and similar wording is to be found in AASB 1013. A simple example shows that the same exchange transaction may also enable the value of internally generated goodwill to be determined reliably.

Illustrative example

Assume for the sake of simplicity that all identifiable assets are reflected at an amount that reflects fair value in the books and accounts of Company S (a listed company). H, also a listed company, which has never made an acquisition before and has no goodwill in its books, acquires S. The net asset (book) value of H is $10 million and its assets and liabilities are such that the carrying value is reasonably regarded as being equivalent to the fair value of those net assets. Its market value is $15 million – and the excess of market value over net asset value is entirely attributable to internally gen- erated goodwill.

H acquires S – (net asset value at fair value equal to $4 million) for $6 million, so that the purchased goodwill is $2 million. H pays for S by issu- ing $6 million worth of shares in H. The entry that H will make in its books on the acquisition is:

Fair value of S's assets	$4,000,000
Goodwill	$2,000,000
To Share capital	$6,000,000

If H acquires the shares in S, rather than the assets, the above would be an adjusting entry on consolidation, but the principle would be unchan- ged.

This entry has recognized the value of the acquired company, including goodwill of $2 million. It has not, however, recognized another fact that has become simultaneously apparent. If the value allotted to the buyer is 'fair', it must follow that the share capital of H is undervalued (or that the owner's equity of H is understated in its Balance Sheet). H's Balance Sheet shows shareholder equity of $10 million pre-takeover (i.e. its net asset value). After the takeover, shareholders' equity would, under normal principles, be shown as $16 million.

It is quite clear that the same exchange transaction which valued S and the H shares exchanged for it at $6 million objectively valued the whole of H at $15 million. This could be recorded in the books of H by the following entry:

Goodwill	$5,000,000
To capital reserve	$5,000,000

Traditionally, the recognition of purchased goodwill has been based on the objective valuation inherent in the purchase. The above example shows that the same objective valuation equally justifies the recognition of previously unrecognized internally generated goodwill on the part of the purchaser. An issue of a substantial number of shares in a listed company for cash or cash equivalent to an independent third party would support a goodwill valuation similar to the above, even in the absence of an acquisition transaction, although the illustration is most dramatic in the context of an acquisition.

This point may be demonstrated further by considering the entries that could be made in S's books consequent upon the transaction described above. S, which had presumably not previously recognized goodwill in its books (on the grounds that it was internally generated) could now seek to make an entry raising goodwill as follows:

Goodwill $2,000,000

To capital reserve $2,000,000

on the grounds that the value of the goodwill had been established by an objective third party transaction.

Assume, which is not unlikely, that the directors of H and S are the same after the takeover. The consolidated accounts of H and the accounts of S would both be their responsibility. It would be difficult for them to justify logically why the identical entry to record the identical facts would be permissible in the case of the former financial statements but not the latter. The goodwill on acquisition is identical: it is the goodwill attributable to S at the date of takeover.

The example given here is a limiting case, in that the fair values of H's assets were deemed equal to their carrying value. The conclusion may be subject to the criticism that, as far as H is concerned, the shares issued to S represent a minority shareholding, and thus would be valued, in practice, without a control element. Because of this, it may not be fair to extrapolate the total value of H on a pure arithmetical ratio basis to the value of the shares issued to S; the true value of H, and hence its internally generated goodwill, may well be greater. Nevertheless, the example highlights the contradictions inherent in the asymmetrical treatment prescribed by AASB 1013, and similar Standards throughout the world, for internally generated goodwill and purchased goodwill.

3.10 Reverse acquisitions

An extreme illustration of this anomaly in practice is seen in the case of reverse acquisitions. The phrase 'reverse acquisition' has not been used in AAS to date, but the concept is contained in the new AASB 3 (corresponding to IFRS 3) 'Business Combinations' (Appendix B, paras B1– B3) adopted with effect from 1 January 2005. It refers to the situation in which the acquirer, for accounting purposes, is the entity whose equity interests have been acquired and the issuing entity is the acquiree. The legal subsidiary is denoted the acquirer if it has 'the power to govern the financial and operating policies of the legal parent so as to obtain benefits from its activities' (e.g. if a large proprietary company is acquired by a smaller public company in order to obtain an ASX listing for the former).

In such a case, the cost of the business acquisition is deemed to have been incurred by the legal subsidiary. The accounting consequences for the issuing entity are as follows (para. B5):

i. the fair value of its assets and liabilities is determined;
ii. the deemed cost of those net assets is obtained by determining 'the number of equity instruments the legal subsidiary would have had to issue to provide the same percentage ownership interest of the combined entity to the owners of the legal parent as they have in the combined entity as a result of the acquisition', and then using the fair value of that notional issue by the legal subsidiary (or acquirer) as the deemed cost of the acquisition;
iii. the goodwill of the issuing entity is then calculated as the difference between the fair value of its net assets and the deemed cost of the acquisition.

On this basis, the issuing entity will revalue its assets and liabilities to fair value and recognize goodwill in its consolidated accounts. The Standard (para. B8) provides that, while reverse acquisition applies to the consolidated accounts, it does not apply to the accounts of the issuing entity itself.

It therefore follows that, in the consolidated accounts of the issuing entity after a reverse acquisition, the internally generated goodwill of that entity is brought to account, whereas normally the goodwill of the legal subsidiary would be recognized in those financial statements. In this case, the fair value of the deemed acquirer's shares is expressly considered to be a reliable basis for calculating the shares of another legal entity. However, the Standard still does not permit the recognition of the goodwill attributable to the deemed acquirer in the consolidated accounts; apparently, the fair value of its shares is not reliable enough for that purpose, despite the fact that it is expressly stated to be reliable enough to make a similar determination for the issuing company. The new International Standard IASB 3 does not attempt a logical justification of this obvious anomaly. (IASB 3 supersedes IAS 22 'Business Combinations', which also contained the concept of reverse acquisitions and prescribed how to account for them. The process was similar, although described in considerably less detail, to that in the new Standard. The procedure has been in vogue, for example, in Singapore, since 1 October 2000 when SRS 22 came into force in almost identical terms to IAS 22.)

3.11 A further anomaly

Purchased and internally generated goodwill are occasionally identical, yet are accounted for in a different manner.

In 1993, Australia's then corporate regulator, the ASC, indicated its 'concern about the disclosure of goodwill and share values in the prospectuses of several recent public company floats'. In each case, a supplementary prospectus had been required by the ASC when:

i. a company acquired a business from a vendor, issuing shares to the vendor, usually at par;
ii. the company, within a very short time, issued shares for cash to the public at a substantial premium.

The ASC contended that:

i. the price to the public, including the premium, was the 'fair value' of the shares as required by the then AASB 1015 'Acquisitions of Assets', because 'the price at which they could be placed in the market will usually be an indicator of fair value';
ii. the prospectuses did not adequately disclose the value of goodwill involved in the issue of shares to the vendor, as required by AASB 1013 'Accounting for Goodwill', which was then in force.

To illustrate the problem using a hypothetical example, assume that the newly formed public company had purchased the business at its net tangible asset value for $10 million from the vendor, satisfying the purchase price by the issue of 10 million shares at $1 each (their par value). The company then issued 5 million shares to the public at $2 each, for cash to raise $10 million for working capital purposes. The company had sought to bring these transactions to account as illustrated in Table 3.1a.

The ASC commented that, in such a scenario:

> Non-compliance with the accounting standards means that investors are not provided with the information they need in order to make an informed decision as required by Section 1022 of the Corporations Law. In addition, the amortization of goodwill over the period of its expected benefit will also impact on profit projections for subsequent accounting periods. The absence of disclosure of material details as required by accounting standards, or lack of information which would provide a true and fair view, will be viewed by the ASC as potentially misleading and deceptive conduct.

Following this strongly expressed view, the ASC required that a supplementary prospectus be issued, showing the position outlined in Table 3.1b.

Table 3.1a Illustrative Balance Sheet no. 1 – Holding company buying an existing business (vendor shares issued at $1 par value)

	$'M	$'M
Business purchased, at cost		10
Net identifiable assets		
Cash		10
Net assets		20
Represented by:		
Issued share capital		
15 million shares		
At par	15	
Share premium	5	20

Table 3.1b Illustrative Balance Sheet no. 2 – Holding company buying an existing business (vendor shares issued at same value as issue to public)

	$'M	$'M
Business purchased, at cost		
Net identifiable assets	10	
Goodwill	10	20
Cash		10
Net assets		30
Represented by:		
Issued share capital		
15 million shares		
At par	15	
Share premium	15	30

Goodwill, in this Balance Sheet, was $10 million which, as the ASC pointed out, would have to be amortized over the period of its expected benefits, whereas there was no goodwill shown in the previous illustrative Balance Sheet.

The paradox resulting from the rigorously enforced Accounting Standards can be seen when Illustrative Balance Sheet No. 2 is compared with that which would have resulted had an existing company, which owned *exactly the same business having the same assets and liabilities and at the same stage of development*, sought a listing on the ASX in order to raise the same amount of capital from the public as that illustrated above.

To simplify the example, assume that, at the date of listing, the net assets of $10 million were represented by 10 million shares of 50 cents par value and accumulated profits of $5 million. The issue to the public, by definition, remains constant at 5 million shares of 50 cents each at a premium of $1.50 to raise the $10 million required for working capital.

Illustrative Balance Sheet No. 3 (Table 3.1c), compiled for a company which, by definition, is identical in substance to that portrayed in Illustrative

Table 3.1c Illustrative Balance Sheet no. 3 – Existing business makes a public issue

		$'M	$'M
Net identifiable assets			10
Cash			10
Net assets			20
Represented by:			
Issued share capital			
Represented by:			
Issued share capital			
15 million shares			
Original shares	At par	5.0	
New shares	At par	2.5	
	Share premium	7.5	15
Retained profits			5
			20

Balance Sheet No. 2, reflects no goodwill at all; Balance Sheet No. 2 shows goodwill of $10 million and reflects the Accounting Standards correctly because it represents the entity resulting from the acquisition of an existing business by a new company, rather than the continuation of an existing company.

It is important to stress that the 'valuation' of the company and the existing business at $30 million is confirmed by the identical transaction, viz. the issue of one-third of the issued capital of the company to public shareholders for $10 million. The assets of the businesses are identical. The number of issued shares is identical. SAC 3 (para. 24), which was issued in August 1990, prescribes that 'if financial information is to be both relevant and reliable it is necessary that the substance rather than the form of transactions or events be reported'. If attention is paid to the substance, rather than the form, of the illustrated transactions, the Balance Sheets should be identical (except possibly for the minor detail of the allocation of subscribed capital between par value and share premium. This distinction would in any event no longer be necessary.)

However, in terms of the relevant 1993 Australian Accounting Standards and their rigid enforcement by the ASC, the newly formed company would have been required to amortize an amount of $10 million against profits over an arbitrarily determined period, whereas the existing company would not have had this requirement; in fact, had the existing company sought to raise goodwill of $10 million in its Balance Sheet, the ASC would no doubt have reacted with equal displeasure to that which it demonstrated when the new company sought not to recognize it. There can be no greater demonstration of the illogicality of the 'Alice-in-Wonderland' accounting rules that have governed the treatment of goodwill.

This is not only a theoretical issue, but a practical one, as Brown observed:

The reduced reported EPS of companies that have acquired goodwill may have a negative impact on those companies' share prices and hence increase the costs of capital to the companies. In turn, this will disadvantage these companies when competing with similar companies who have internally generated goodwill. The industries where this problem will be most noticed are those dominated by companies which tend to be priced at a substantial premium to their net tangible assets such as service industries.

Brown (1988: 4–5)

It is true that forecast cash flow, rather than 'reported EPS' (earnings per share), is the major determinant of the company's value. Nevertheless, by reducing reported profits, unwarranted and substantial amortization of goodwill may impact adversely upon a company's ability to pay a dividend, making it less attractive to investors. EPS itself is a widely quoted measure, and directors are generally averse to reporting items that reduce earnings and hence EPS. At best, the consequence noted by Brown will be negligible; at worst, his tentative conclusion may have some validity.

3.12 The link between purchased and internally generated goodwill

Ma and Hopkins (1988) extended this argument significantly. They contended that 'a meaningful economic interpretation can be developed for internally generated goodwill but not for purchased goodwill'. There is an inability to identify the stream of benefits specifically associated with goodwill arising on acquisition' (ibid. 75). The following argument is based heavily on the Ma and Hopkins article.

Under historical cost principles, it is generally assumed that cost, in a third party transaction, establishes a fair value for the assets concerned at the time of the acquisition. In the case of the acquisition of a parcel of assets, their total cost may have to be allocated for accounting purposes over the individual assets in accordance with a discretionary determination.

Ma and Hopkins (1988) examine goodwill in three situations:

i. internally generated goodwill;
ii. purchased goodwill where the acquired company is expected to continue to operate autonomously;
iii. purchased goodwill where the operations of the acquired company are wholly or partially integrated with those of the purchaser.

a. Internally generated goodwill

A firm is a dynamic open system in that its productivity is generated by transactions between the firm and its environment. In such a system, '[an] enterprise's earnings may well exceed the normal return on an identifiable assets investment base and enterprise value may exceed the total value of those net assets' (ibid. 77). The excess of those earnings over the normal level of return is, of course, the super-profit, as described by Leake (1948), and goodwill, mathematically, is the present value of that projected stream of super-profit returns.

The value of goodwill can therefore be attributed, in total, to two synergistic interactions:

i. the interaction of assets and other sub-systems of the enterprise with each other (the enterprise is a *dynamic* system); and
ii. the interaction of the enterprise itself with its environment (the enterprise is an *open* system),

and mathematically quantified as the sum of the super-profit generated by those interactions. This is equal, of course, to goodwill quantified in the more conventional manner as the difference between the total value of the enterprise and the total fair value of the identifiable tangible and intangible net assets. If goodwill has never been purchased, either quantification serves to define internally generated goodwill.

b. Goodwill on acquisition of an entity designed to operate autonomously

In this case, price is initially substituted for value (i.e. value has been subjectively determined), but otherwise the basic equations are no different from those affecting internally generated goodwill. The implicit assumption is that no new synergies arise as a result of the acquisition. The goodwill of the acquired enterprise is still equivalent to the sum of its internal and external synergies existing at the time of the acquisition; equally, the goodwill of the acquirer is not affected.

c. Goodwill on acquisition of a wholly or partially integrated entity

Years of experience as a public accountant in practice, dealing with significant acquisitions by both public and private companies, have shown me that it is rare for an acquisition to be designed so that the newly acquired entity continues to operate as a totally separate unit – certainly in any period beyond the short run. Nearly all acquisitions are made with a view to partial or total integration with the operations of the purchaser. Even if physical integration does not take place, the entity acquired is seen to be compatible in other ways, such as increasing the size or range of the group's operations, so that overall group profits will be increased beyond the sum of the previous individual parts.

Once integration is proposed, the expected synergies expand. They are:

i. new synergies arising between the interaction of the assets and sub-systems of both companies;

ii. increased synergies arising between the interaction of the enlarged group with its environment; and

iii. direct benefits to the acquirer arising from the acquisition, such as control of a source of supply or an outlet, or diversification which may be viewed as reducing the appropriate risk factor to apply to the acquirer's earnings.

The synergies set out above cannot be merely aggregated with the first level of synergies available at the level of internally generated goodwill prior to the acquisition. The interactions that arise between the assets of the merged groups in fact replace those previously existing independently in the purchaser. Similarly, the interaction of the merged group with its environment may release synergistic benefits (or disadvantages) arising out of the combination itself. To illustrate this, Ma and Hopkins (1988) cite a possible benefit (easier access to capital markets) and possible disadvantages (increased control problems, potential anti-trust problems, more difficult employee relationships).

d. Determination of the purchase price of an entity to be merged

The shareholders of the target will theoretically not accept less than its existing fair value, i.e. its value as an enterprise that will not be merged. It may be assumed that this is the minimum purchase price. The purchaser is theoretically prepared to pay up to the difference between the value of its own capitalized earnings (i.e. without the acquisition) and the expected value of the merged enterprise. This is based on the combined earnings, including synergies arising from the merger and any improvement expected in the fair rate of return on assets applicable to the merger (i.e. any market re-rating of the acquirer following the merger).

The actual price struck will fall somewhere between these values, depending on the relative bargaining strength and knowledge of the parties. To the extent that the purchaser actually pays less than the maximum amount it was prepared to pay, it has made an apparently advantageous purchase. The advantage increases the lower the purchase price, i.e. the closer the purchase price to the minimum purchase price as defined above.

e. Quantum of goodwill paid in the case of an entity acquired to be wholly or partially merged

In accordance with normal accounting practice, goodwill on acquisition is accounted for in the same way whether the goodwill relates purely to the acquired benefits (the acquired entity is to operate autonomously) or whether a portion of the goodwill relates to expected synergistic benefits arising from combination with the acquirer. This has two logical flaws:

i. some part of the 'goodwill' is not due to pure economic factors (i.e. earnings related) but due to 'non-economic considerations such as relative bargaining skills and knowledge asymmetry' (ibid. 81);
ii. the pure goodwill of the acquired entity as an autonomous unit is not relevant to the acquirer; what is relevant is the total addition to earnings and the capital value of the merged enterprise. In the extreme case, all earnings previously generated by the acquired company in that form may cease, e.g. following total integration.

One could imagine a case in which the only purpose of making an acquisition is to close it down and dispose of its identifiable assets in the expectation that elimination of a competitor would of itself increase the earnings of the acquirer to an extent sufficient to justify the cost of the acquisition. As the identity of the acquired entity becomes lost, post merger, the distinction between internally generated goodwill and purchased goodwill is more difficult to sustain. The acquiring entity can be viewed in either case as having incurred expenditure in order to increase its own future profit (i.e. as distinct from the profit of the acquired entity). To be consistent, it would appear that, in such a case, goodwill on acquisition should be written off immediately; indeed, having regard only to the fact that the acquired entity had been closed down, this might appear to be a logical accounting treatment that would be followed by a number of reasonable accountants, notwithstanding the increase in expected earnings consequent on the elimination of the competitor, and the current requirement to allocate goodwill viewed as synergistic across the appropriate cash generating units of the acquirer.

The difference between that case and normal internally generated goodwill is that the amount paid to acquire or to develop the potential increase in earnings (and hence value) of the acquirer is immediately ascertainable, i.e. it has a specific cost, unlike the myriad of costs incurred to build the synergies that normally give rise to internally generated goodwill. However, there are some commercial examples of similar costs, such as the purchase and installation of a large computerized programme, excluding hardware costs, and accompanying expenditure on staff and systems aimed at contributing to future profit by improving customer relations management or factory efficiency. Costs of this nature are conventionally either written off immediately or amortized over a comparatively short period.

f. Ma and Hopkins' (1988) comments on AAS 18

It should be noted that these comments (ibid. 82) relate to the version of AAS 18 issued in 1984:

> The examination of goodwill from a dynamic open system perspective makes it possible to view goodwill as a product of the synergistic benefits

generated by interactions of assets and other sub-systems within the firm and between the firm and its environment. However, the effective valuation and reporting of the capitalized value of the expected earnings flows associated with such activities clearly presents problems for accountants, specifically in the lack of identification of the flows with specific assets or entities. Attempts to solve these problems within the formal double entry framework have ranged from no recognition and hence no identification of flows in the case of internally generated goodwill, to a 'forced' identification of flows with the acquired entity in the case of goodwill arising on an acquisition.

Ma and Hopkins (1988) continued by pointing out that internally generated goodwill can thus be given an understandable economic interpretation. Despite this, AASB 1013 forbids recognition of this source of benefits 'since, it is argued, no asset acquisition has taken place'. This is a little simplistic with regard to the version of AASB 1013, updated in 1996, which prohibits recognition on two grounds: the difficulty of identifying transactions generating internally generated goodwill and the difficulty of measuring the value of the resultant benefits. On the other hand, purchased goodwill 'does not admit of any simple economic explanation (in terms of a relationship to a defined stream of benefits)' (ibid. 82).

Logically, as purchased and internally generated goodwill represent benefits with similar risk characteristics, they should be accounted for in the same way. Equally, as purchased goodwill often cannot be associated with a specific stream of benefits, its systematic amortization is difficult to justify.

The authors conclude:

> By choosing to identify this latter category of goodwill (i.e. purchased goodwill) exclusively with the purchased entity, accountants have opted for convenience rather than reality. The manifest danger is the practice of Alice-in-Wonderland accounting, which will lead inescapably to a loss of professional credibility in the business community ... the search for a correct method of recording and amortizing goodwill within the historical cost framework is unlikely to succeed.

The problem identified by Ma and Hopkins (1988) may be seen as a special case of that examined by Thomas (1969) in his consideration of the 'allocation problem'. Thomas points out the difficulties experienced in achieving a theoretically justifiable basis of allocating inputs of depreciable assets and other non-monetary goods (including many never reported as assets) over a number of accounting periods. He concludes:

> When the entity's revenue function incorporates interaction effects, the net-revenue-contributions approach usually will find *all* non-monetary inputs hopelessly entangled, blurred together. ... Insofar as

cost-accumulation and matching involve allocations of nonmonetary economic goods, these allocations are almost always arbitrary; no general solution to this problem is possible within the framework of present allocation theory and present conventional rules.

Thomas (1969: 76–7)

The following chapter examines the attempts to find 'a correct method of recording and amortizing goodwill' in the limited context of purchased goodwill.

4 Purchased goodwill

Historical treatment

Confusion over goodwill was one of the principal reasons for setting up the ASC (Accounting Standards Committee), yet that committee grappled with it for nearly fifteen years. All that time, they were driven into two competing factions with mutually incompatible views about how to treat the topic, so that SSAP 22 finally allowed two incompatible methods as alternative options and did not even insist that either one be used consistently by a single reporting entity.

(K. Wild, as cited in Brown and Chrispin 1998)

4.1 Introduction

While accounting for internally generated goodwill has been shown to have received only limited attention from accounting theorists and standard setters, this has not been the case with respect to purchased goodwill. The reason for this is clear. The purchase of goodwill is an identifiable transaction, unlike the development of internally generated goodwill. It results in identifiable expenditure, often substantial, which requires to be accounted for in some way because it fits within the historical cost framework. This chapter examines the previous attempts to account for purchased goodwill. The following chapter examines the prescriptions of the current Australian and comparable international Standards.

Under historical cost accounting, the purchase of a trading, non-corporate entity generates goodwill in the accounts of the purchasing entity itself. On the other hand, the purchase of one company by another generates goodwill only in the group, or consolidated, accounts of the purchaser or its holding company. It is not necessary to distinguish between these two cases, other than to note that, in the latter case, the consolidated financial statements are relevant rather than those of the purchasing entity itself.

In the great majority of cases, goodwill is positive. It is calculated (AASB 1013: 5.7) as 'the excess of the cost of acquisition (i.e. the purchase consideration plus any costs incidental to the acquisition) incurred by the entity over the fair value of the identifiable net assets acquired'. 'Identifiable net assets' are not restricted to tangible net assets, but include all assets that are capable of being both individually identified and specifically recorded in the books of account.

Having arrived at a residual balance asset, the issue then arises as to whether it needs amortization. In earlier times, such a decision was largely driven by the desire to match expenses against income received. This issue is now examined in more depth.

4.2 To amortize or not to amortize?

As Hughes observes, this is one of the longest running debates in accounting history:

> In 1909 Henry Rand Hatfield listed an illustrious group of contemporary accounting authorities who supported amortization and then listed an equally illustrious group who advocated permanent retention. In 1946 an Australian writer used the same approach listing several current authorities on both sides of the issue. (Norman S. Young, 'Valuation of Goodwill and its Treatment in Accounts', The Australian Accountant, November 1946, pp. 532–33). In the almost forty years separating the two writers, little had changed except the names of those involved in the controversy.
>
> Hughes (1982: 115)

The AIA commented, in 1952, that 'with the change from increased net worth to the realization test of income (circa 1920 in the United States), it became common to speak of income determination as being essentially a process of matching costs and revenues' (AIA 1952: 28, cited in Chambers 1995: 587). This process may be defined as the allocation of expenses incurred by an entity to the period in which revenues generated by those expenses have been recognized in the accounts of the entity.

While the matching process has long been generally accepted as an accounting process, it has not lacked critics. It results in items being carried on the Balance Sheet that are neither assets nor liabilities, but rather deferred items of expenditure or income that are being 'carried forward' until an appropriate accounting period in which they can be recognized in the Profit and Loss Account in terms of the relevant Accounting Standards. Despite this, the so-called 'primacy of the income statement' ensured that the matching process, which aims at the most meaningful and accurate statement of income, remained the prevailing wisdom from about 1930 and for most of the twentieth century. (SAC 4, reissued in March 1995 to replace an earlier version in March 1992, gave a lukewarm endorsement to the matching principle, expressly refusing to regard it as an 'overriding concept'. A strong dissenting view was expressed by Lonergan (1995), who believed it to be 'a fundamental accounting concept'.) Paton and Littleton put it succinctly as early as 1940: 'The primary purpose of accounting ... is the measurement of periodic income by means of a systematic process of matching costs and revenues' (Paton and Littleton 1940: 123, cited in Chambers 1995: 367).

Leake (1930) put the case for amortization in the light of his super-profit theory, arguing that a payment of goodwill represented a purchase of super-profits and that, accordingly, it should be amortized against those profits as a cost of acquisition. In answer to one of the most frequently voiced objections to goodwill amortization, Leake replied:

> It is urged against the writing off of the cost of goodwill – and often it is a fact – that the goodwill of a prosperous undertaking earning large surplus profits is worth no less now than it was when it was purchased ten or twenty years ago. The question is asked: 'Why, therefore, should the goodwill be written off?' The answer is that the present goodwill is, in the main, not the goodwill which was bought ten or twenty years ago.
>
> Leake (1930: 77)

Leake's position was supported by Paton and Littleton:

> ... purchased goodwill represents an advance recognition of a debt for a portion of income that is expected to materialize later. It follows that the amount expended for goodwill should be absorbed by revenue charges during the period implicit in the computation on which the price was based in order that the income not paid for in advance may be measured.
>
> Paton and Littleton (1940: 92–3)

The strength of the 'matching principle' is evident in the reasoning of these authors. On the other hand, there were some who merely wished to write off goodwill even without regard for any matching principle, such as Sanders, Hatfield and Moore (1938):

> The writing off of such intangible assets as goodwill evokes scarcely any protest, even when it is recognized that substantial goodwill exists ... when actual consideration has been paid for goodwill, it should appear on the company's balance sheet long enough to create a record of that fact in the history of the company as presented in the series of its annual reports. After that, nobody seems to regret its disappearance when accomplished by methods which fully disclose the circumstances.
>
> Sanders, Hatfield and Moore (1938: 14)

This view is supported, to some extent by a comment in an article (Alfredson and Murray 2002: 221–2) appearing in *JASSA*, the *Journal of the Australian Society of Securities Analysts*, 'When analysts are asked about goodwill amortization expense, a common response is that they add it back to profit', indicating that analysts are not concerned with meticulous calculations of goodwill amortization, but rather with estimates and analysis of future cash flows. These are not affected by goodwill amortization, which is a cash neutral book entry.

However, Walker (1964: 210–16), in a thoughtful article from which a number of quotations in earlier chapters have been cited, draws on the 'matching' process to come down firmly in favour of systematic amortization: 'In accordance with a primary function of accounting to match costs and incomes, the cost of purchased goodwill should be amortized as a means of matching the cost of securing the income against the income actually received'.

To summarize, those pro-amortization have always argued that the principle of matching costs and revenues demands it, and that this argument takes precedence over any resultant distortion of the Balance Sheet. In any event, the Balance Sheet is not viewed as a statement of value in any real sense.

Esquerre set out his opposing position:

> The importance of the asset goodwill, when it has been acquired by purchase, cannot be overestimated. There is no other asset of a concern, the sale of which would be so effective in bringing operations to an end.
>
> Why goodwill, having been acquired at a cost which is somewhat considerable, and constituting in some instances the only truly valuable asset of a concern, should be outlawed, and sentenced to gradual expulsion from respectable books of account, is one of the perplexing puzzles which accounting offers to its students. Accountants who would never permit the reduction of a physical asset by the estimated amount of depreciation which it may or may not have suffered during a given period have no scruples at all when it comes to goodwill. Still, it seems that if a concern has paid a large sum to acquire the goodwill of another, and has not only retained it, but even increased it, there is no apparent reason why so-called conservation (sic) should demand the writing off of the asset, to the detriment of the very profits which its purchase gave the right to expect.
>
> Esquerre (1913/1965: 482)

However, Esquerre also notes: 'One of the reasons frequently advanced in favor of this writing off policy is that the valuation of goodwill, being based on a given number of years' average net profits of the vendor concern, less a fair return on capitalization, its cost is consumed concurrently with the effluxion of the period for which it has been purchased. This is, indeed, an extreme view. It is unequivocally expressed in *Day's Accounting Practice*: "Goodwill is a legitimate asset in an industrial enterprise and the most accepted method of computing the amount of goodwill is to take the total profits for the last five years and deduct from them five years' interest on the capitalization at seven per centum per annum, the balance is goodwill. The rate of interest is based on the assumption that no capitalist would invest in an enterprise unless he were assured at least seven per cent annual return. Goodwill should be written off the books during five subsequent years, by charging off one-fifth against each succeeding year'".

Some writers have embraced the 'value' concept, although in a guarded way. Sanders, Hatfield and Moore (1938: 17) fall into this camp: 'While exact agreement with real values cannot be attained, yet accounts will be more respected in proportion as they avoid arbitrary or fictitious values, and reflect real values as nearly as possible'. Finney (1934: Vol. 1, 317) put the view for retention of goodwill simply, although, by 1946, he had changed his mind in favour of systematic amortization: 'If profits have continued or increased, the goodwill has not diminished; to write off the goodwill creates a secret reserve, understating the net worth and accumulated profits, a procedure that may be prejudicial to the interest of stockholders wishing to market their holdings'. Staub approached the issue from another angle:

> ... there is no basic reason for, or scientific method of, writing off or amortizing the cost of Type B intangibles (including goodwill), the value of which is continuing. To require the compulsory amortization of intangibles, the value of which is being currently maintained or even enhanced, seems a departure from the 'going concern' concept of financial statements and an attempt to provide for losses which may be sustained on termination or liquidation of an enterprise at some time in the future.
>
> Staub (1945: Chapter 8: 5)

With small variations, which will be traced in the remainder of this chapter, the argument has continued along much the same lines to the present day.

Consensus has fortunately been reached on at least one point. Writing goodwill off during the good times while providing no amortization in the bad times was discredited fairly early. This afforded one of the few examples in which the debate about goodwill has generated both humour and impeccable logic. As Couchman said, 'To put it briefly, if you can write it down, you need not; if you cannot, you should!' This may be the single most quoted comment about goodwill (Couchman 1924: 138, cited in Hughes 1982: 51). Or, as noted in *The Accountant* ('Goodwill: Its Nature, Value and Treatment in the Accounts', December 6, 1913: 817 (author not identified), cited in Hughes 1982: 51), 'After once placing a value upon your books, if you actually have it, write it off; if not, then continue it and make a show of having it. If you have a thing, you haven't; if you haven't, you have'.

4.3 Momentum, super-profits and matching costs with revenues

a. Momentum theory

While most writers in this genre based their comments on the 'super-profit' theory of writers such as Leake and Paton, Nelson (1953) proposed the 'momentum theory of goodwill'. This suggests that, in purchasing an existing business, businessmen are focused not so much on a revenue enhanced stream of annuities, but on a marketing or promotional 'push'. Although Nelson limited his examples of the advantage of such a push to the marketing advantage, in fact there are many other practical advantages attached to purchasing an existing enterprise rather than starting one from scratch. Examples of these are the presence of an existing, trained staff, established production and administrative procedures and even mundane advantages such as existing telephone connections and, for example in the case of a restaurant, necessary Council permission to carry out the operation. Indeed, many of the cases being made for a specific recognition in financial accounts of 'intellectual capital' in the form of employee knowledge and skills depend on arguments inherent in Nelson's momentum theory.

Nelson (1953: 492) comments that this 'push' is not everlasting, but rather like a momentum or running start to which the purchaser must continually add his own energy in order to keep the business in existence. The investment ought therefore to be charged against the income of the period during which the original 'push' will exert its influence. Owing to the nature of this momentum, its amortization would in most cases be over a life of from two to ten years, and should be carried out by the straight line method. The estimate on which amortization is based should be the one on which the purchaser originally based his bid for the business, and ought not to be adjusted in the light of later events.

Under this theory of momentum, it is not necessary for the enterprise to have made a profit, or even to demonstrate the likelihood that it will earn super-profits in the future. It is only necessary that an entity should be able to offer prospective buyers a marketing, promotional or other 'push', which makes it more attractive than the prospect of developing a similar organization from scratch. A client company had operated for some three years and had incurred substantial operating losses. During this time, however, the company had built up a substantial organization, involving:

i. a mailing list of several thousand potential customers for its product (tapes and compact discs, predominantly in the musical arena);
ii. detailed systems for updating and maintaining the list;
iii. systems for handling the receipt of money via the mail and by direct bank transfer from its list customers;

iv. well developed purchasing procedures, linked to demand from its customers, and contacts with major suppliers;
v. effective means of attracting additional subscribers to its list;
vi. a well trained and effective staff.

Despite its lack of past profitability, the company was acquired, at a goodwill of several million dollars, by an international corporation seeking to
establish a presence in Australia. It should be stressed that the goodwill
payment far exceeded the value of the customer list taken in isolation (a
value that could be established by reference to the prices of lists available
from commercial list brokers). Clearly, in this case, the past transactions or
events that had created value for the company concerned were the development of the items listed above. It became clear during the negotiations that
the overseas purchaser was concerned primarily with the time saving offered
by the purchase of an existing enterprise as against the delay and incon-
venience of building a similar enterprise as a start-up.

The momentum theory does not seem to have been widely discussed in
the literature on the goodwill issue, although, as indicated, it does offer a
practical explanation for the payment of goodwill that is not linked to a
'super-profit' concept. Insofar as momentum results in a saving of time,
adherents of the matching principle would support amortizing the payment
over the time saved; opponents of amortization would argue that, while
companies continued to produce super-profits, there is no need for such
amortization.

b. Super-profits

Leake's definition linking goodwill with the prospect of the entity's earnings of
a super-profit has been set out briefly in Section 4.2 above. He considered that:

> ... the purchaser is in the position of having already paid away a share
> of each future year's estimated super-profit. For this reason the pur-
> chaser must make some annual provision out of super-profit earned to
> refund this share before he can safely enjoy the remainder.
>
> Leake (1948: 24)

and, accordingly, he recommended writing off the cost of the super-profit in
the period over which it was expected to be earned. He noted that purchased goodwill would always be eroded by factors such as competition,
innovation by others and technical obsolescence of the acquired assets.
Notwithstanding this, the overall value of goodwill owned by an enterprise
might increase, but he claimed that this was due to internally generated
goodwill arising after the goodwill was purchased in the acquisition. The
prohibition against the recognition of internally generated goodwill meant
that the requirement to amortize remained valid, despite the apparent

maintenance of goodwill; he did not question the principle that internally generated goodwill should not be recognized.

The intellectual justification of the positions espoused by both Nelson and Leake is based on the desirability of matching costs with the anticipated revenue produced, or the future expenditure saved, by such costs. For Nelson, the expenditure concerned is justified by the time saved by the purchase of an existing enterprise and should be written off over that time: in the momentum model, the enterprise will be expected to earn higher profits in that time than would have been earned by a new business. The Leake model is more explicit: super-profits have been purchased at a cost that is *ipso facto* required to be offset against those super-profits when they were planned to arise. The writing off of goodwill over the period of greater profits will match costs and revenues, if accurately computed, during that limited period. After that period has expired, any increased profits will presumably have been due purely to self-generated goodwill.

As noted earlier, this theoretical position was strongly supported by Paton and Littleton, among others, at the time. However, the formulation of the super-profit concept results in the need to amortize goodwill over a limited period, due to the formula adopted and the need to utilize a high rate of return. This meant that material expenditures on goodwill were followed by material charges against profits, which in turn aroused opposition from those who considered such charges to be illogical at a time when goodwill was being maintained or increased, and for whom the 'matching' argument was less important than the distortions that they considered resulted from the strict application of the principle.

c. Possible analysis of goodwill into sub-categories

Lonergan (1995: 6–7) concurs that purchased goodwill should be written off because it depreciates in value over time, although he does not specifically cite the 'matching' principle. However, he attempts to remove the effect of an arbitrary period of amortization for goodwill by differentiating between its constituents. His list of items constituting goodwill is referred to in Chapter 2.3 above. He further analyses goodwill on acquisition into a number of different categories, being those having a short life (0–3 years), a medium life (3–7 years), a long life (7–10 years) and a very long life (10–20 years). Examples of items of goodwill falling into each category are:

- qualities of marketing team, marketing expertise (short/medium);
- consumer preference loyalty (medium/long);
- economies of scale (medium/long);
- know-how (short/medium);
- technical skills (short/medium);
- individuality/uniqueness, monopoly position (short/long).

This analysis adds a level of sophistication missing in the earlier expositions, by isolating the components of purchased goodwill and attaching a defined life to each of them. It does require a series of decisions, likely in practice to be fairly arbitrary, as to how to allocate the aggregate amount of goodwill to its components.

This approach is in line with that advocated in AASB 1013 (para. 5.6.1.):

> In determining the amount of purchased goodwill, the purchaser needs to recognize all the assets acquired, whether of a tangible or intangible nature. This might involve recognizing some intangible assets which, if internally generated by the purchaser, would not normally be recognized as assets because the absence of an exchange transaction prevents them from being measured reliably.

It accords with similar provisions in the existing comparable Standards in the US, the UK, Canada and New Zealand, as well as the IASC, although all of these refer to 'identifiable' assets acquired in the context of an acquisition of assets rather than 'tangible or intangible' assets. (See review of comparable standards in AASB Financial Reporting Council 2000.)

It had also been recommended by Tearney (1981), who claims that, as far as possible, the term 'goodwill' should be eliminated, and that the excess of the purchase price over net identifiable assets needs to be further broken down to identify its constituent elements. He cites with approval an article appearing in the January 1964 *Journal of Accountancy* describing how goodwill arising on one particular acquisition was dealt with in the accounts of the acquirer. Initially, the excess purchase price was allocated in part to the cost of patents (which would today be treated in terms of AASB 138 as an identifiable intangible). Another asset identified was 'partially completed drawings and designs for new products', which were amortized over three years, having regard to the normal obsolescence for the company's products and the estimated profit contribution of the new products in question. The asset 'engineering staff' was identified and valued; the amortization period allotted was seven years, this being the normal period of staff turnover in the industry. (The new Accounting Standards do not permit the recognition of an assembled workforce as an asset.) After these allocations, a comparatively small unidentified excess remained to be treated as conventional goodwill, although even this amount could have been allocated to asset descriptions such as 'high quality product' and 'good customer relations'. He concluded:

> Valuation techniques have been developed to a point where goodwill no longer need appear on financial statements. All assets acquired in business combinations, regardless how intangible they may be and whether or not they appear on the acquired entity's Balance Sheet, should be

identified, valued and disclosed, thereby removing one of the thorns in the accountant's side.

Tearney (1981)

Tearney's view about the development of valuation techniques was expressed in 1981, but few, if any, of the Accounting Standard setters appear to have shared it until comparatively recently.

If valuations were regarded as sufficiently reliable to serve as a basis for goodwill impairment calculations, one of the major barriers to the recognition of internally generated goodwill would be removed. The current Standards dealing with the recognition of goodwill on an impairment basis implicitly concede that valuations carried out on a prescribed basis are at least reliable enough to support the existing book value of goodwill in a company's Balance Sheet or indicate the degree to which such goodwill is impaired and should be written off (see Chapter 5).

4.4 The 'double counting' problem

One major criticism of the amortization principle is enunciated by those who point to the well known 'double counting' problem. During the amortization period, the acquirer will also be incurring expenses in order to maintain goodwill. These will be written off against profits at the same time as the purchased goodwill is being amortized, thus creating a 'double charge' against profits for the period in question.

This point was clearly set out (in an Australian context) by Lonergan (1995):

> The real issue in the goodwill debate is not whether acquired goodwill (ie, the goodwill arising in a takeover that AASB 1013 requires to be amortized) depreciates in value over time. Clearly, it does. And, because it does depreciate, it is also clear that it should be written off over its expected useful life. Indeed ... it is apparent that the maximum 20-year write-off period for acquired goodwill permitted in AASB 1013 is actually generous.
>
> What is arguably unfair about the Australian accounting standard requirements is that the reported profits are reduced not only by the write-off of acquired goodwill but also by the write-off of internally generated goodwill (that is, replacement goodwill, being the annual expenditure by companies to maintain, replace or expand their goodwill).
>
> Lonergan (1995: 6–7)

Note that Lonergan defines internally generated goodwill in this paragraph in terms of its cost, not in terms of its addition to the value of the enterprise. He justifies the need for writing off these costs as follows:

In a successful business, goodwill is nurtured and grows. Yet accounting standards worldwide preclude the recognition of this internally generated goodwill. The reason for forbidding the recognition of internally generated goodwill is simple. If its recognition were permitted it would lead to widespread overstatement of reported results. Simply put, the value of internally generated goodwill is so difficult to measure that its recognition is forbidden in all major countries of the world.

This, of course, emphasizes that the cost of internally generated goodwill is not only difficult to isolate, but also has little or no direct relationship to incremental value.

He also maintains: 'Despite what accountants may write into the books, investment analysts, smart investors and takeover merchants all over Australia will simply add back the amortization of goodwill in their analysis, on the basis that it has no cash effect' (Lonergan 1988: 26). This is supported by the fact that the ASX, as part of its Standard Form of Report, routinely required listed companies to disclose profits both before and after amortization of goodwill prior to the introduction of the new Accounting Standards.

Gynther (1974), as noted previously, draws a very strong distinction between the attributes of goodwill on the one hand and how it is measured on the other. Taking a different view, he concludes:

> ... the purchase price of goodwill (assuming that an attempt has been made to give present values to all assets purchased) must be treated for what it really is, and goodwill must at least be left intact as long as the earning power of the entity is unimpaired. Consideration must be given to amortizing goodwill only when and if earning power diminishes.
>
> Gynther (1974: 228)

Gynther, unlike Lonergan, does not draw the distinction between the value of the purchased goodwill at the time of purchase and the value generated by subsequent internally generated expenditure on the part of the acquirer; he is concerned with the fact that it is illogical that an asset whose value has been preserved should be written off, thus implicitly equating purchased goodwill with its internally generated counterpart.

His 1974 comments look prescient in the light of the goodwill impairment review policies now enshrined in Accounting Standards. In some ways, it is surprising that his recommendation has taken so long to become mainstream, especially given the fact that the argument he presents has great appeal to businessmen. Company directors have long considered it illogical to amortize goodwill, especially when its value has demonstrably increased; the accountants' traditional devotion to historical cost and the carefully drawn distinction between the two types of goodwill has little pragmatic appeal.

4.5 Other arguments against amortization

a. *Effect on the cost of equity capital and acquisitions*

Brown (1988: 4) pointed out that the introduction of the Accounting Standards Review Board (ASRB; now AASB) 1013 in Australia, which forced companies that had purchased goodwill to amortize it, created a dichotomy between those companies and companies with self-generated goodwill; the former group would be at a disadvantage. It was postulated that this rule might increase the cost of equity capital for those companies forced to amortize goodwill.

In practice, it is by no means certain that the suggested effect would eventuate. The profits of companies with internally generated goodwill were depressed in the past by the writing off of expenses that generated goodwill; the profits of those who purchased goodwill will be depressed in the future by its amortization. For example, assume two companies with identical goodwill factors, acquired at an identical cost, one purchased and the other internally generated. The relative degree to which the cost of raising equity capital would be affected is difficult to predict. It would depend on the extent to which the market viewed the reduction of future profits as against the reduction of past profits as being more important in setting the appropriate equity price for the companies in question.

In similar vein, it has often been pointed out that the accounting treatment of goodwill amortization, because of its depressing effect on reported profits in the future, could thwart takeovers and acquisitions that would otherwise be beneficial. In this connection, in a 2001 article originally contained in the *Princeton Business Journal* and reissued on the Internet, (obtained via http://www.fleet.com/m_and_a_advisors/article_1.pdf), George Moosburner, the managing director of Fleet M&A Advisors, commenting on the recent change to an impairment review of goodwill rather than compulsory amortization, noted:

> Opponents (of purchase accounting, as against pooling) argued that companies could not have completed many recent mergers – and achieved the efficiencies they produced – if they could not use pooling. Amortization of goodwill, they said, reduced earnings per share, making the transactions unattractive to shareholders.

Perhaps the feature of pooling accounting most attractive to businessmen is that, where adopted, it eliminates the need for goodwill to appear on the Balance Sheets of the pooled companies or to be amortized in their Profit and Loss Accounts. Moosburner also commented: 'Eliminating goodwill amortization (under the new rules) may make deals economically viable for buyers, helping them justify higher prices. It also puts US buyers on equal footing with many foreign buyers, who have not had to recognize or amortize goodwill'.

The impact of accounting methods on business acquisitions arouses strong comment, such as the following, written while pooling was still permitted in the US, unlike Canada:

> Canadian firms face a huge competitive disadvantage from the perspective of their investors. ... This is because U.S. firms do not have to value their acquisitions at fair value and as a result do not have to allocate a large amount to goodwill (so basically it is hidden). Whereas Canadian firms on the other hand are forced to amortize goodwill and consequently their future earnings are reduced and the all-important 'earnings per share' figure declines.
>
> Some Canadian companies are discouraged from undertaking acquisitions, since they would be at an accounting disadvantage to their American counterparts. ... We understand that a number of ... investment bankers and venture capitalists are encouraging Canadian firms to set up shell companies in the U.S. to avoid this problem.
>
> CATA Alliance discussion paper (undated; www1.cata/advocacy/accounting.pdf)

In an Australian context, Ernst & Young responded to the introduction of the new US Standard SFAS 142, and its contrast to the Australian requirement to amortize goodwill, with a similar series of comments and suggestions to enable local clients to 'narrow the competitive disadvantage' with US companies. These included the formation of a US subsidiary and the structuring of transactions to minimize goodwill. Another recommendation was to allocate the purchase price in an acquisition to maximize other intangibles that could be amortized over a long time, pointing out that, under the US Standards, the impairment test for other identified intangible assets is far less onerous than that applied to goodwill (Ernst & Young 2001: section 2).

There has been some research on whether some companies have suffered a competitive disadvantage because of goodwill accounting standards. A 1991 study by Choi and Lee (1991: 219–40) compared takeover premiums paid for US companies in the UK, where firms at the time could take a direct write-off and therefore avoid periodic amortization charges, and the US, where firms predominantly operated under an amortization regime. The firms based in the UK were found to pay higher acquisition premiums.

The effect of goodwill amortization on reported profits is heightened in countries where, like Australia, the charge is not tax deductible. At the Australian corporate tax rate of 30 per cent, for example, pre-tax earnings of AUS$143 are required to cover a goodwill amortization charge of AUS $100. Some countries, such as the US and Brazil, do allow limited tax deductibility for goodwill amortization.

In extreme cases, amortization of goodwill might reduce profits to an extent that materially reduced the ability of the company to pay a dividend, despite the fact that the company might have ample liquidity to do so. This is especially true if the acquired company has a high ratio of purchased goodwill to identifiable assets, as is typically the case for an acquisitive service company (although it should be noted that goodwill arising only on consolidation would not cause this problem, as dividends are payable from reserves of the holding company). An accounting policy or convention should not be allowed to frustrate events that would otherwise be economically advantageous. Share buy-backs might be used to alleviate this problem. They can, however, never replace a regular dividend programme because they are more complex to execute, have differing tax consequences and affect accepting shareholders in a different manner from those who choose to retain their shares.

It is likely that commercial imperatives, driven by considerations of this nature, have led the current trend to replace amortization of goodwill with a policy that does not require amortization if the value of purchased goodwill has not been impaired.

b. Goodwill should not be amortized on a time basis

A further argument against a rigid programme of goodwill amortization is that it appears to suggest that loss of value is time based, in a similar way to that by which the provision of depreciation of plant and machinery reflects the loss of value of that asset in normal circumstances. A key difference is that goodwill, unlike plant, is not consumed in the process of production; indeed, it could be argued that, in the absence of unusual circumstances, every sale tends to increase goodwill.

One variation, briefly employed by a number of companies in Australia in the early 1990s, was the amortization of goodwill on a 'reverse sum of digits' basis. (Companies using this method included Southcorp Holdings, Pacific Dunlop, Mayne Nickless and Amcor.) This satisfied a requirement that goodwill had to be systematically amortized, and had the advantage for businessmen that the amortization charge was extremely low in the early years. Although there was some logical support for this method of amortization in that purchased goodwill might well maintain the greatest proportion of its value in the early years after acquisition, the method aroused the ire of the then Australian Securities Commission (ASC), which effectively outlawed the procedure in November 1993 (ASC Practice Note No. 39 'Accounting for Goodwill').

c. Distortion of profit resulting from acquisition cost

The value of goodwill is set by the purchase price of the acquired company (and, possibly, if shares are used, the valuation of the acquirer at the time of purchase). This could introduce considerable distortion, depending on market sentiment at the date of the acquisition. Amortization would distort profits, either positively or negatively, according to whether a company had been acquired cheaply or at an unusually high cost.

Lonergan (2004: 85–90) also notes that the consideration paid in an acquisition that consists largely of the offeror's shares can be valued at very different amounts, depending on the date chosen to determine the market price of those shares. He quotes an illustrative case in which the consideration could be valued at a very wide range, as follows:

$1.44 billion based on the share price specified in the offer, which was actually lower than the price range over the bid period;

$1.76 billion based on the offeror's share price at the offer date;

$2.16 billion based on the price at the end of the offer period, when the market had presumably factored in the likelihood that the bid would succeed, as well as the anticipated synergy benefits.

As he points out, accounting for the acquisition which was (almost certainly) incorrect was based on the lowest of the above prices. Adopting either of the higher prices would have increased the purchased goodwill figure very materially, with important effects on annual amortization and profit.

The recently adopted AASB 3 defines 'acquisition date' as 'the date on which the acquirer effectively obtains control of the acquiree', with 'control' in turn being defined as 'the power to govern the financial and operating policies of an entity or business so as to obtain benefits from its activities'. Normally, fair value is measured at the acquisition date, although the Standard also makes provision for acquisition by successive, or serial, share purchases. These provisions substantially maintain the provisions of AASB 1015, which were introduced in November 1999. As Lonergan notes, the US currently specifies that it is the value on the offer date that is to be used for the purpose of accounting for the acquisition, but it is expected that the US will modify its rules to conform with the international and Australian position.

The more that is paid for a company (given its net tangible assets), the less will be the future profit reflected by the merged entity under an amortization policy. The rate of return provided by a given level of profit will, of course, vary inversely with the price paid. On the other hand, goodwill amortization will cause a greater distortion of the amount of reported profit (as against the rate) if the value of goodwill is maintained or increased. While this would appear obvious to an intelligent businessman not steeped in accounting principles, an accounting technician drawing on traditional cost based logic could counter this argument, as did Walker.

It is as incorrect to relate amortization to the value of intangibles as it is to relate depreciation to the value of fixed assets.

The basis for the most confusion on the question of amortizing goodwill can be traced to the word 'value'. Though accounting is not a process of valuation, writers continue to reach conclusions with reference to the treatment of goodwill on the thesis that its present value has changed or has not changed. Depreciation charges are not made in an attempt to show present value, but as a means of allocating the cost of the asset over the period of its estimated usefulness. Goodwill amortization charges are of the same nature. The fact that the value of the building or the goodwill has increased during the year is beside the point. In general, asset values have skyrocketed during the past fifteen years, but this increasing of values did not eliminate the need for depreciation charges on buildings and the systematic amortization of purchased goodwill.

Walker (1964: 234)

Comments such as these are interesting, because they show a devotion to form over substance that is a feature of much accounting literature. Walker's comments were originally made in 1953, when it was not common to advocate any form of 'value' recognition. The demand by users of financial statements that they should be relevant and useful has led to some breaches in the hitherto impenetrable wall of historical cost accounting. For example, 'skyrocketing' asset values, particularly in the fixed property area, have now led to mandatory depreciation charges for buildings in the financial statements co-existing with accounting recognition of regular asset revaluations. Some companies, in particular banks and insurance companies, now reflect operating investment assets on a 'mark to market' basis. Even today, however, no Standard permits upward revaluation of goodwill; at best, amortization charges can be avoided if goodwill values are not impaired.

Walker himself cites three powerful arguments furnished against amortization:

i.   to write off goodwill when it has not depreciated is overconservative and creates a secret reserve, which is bad accounting. Goodwill suffers no decline in value so long as the earning capacity of the enterprise is maintained;
ii. the degree to which goodwill exists is shown by the maintenance of profits. Amortization is not required, although it is permissible to write goodwill down when it is declining in value;
iii. since appreciation of goodwill is not permitted to be recorded, neither should depreciation, especially as the extent of the depreciation cannot be accurately measured. Walker (1964: 238)

d. *The view of the Securities Institute of Australia (1989)*

The views of the Accounting for Intangibles Subcommittee of the Securities Institute of Australia are interesting, coming, as they do, from a body relying heavily on published financial statements for the purposes of investment analysis. As such, the Securities Institute has a clear vested interest in the reliability and relevance of accounting data. They commented (IASC 1989: 26) in relation to a draft goodwill Standard (later to be issued as AAS 18):

> It assumes that goodwill is a wasting asset in all circumstances. This is clearly open to question. The standard does not recognize that goodwill may be maintained, increased or dissipated through good or bad management, ongoing expenditure or market forces. Further, it ignores the fact that some intangible assets have a life in excess of any arbitrary write-off period.

This is typical of the objections that have led to the adoption of impairment criteria for writing off goodwill, rather than arbitrary amortization. However, the criticism, when expressed in 1989, was not effective in having the draft Standard modified; as mentioned previously, the amortization principle expressed in AAS 18 lasted until 2005.

Highlighting the problems faced by analysts under the amortization regime, a number of further problems were also raised in the same article in connection with the proposed Standard:

> It distorts the rate-of-return analysis by affecting both the numerator and denominator.
>
> It encourages avoidance techniques such as revaluing licences or making selective revaluations.
>
> It ignores the corresponding goodwill of the purchaser issuing shares with a goodwill element in their price. This aspect appears to have been largely ignored in the literature, but is important. It has been explored in Chapter 3 above.
>
> It encourages inconsistent treatment between companies and over time.
>
> It distorts the matching of costs and revenue (e.g. 'maintenance expenditure' on advertising).
>
> It fails to acknowledge that accounting concepts do not recognize some fundamental valuation issues (such as NPV) and this failure is partly reflected in goodwill.

4.6 The Financial Institution Accounting Committee (1999)

Having reviewed the arguments for and against amortization, it is instructive to consider the widely contrasting views expressed by the Financial Institution Accounting Committee (FIAC) of the US in a letter dated 15 July 1999, commenting on the draft proposals on 'Accounting for Goodwill' issued by the FASB prior to the adoption of the 'impairment' method. The majority view concluded:

> The financial statements cannot show an investor the return on investment that a company has achieved on its investment unless the

amortization of goodwill is reflected in the income statement. Rate of return analysis (return on assets and return on equity) is a meaningful technique, a measure of an institution's performance which should include all elements of both the return and the investment to prevent misleading interpretations. The asset base should omit expenditures that have been consumed or impaired at the end of the fiscal period. Absent more compelling evidence of consumption or impairment, the goodwill asset should be amortized systematically and consistently from company to company. Similarly, the equity base should reflect the reduction for the portion of goodwill consumed or allocated systematically.

The income of an institution is not properly stated unless all costs are deducted from related revenues. Unless amounts paid for goodwill in a business combination are charged to future revenues, the income of the continuing company is overstated. Goodwill is similar to most other assets of a business. Because goodwill is a cost incurred in anticipation of future income, the cost should be amortized in the periods that future income is realized.

The amortization of the goodwill asset does not necessarily imply that the goodwill asset can be accurately measured subsequent to the combination. Instead, it implies that some form of amortization is preferable to no amortization and is preferable in reporting return on investment and return on equity than immediate and total write-off.

On the other hand, a minority of the members of FIAC argued, *inter alia*:

The amortization of an arbitrary amount of purchased goodwill in the determination of income does not accurately represent the cost of resources consumed to produce that income.

Most analysts and creditors remove goodwill amortization in their calculation of earnings per share, return on assets and return on equity. If financial statements are to be meaningful to users, the periodic amortization of goodwill should not be reflected in the income statement.

These contrasting attitudes resulted in widely differing recommendations by the majority and the minority members of FIAC. The majority recommended:

Although the goodwill asset should be systematically amortized to income, the amount of earnings before amortization should be highlighted in the income statement. Earnings per share should be calculated both including goodwill amortization and net of goodwill amortization. Both EPS calculations should be mandatory requirements. This requirement would permit comparability between financial statements and would assist the work of analysts, who normally deduct goodwill amortization from earnings.

The minority took a predictably different pragmatic view:

> A viable solution adopted in the United Kingdom is to treat goodwill as contra-equity instead of an asset, charging it off immediately against equity and completely avoiding the income statement. This removes goodwill from the statement of condition, outside the income statement, and creates more comparability of earnings.
>
> For decades accountants have argued over the existence, value, and write-off period for goodwill. It is time to end the debate and recognize conservative reality. Just as in the fairy tale, 'The Emperor Has No Clothes', goodwill cannot be consistently valued or reliably measured and should not be placed on the Balance Sheet. Income statements should not be burdened with arbitrary amounts of goodwill amortization for extended periods of time. (The proposed MCS would satisfy this recommendation.)

Finally, in concluding its letter, FIAC ensured that it had covered all bases: 'We also acknowledge that a third recommendation would be to record goodwill and periodically test it for impairment'.

Plus ça change, plus c'est la même chose ('The more things change, the more they stay the same'). The confusion exhibited in 1999 by FIAC after so many years of accounting analyses and disputation on this issue is a prime example of the validity of Sterling's lament that accountants recycle ideas rather than resolve problems. In this connection, it is instructive to review some of the major prior authoritative accounting pronouncements and developments.

4.7 Nominal value

There have been times when the practice of reflecting goodwill in the Balance Sheet at nominal value was generally accepted. In the US, ARB 43 'Restatement and Revision of Accounting Research Bulletins' was issued in 1953. It disapproved of goodwill write-offs against retained surplus. The 1951 Annual Reports were the last reports published in the US before the contemplated changes were widely published. Leonard Morrissey (Backer 1966: Chapter 9) quotes a sample of 600 industrial and commercial corporations that was surveyed in 1951 by *ATT*, an annual publication of the American Institute of Certified Public Accountants. Of that sample, 161 reflected goodwill in their 1951 Annual Reports, and 82 per cent of that number chose to show goodwill at a nominal value.

By 1963, 153 out of the 600 companies surveyed by *ATT* reflected goodwill, but the percentage reflecting goodwill at a nominal value had fallen to 30 per cent. It is interesting to note that the balance was almost equally split between those that amortized goodwill (33 per cent) and those that carried it unamortized (37 per cent). (These statistics are obtained from the sixth (1952) and eighteenth (1964) editions of *ATT*, at p. 86 and p. 78 respectively.)

Morrissey notes that reflecting goodwill at nominal value could result from either a lump sum write-off at a prior date or a reduction to nominal value as a result of systematic amortization. In most cases, a nominal carrying value indicated an earlier write-off against surplus, as permitted prior to the issue of ARB 43; it was probably an effort to indicate that goodwill did exist, despite the fact that prevailing accounting practices mitigated against its continued recognition as a substantial asset.

A similar situation existed in Canada at that time. CICA (*Financial Reporting in Canada*, sixth edition) reported that, of the 103 companies surveyed that reported intangible assets, thirty-six recognized them at nominal value. The survey was not limited to goodwill, but goodwill was the most frequent intangible asset recognized.

Hughes (1982: 99) states that, as late as 1927, the fourth edition of Montgomery's *Auditing* made virtually no mention of nominal valuation of goodwill but, by 1934, the practice was popular enough for the fifth edition, published in that year, to comment specifically on it. Montgomery pointed out that nominal valuations were usually defended on the grounds that no one was misled, and the reader was put on notice that the cost of goodwill bore no relationship to its value at balance date. This might be conservative and more justified for intangibles than for other assets. However, Montgomery did note that minority shareholders and uninformed readers might be misled as to the real value of their stock. Hughes notes further:

> The practice of nominal valuation of goodwill might be viewed as part of the general trend toward conservatism then present. The write-down to $1.00 was only a slight modification of complete write-off of the account, offering the advantages of write-offs while testifying to the presumed existence of the asset. In the case of tangible fixed assets and intangibles whose usefulness was limited in duration, the practice relieved current and future income of charges that otherwise would have been necessary and was criticized for so doing. Goodwill's duration had constantly been a point of contention, however, and the same criticism directed toward goodwill did not carry nearly the same significance.
>
> Hughes (1982: 100)

Hughes' point regarding 'testifying to the presumed existence of the asset' has some validity, particularly in the context of internally generated goodwill. It could be argued that only a very unsophisticated reader of financial statements would be totally unaware of the possibility of goodwill, even if there were no mention of it in the financial statements. Nevertheless, it would seem to do little violation, even to traditional accounting principles, to carry goodwill at a nominal value in traditionally prepared financial statements, with an appropriate note to guide readers as to its valuation. Inasmuch as it at least forces the reader to confront the existence of goodwill, this treatment is a marginal improvement on the total write-off of goodwill, as discussed below; this would apply whether goodwill is internally generated, purchased or a combination of the two. However, as discussed in later chapters, it would certainly not represent the preferred treatment.

4.8 Significant developments in the US

a. ARB 24

In December 1944, the AICPA Committee on Accounting Procedure issued ARB 24, which dealt only with purchased intangibles. Intangibles (including goodwill) were classified into type (A), in which by law, regulation, agreement or intrinsic nature, there was evidence of limited duration, and type (B), in which there was no ostensible limited term of existence, such as goodwill in general. (ARB 24 actually referred to these classifications as (a) and (b); the font has been changed to eliminate confusion with the designation of sub-headings.)

While both types (A) and (B) were initially to be recorded at cost, the former was to be amortized over the estimated limited duration period of benefit. Two options were allowed for type (B) intangibles:

i. retain indefinitely at cost;
ii. systematic amortization in the income statement.

The previous practice of writing off type (B) intangibles against surplus (particularly capital surplus) even though unimpaired, described as 'a long-established and widely approved practice', was discouraged, but not totally forbidden.

These options obviously afforded a wide discretion, although, if circumstances changed to indicate that the life of the intangible had become limited, the company was required to adopt:

i. systematic amortization in the income statement; or
ii. partial write-down to earned surplus, followed by systematic amortization via the income statement.

A type (B) intangible that became worthless could be written off to either earned surplus or the income account. It is evident that the treatments permitted covered most of the accepted methods at the time.

b. ARB 43

In 1953, the AICPA issued ARB 43, which retained the classification of intangibles into types (A) and (B). However, a major change was the fact that the immediate write-off of purchased goodwill on acquisition against either earned or capital surplus was now prohibited; it was still permitted to retain goodwill at cost or write it off against future profits via systematic amortization. Interestingly, if changing circumstances resulted in an intangible previously viewed as type (A) changing its category to type (B), there was no mandatory requirement to amortize it, although amortization via systematic charges to income was encouraged. In fact, the Bulletin specifically notes: 'Where the intangible is an important income-producing factor and is currently being maintained by advertising or otherwise, the period of amortization should be reasonably long'.

Only when it became reasonably evident that an intangible was worthless did ARB 43 require it to be written off, and then preferably in the income statement rather than against earned surplus.

c. *Writing goodwill off against owner's equity – ARS 10*

The argument for this method of accounting for purchased goodwill was notably put, in a US accounting context, by Catlett and Olson (1968) and supported by Spacek (1969).

In the US, in particular, there has been a long, protracted and heated debate as to the relative merits of using the pooling or purchase methods to record acquisitions. (See, for example, discussion of this issue in Zeff (1972).) The former merely aggregates the assets and liabilities of the acquired entity with those of the acquirer, bringing them to account at their existing book values. The purchase consideration is adjusted to record the acquisition at net book value. By definition, pooling does not bring any additional goodwill into the financial statements of the purchaser. The intellectual justification of pooling lies in the assumption that, once two enterprises are effectively combined, each party is entitled to carry its cost base and retained earnings into the merged enterprise, rather than allowing this privilege to the acquirer only.

The purchase method of accounting, on the other hand, has as its base premise that the purchase is to be accounted for on the basis of its realistic cost to the purchaser and with regard to the fair values of the assets and liabilities acquired. It requires the purchaser to account for these factors, with the result that, unless the realistic purchase price can be accurately allocated in total to the fair values of identifiable assets and liabilities, there will be a residual in the form of either positive or negative goodwill.

However, once immediate write-off of goodwill was outlawed, the distinction between purchase and pooling accounting became very important. Previously, it had been possible to avoid the impact of purchase accounting, as far as goodwill was concerned, by writing it off immediately to earned surplus. Now that this was no longer possible, the attractiveness of keeping goodwill entirely off the Balance Sheet via pooling was enhanced. It is interesting to contrast this with the contemporaneous position in the UK and Australia where the immediate write-off of goodwill continued to be an option so that there was little pressure in favour of the pooling alternative.

Perhaps for expediency, the issue of ARB 48 in January 1957 considerably relaxed the criteria under which pooling had been permitted. For example, in the wake of the popularity of conglomerates, the previous requirement that pooling required a 'similarity of activities' criterion fell by the wayside, as did the requirement that the size of the enterprises concerned be comparable. Broadly, any business combination that resulted in the exchange of stock for other stock or for property could now be accounted for as a pooling as well as a purchase.

Pooling was attacked on many grounds, notably because it effectively permitted goodwill to be written off against capital surreptitiously, by the simple expedient of understating the value of shares issued in connection with a business combination, thus effectively frustrating the express prohibition of such write-offs established in ARB 43. In so doing, it also appeared to violate the accounting principle that all charges should be reflected in the income statement. Catlett and Olson (1968) specifically rejected the pooling method of accounting for an acquisition, placing their recommendation to write goodwill off against Owners' Equity (via retained surplus) firmly in the context of purchase accounting and the consequent goodwill figure arising as described in the previous paragraph. It should be mentioned in this context that the pooling method is now expressly forbidden in the US, in terms of SFAS 141 'Business Combinations', issued in 2002. Pooling has been banned in Australia, Canada, Hong Kong and New Zealand, and the IASC also now insists on the purchase method of accounting for acquisitions, per IFRS 3.

The reasons given for their recommendation to write goodwill off against owners' equity, as drawn from Chapter 10 of their study (the Summary), may be summarized as follows:

i.   The role of accounting is to provide information which the investor can use in arriving at his opinion of the value of a business; accounting does not determine that value.

ii. The principal test of the soundness of accounting principles lies in the usefulness of the resulting information.

iii. The Balance Sheet provides information useful to investors and creditors, about the separable resources and property rights of a business, subject to the limitations of the cost basis. The cost basis is 'necessary in accounting even though it may restrict the usefulness of financial statements', acknowledging that the Balance Sheet is more useful the closer the amounts ascribed to individual resources and property rights are to their current values determined objectively.

iv. Financial information is most useful when prepared on a comparable basis.

v.   Goodwill differs from the elements of a business. It is not consumed or utilized in the production of earnings; it is a result of the expectation of earnings.

vi.   It exists only as part of the value of the business as a whole, and is not separable.

vii.   Its value is not cost related and is subject to sudden and wide fluctuations.

viii. The record of past earnings primarily governs the market price of the company's stock and the value of the enterprise as a whole.

ix.   The then existing practices of accounting for goodwill were inconsistent with the matching of costs and revenues and hence distorted reported profits.

x.   Expenditure on goodwill represents expenditure of a company's reserves, which can be restored and augmented only if earnings are realized later. It is accordingly a reduction in stockholders' equity and should be accounted for as such. Accounting for purchased goodwill in this manner is also consistent with the accounting (or, more precisely, the non-accounting) for the goodwill value of the continuing entity with which the purchased goodwill has in fact been merged.

xi.   Purchased goodwill does not belong as an asset in the Balance Sheet, the objective of which is to show the separable assets and resources used in the production of earnings. It is 'the value at one point of one segment of the business' and can have no continuing significance.

xii.   Goodwill is a result of earnings or of the expectations of them; amortization has 'an improper circular effect' because it 'may affect the values those earnings are designed to measure'.

The MCS treatment of goodwill proposed here, involving, as it does, the immediate writing off of purchased goodwill against owners' equity, retains all the advantages cited by Catlett and Olson (1968).

The study was subjected to some trenchant criticism. Philip L. Defliese, in a commentary on (and attached to) ARS 10, stated that the best that could be said of it was that it was 'a pragmatic approach to "Non-Accounting for Goodwill"'. It avoided the problem by getting rid of a troublesome item, rather than solving it. 'Resurrecting the spirits of the late 20's and early 30's, when in the interests of conservatism, it was popular to write off anything that might embarrass future reported results, just won't do'.

Defliese also made the point that, if purchased goodwill has a limited life and is to be amortized against earnings, thus diminishing those earnings, a purchaser would be as well off buying municipal bonds. He stated further that shareholders need to know what was paid for the asset and whether the company still considers it valuable, and whether the company's earning power was self-developed or purchased. If goodwill is immediately written off, readers of the financial statements would have no way of ascertaining directly whether the purchased goodwill still continued to have a value and, if so, how much.

Paton's contemporary commentary described the proposal as 'fundamentally objectionable', pointing out that an asset was not inherently tangible or physical, but was an economic quantum. 'A brick wall is nothing but mud on edge if its capacity to render service has disappeared; the molecules are still there and the wall may be as solid as ever, but the value is gone'. Paton contended that, in fact, the proposal was not consistent with the manner in which self-generated goodwill was treated. In that case, the expenditure giving rise to goodwill was routinely charged against operating expenditure over a number of accounting periods, rather than being charged against shareholders' equity as a lump sum. On this reading, amortization of goodwill against earnings over a period would be a more consistent treatment. (A similar point was made in the commentary by Reed Storey, the Director of Accounting Research at the APB.)

Spacek (1969) was the leading supporter of the Catlett and Olson (1968) proposal. Perhaps it is no coincidence that he headed the firm of Arthur Andersen, in which the authors of the study were partners, so that the proposal may well have represented a 'house view'. In commenting on ARS 10, Spacek based his defence on the need to make financial statements useful to investors and creditors, rather than management. He pointed out that goodwill was not consumed in the profit-making process, but can grow or cease to exist instantly, sometimes in the opposite direction from current profits. Its value was dependent upon a vast number of factors, many independent of the business itself. Goodwill value is 'the child from the marriage of the current net income with the investors' state of mind. Accountants do not create values and it is not their job to "second-guess" market prices'. The basic concept that must govern the accounting for goodwill is that it is not an asset that can be reflected in financial statements because it is based upon an 'opinion value' continually determined by investors. The MCS accommodates Spacek's view by reflecting goodwill in a complementary statement that reflects his 'opinion value' precisely.

Backer's comments are reproduced at length because they are a good summary of the arguments in favour of and against ARS 10.

> Strong arguments can be raised against this procedure. Since goodwill constitutes a payment for anticipated excess earnings it is not unlike other assets from which future benefits are expected to be derived. Thus, failure to reduce earnings by an amortized portion of goodwill produces a mismatching of revenue and costs, and an over-statement of income and return on stockholders' equity. It may also be difficult for stockholders to understand why a dilution of equity immediately takes place as a consequence of the purchase of goodwill. Nor does it seem correct to compare a write-off of purchased goodwill with internally generated but noncapitalized goodwill resulting from advertising, marketing and similar expenditures since these expenses were charged to income rather than surplus.

Nevertheless, as a pragmatic solution to the problem, writing off goodwill to earned surplus has much to commend it. Although our interviews with security analysts, bankers and corporate executives were concluded prior to the issuance of Research Study No. 10, the author's recommendation in regard to the write-off of goodwill is consistent with the views of the majority of those interviewed. As has been indicated, bankers routinely delete goodwill from customers' Balance Sheets. Security analysts also would regard implementation of this recommendation as an improvement in financial reporting practices since it would enhance intercompany comparisons. In effect it would equate business combinations accounted for on a purchase basis with those handled as a pooling of interests. It also would eliminate the effect on income comparisons of disparate amortization policies. As has been noted, many company managements also would welcome the opportunity of eliminating an elusive assets (sic) of questionable value from the Balance Sheet without impairment of reported earnings.

Backer (1970: 152)

Hughes quoted some further interesting arguments against the Catlett and Olson position.

Setting up goodwill as an asset and subsequently amortizing it resulted in charges in the income statement for cost of earning power that, according to Spacek, were wrong and potentially misleading. Hylton (1964: 30) countered this opinion with 'What charges are there on an income statement which do not represent the cost of earning power?'.

One writer felt that immediately writing off goodwill was 'tantamount to saying that someone deliberately threw his money away'.

In addition to inferring that goodwill was not an asset, the direct write-off method also implied that it did not subsequently become an expense and should not be deducted in the income statement. Thus, income for which an expenditure was made will appear on the income statement with no indication that an expenditure was made to acquire this income. Should the expected income not be realized, again, income will not be offset by the cost incurred in hope of that future income. ... The hallowed directive to 'match revenue with related expense' seems to be ignored by the direct charge-off.

If goodwill was considered neither an asset nor an expense, then the write-off presumably represented some sort of capital contraction. After evaluating and discarding the available alternatives of goodwill's treatment as a dividend, a gift, a capital contraction, and a correction of prior years' income, Hylton concluded that implications of the treatment appeared to cast serious doubt on the propriety of any such entry.

Hughes (1982: 143)

The MCS treatment of goodwill also accommodates these criticisms of the Catlett and Olson recommendations. While charging purchased goodwill immediately against owner's equity, the review provided by the MCS enables a reader to ascertain whether MCS goodwill exceeds purchased goodwill, thus offering *prima facie* evidence as to whether the value of purchased goodwill has been maintained. Certainly, if MCS goodwill is less than purchased goodwill, there is a strong indication that this is not the case. By avoiding the writing off of goodwill via the Profit and Loss Account, the question of accurate matching of revenue and expenses is eliminated – a question only given validity if goodwill or its subsequent amortization is regarded as an expense. Indeed, one of the major advantages of the MCS is that it is not necessary to decide whether goodwill is an asset, an expense or a capital contraction for the treatment to make sense from an accounting point of view.

The procedure recommended by Catlett and Olson was never adopted in the US; the criticism levelled against it proved persuasive. This was in contrast to the UK and Commonwealth countries whose legal system followed the UK Companies Act. In those countries, the writing off of purchased goodwill was far more widespread. (See Section 4.9b below for an analysis of UK practices in this regard.)

d. Survey of US amortization practices

In 1970, Morton Backer carried out a Research Study into goodwill published by the National Association of Accountants (New York). As has been noted, the rules for amortization under ARB 43 were flexible. In his study, Backer referred to a sample of the 1966 accounts of seventy companies, of which forty had goodwill on their books. The accounting treatment in respect of these forty is shown in Table 4.1 (Backer 1970: 148).

He commented that 'when goodwill is large, there is a distinct reluctance to amortize it or a tendency to extend the period of amortization well into the future'. It is intriguing to note that the company with the highest ratio of goodwill to total assets analysed by Backer was Bristol Meyer, at 10.3 per cent, a far cry from figures achieved recently by 'high-tech' companies (see Chapter 7).

Table 4.1 Goodwill amortization practices of a sample of forty US companies in 1966

Did not amortize		22
Amortized over	5 years	8
	10 years	6
	20 years	3
	40 years	1
		40

Some of Backer's observations have been quoted previously. In general, bankers were little concerned with goodwill accounting, as their prime concern was liquidity. Security analysts were most perturbed about the variety of treatments and the resultant lack of comparability in earnings per share figures (in the US, this was heightened by the controversy between advocates of pooling accounting and those recommending purchase accounting). A large majority of corporate executives favoured writing off purchased goodwill against earned surplus to avoid high future charges against income.

e. ARB Opinion No. 17

In August 1970, the APB issued its Opinion APB 17, which superseded ARB 43. The major tenet of this Opinion, insofar as purchased goodwill was concerned, was that, like other intangibles, it was to be treated similarly to other long life assets. Accordingly, it was to be accounted for on the normal pattern, viz.:

i. fix its initial carrying value;
ii. in normal circumstances, amortize it over its normal life;
iii. write it off appropriately to account for evident partial or complete falls in value occurring before the end of its normal life.

The opinion reinforced a trend in many similar pronouncements, which was the acceptance of value restatement in the case of a partial or total diminution in value, combined with an asymmetry in that revaluation was not permitted.

APB 17, as far as goodwill was concerned, was predicated on the belief that no asset had an indeterminate or permanent existence so that the previous 'type (B)' classification no longer applied. The asset's life was to be subject to continuous review. A maximum amortization period of forty years was arbitrarily set, although there was a requirement, when possible, to estimate the actual life of purchased goodwill and amortize it over that period. The disappearance of the 'type (B)' classification meant that the possibility of permanent recognition at the cost of acquisition was no longer permitted. The recommendations of Catlett and Olson in ARS 10 in favour of immediate total write-off of goodwill to reserves were also rejected; not surprisingly, Catlett, who was a member of the Accounting Standards Board at the time, strongly dissented. (Four more of the Board's eighteen members voted against the opinion, on the grounds that amortization was inappropriate when the facts indicated that the value of goodwill had been maintained or enhanced. Philip L. Defliese subsequently defended the Opinion on the grounds that the long amortization period at least partially mitigated the double counting involved in amortizing goodwill and writing off the expenses required to maintain it, while also recognizing the fact that acquired goodwill could never be an asset existing in perpetuity.)

f. Diversity of practice: 1958–1979

A good indication of the diversity of US practice over a period of twenty years is found in Table 4.2. The data analysed covered 600 companies.
Hughes (1982) notes:

> Interestingly, while amortization had been mandatory for nine years by 1979, nonamortization was being utilized about as often as it had been in 1970 – the year the opinion excluding nonamortization was issued. Presumably the nonretroactive provisions of the Opinion, allowing goodwill purchased prior to November 1, 1970, to be retained permanently and thus obtain the treatment's generally favourable effect relative to amortization, explains its lingering popularity.

Table 4.2 Goodwill amortization practices of 600 US companies: 1958–1979

Years	Amortized (1)	Not amortized (2)	Total of columns 1 and 2	Nominal valuation
1958	48	35	83	91
1959	51	43	94	84
1960	55	46	101	82
1961	60	52	112	71
1962	59	46	106	64
1963	51	46	97	57
1964	44	51	95	55
1965	50	64	114	46
1966	43	72	115	35
1967	43	72	115	31
1968	46	108	154	24
1969	47	138	185	20
1970	70	166	236	11
1971	129	162	291	5
1972	217	207	424	6
1973	250	197	447	4
1974	262	187	449	0
1975	261	182	443	0
1976	253	174	427	0
1977	288	175	463	0
1978	296	165	461	0
1979	285	156	441	0

4.9 Accounting for purchased goodwill – UK and Commonwealth countries

a. Against the Share Premium Account

In the UK, the practice of writing goodwill off against shareholders' equity was not unusual, prior to the introduction of the 1948 Companies Act. For example, in 1944, The Institute of Chartered Accountants in England and Wales (Cohen Committee *Minutes of Evidence* 1944, head 16(B)) stated, with respect to possible uses of the Share Premium Account (which, of course, did not exist in the US, where shares traditionally had no par value):

> The Institute suggest that they should not be capable of distribution in dividend or use, without the sanction of the Court, in relief of losses whether of a capital or revenue character. There would, however, be no objection to their use for writing down assets or expenditure, for example goodwill and preliminary expenses, the amortization of which does not form an essential charge against profits.

No issue was taken on this point by the Joint Committee of Chartered Accountants of Scotland.

In the end result, however, the 1948 UK Companies Act only permitted the writing off of preliminary expenses or expenses incurred or discount allowed in issuing shares or debentures. It did not permit the writing off of goodwill.

New Zealand permitted goodwill to be written off against the Share Premium Account until 1955, when it was outlawed by the Companies Act introduced at that time. That new Act took a very strong line against the practice, requiring entries previously made writing off goodwill against the Share Premium Account to be reversed, so that the Share Premium Account would be fully reinstated to be used only for the limited purposes permitted by the new Act.

The practice of writing off purchased goodwill was also widely followed in South Africa, where it was permitted by the Companies Act provided it could be written off against the Share Premium Account. It was standard practice to structure acquisitions using shares whose value included a substantial Share Premium over par value, precisely to enable this write-off to be made.

In Australia, the Companies Act 1961 (Section 60) ended the previously permitted practice of writing goodwill off against the Share Premium Account. Johnston, Jager and Taylor (1973: 171) note that the previous practice of writing off goodwill against the Share Premium Account could no longer be followed without involving the procedure for reduction of capital. This mirrors the New Zealand treatment, but without the requirement to reverse entries previously made following this practice.

In countries which fell predominantly within the legal framework established by successive UK Companies Acts, the procedure of writing off goodwill against the Share Premium Account, while those Acts permitted it, seems to have been governed by a theory of capital maintenance. Once a share could be issued at par, capital had been maintained as far as the original shareholders were concerned. Any excess over par, as expressed by the Share Premium Account, was therefore deemed to be available for writing off goodwill. The procedure also had some internal logic, in that the building up of internally generated goodwill could be deemed to be a significant contribution to the fact that the company concerned was able to issue shares at a premium over par in the first place. In a sense, therefore, although it was accepted that internally generated goodwill could not be brought to account directly, it seemed reasonable to utilize its benefit, as expressed in the Share Premium Account, to achieve consistency in treatment by writing off purchased goodwill.

The abolition of par values for shares has long been followed in the US, and Australia has followed suit. This must be viewed against the legislative requirement, still contained in section 254T of the Corporations Act 2001, that dividends can only be paid out of profits. A discussion paper, issued in 2002 by the Legislation Review Board of the AARF (2002: para. 3.5.2) stated:

> In general terms, a company has maintained its capital if it has as much capital at the end of the period as it had at the beginning of the period. Any amount over and above that required to maintain the capital at the beginning of the period is profit.

The Corporations Act 2001 now contains regulations enabling companies to buy back share capital and reduce capital, with strict safeguards to maintain liquidity and solvency, so that the interests of creditors are not prejudiced.

The discussion paper pointed out that, in recent years, solvency (i.e. whether a company was able to pay its debts as and when they fell due) was the prevailing philosophy of the Corporations Act in evaluating share buybacks and capital reductions, rather than adherence to a formal capital maintenance principle. It argued that a similar principle should be followed with regard to the payment of dividends, as is already the case in Canada and New Zealand; furthermore, there is already case law supporting the payment of dividends out of current profits even though past losses are not made up, provided the ability to discharge third party liabilities is not impaired.

Were the Australian Corporations Act to be formally changed to make solvency, rather than any capital maintenance based principle, the criterion for payment of dividends, this would facilitate writing off goodwill in the manner deemed most suitable by accountants. Such a write-off, whether immediate or over a period, is an accounting entry that has no practical effect on a company's ability to meet its liabilities as and when they fall due.

b. Against revenue reserves

The UK traditionally allowed the writing off of goodwill against reserves other than the Share Premium Account, a similar position to that espoused by Catlett and Olson. It has had a relatively short history with regard to prescriptions for the treatment of goodwill. Ken Wild, the National Director, Assurance and Advisory Services of Deloitte & Touche, noted that:

> Confusion over goodwill was one of the principal reasons for setting up the ASC (Accounting Standards Committee), yet that committee grappled with it for nearly fifteen years. All that time, they were driven into two competing factions with mutually incompatible views about how to treat the topic, so that SSAP 22 finally allowed two incompatible methods as alternative options and did not even insist that either one be used consistently by a single reporting entity. SSAP 22 has been the least defensible of the UK Standards, and, not surprisingly, has been criticised continuously.
>
> Preface to Brown and Chrispin (1998)

SSAP 22 'Accounting for Goodwill' was only issued in 1984. The two alternative procedures referred to were those foreshadowed in an 1980 Exposure Draft, viz.:

i. capitalization with amortization over a maximum twenty year period; and
ii. immediate elimination against reserves, with the latter being traditionally favoured.

One variation that was used in the UK over some years but does not seem to have attracted much attention elsewhere was the writing off of goodwill to reserves, but continuing to show the write-off as a separate deduction from reserves. Lee (1976: 106) furnished the statistics shown in Table 4.3, in relation to companies that had written off goodwill to reserves:

Table 4.3 Goodwill amortization practices of UK companies: 1962–1971

Years	No. of companies analysed	% of companies with disclosure of goodwill	
		Separate deduction from reserves	Write-off to income retained or reserves
1962	45	18	49
1963	43	19	44
1964	45	22	40
1965	46	22	50
1966	52	21	42
1967	58	16	57
1968	60	12	55
1969	66	9	62
1970	66	9	62
1971	66	9	58

The balance of the companies analysed by Lee adopted alternative methods of dealing with goodwill, such as reflecting it as either a fixed asset or a separate category of asset. The figures in Table 4.3 are also to be read in the context that it was compiled on the basis that certain companies adopted more than one basis of accounting for goodwill, in which case the table acknowledges all bases. Nevertheless, it is clear that, in Lee's limited sample, a large majority of companies chose to write off goodwill against reserves, and a significant number of these originally continued disclosures of the write-off in years after it was made. By 1969, however, the practice appears to have had relatively few adherents.

In Australia, too, the position was very flexible prior to the introduction of the first version of AASB 1013 in April 1988 (see Section 4.12 below).

Just over twenty years ago, the Australian National Companies and Securities Commission (NCSC) issued a paper (1983: 81–2), prepared for consultative purposes, in which the following points were made with regard to the treatment of 'goodwill' and 'premium on consolidation':

A range of accounting treatments is practised in Australia. The adjusting item may be shown as an asset, either at 'face value' (the figures originally calculated at acquisition) or amortized; it may be 'written-off' against reserves (so that it does not appear as a balance sheet item at all); or it may be shown as a deduction from aggregate shareholders' equity.

The NCSC paper also pointed out:

i.   the UK Companies Act 1981 provided for goodwill on consolidation to be reported as an asset, and prevented its deduction from shareholders' equity. This treatment appeared to be the product of efforts to standardize EEC reporting, rather than a firm commitment to the principle espoused.
ii. APB 17 appeared to require the writing off of goodwill.

The paper sought comments on whether the goodwill should be deducted from shareholders' equity, offset against reserves or other components of retained earnings or shown as an intangible asset to the extent that the fair value of the shares in the subsidiary acquired exceeded the fair value of its net assets.

It has not been possible to trace any responses to the paper in question. However, an indication of the diversity of Australian practice at that time is furnished in an article by Goodwin (1986: 15 *et seq.*), who surveyed 133 listed companies between 1980 and 1983.

Over this period, the favoured treatment was to record goodwill on consolidation as a negative component of 'Capital and Reserves', although the percentage of companies favouring this method fell from 51 per cent in 1980 to 41 per cent in 1983. The other common treatments were to write goodwill off in the year of acquisition (20 per cent in 1980: 26 per cent in 1983) or to record it as an asset (28 per cent in 1980: 33 per cent in 1983). This confirms that there was no consistent treatment, and explains the NCSC's range of options.

The introduction of the Accounting Standards requiring amortization of goodwill led to a virtual abandonment of other alternatives. In a study of financial statements from 1993 to 1997, Wyatt, Matolcsy and Stokes (2001: 23) found that, of 810 Australian companies that disclosed their policies on accounting for goodwill, virtually all (783) capitalized goodwill and subsequently amortized it, with 649 using a basic twenty year programme and 134 using shorter periods. Only seven wrote off goodwill on acquisition.

4.10 Europe

In Europe, procedures governing accounting for purchased goodwill were laid down in the Fourth Directive (see Articles 34 and 37), which permitted purchased goodwill to be written off to reserves, but also allowed for amortization. There was a rebuttable presumption that the maximum period of amortization should be five years; if a longer period was chosen, the reasons for this were required to be specifically disclosed. Nobes and Parker (2000: 334) described some European prescriptions with regard to goodwill. In the Netherlands, it was customarily written off immediately against reserves. If amortized, the period was normally not longer than five years, unless special circumstances could be shown to extend this period to ten years. In Germany, goodwill was traditionally determined by recalculating goodwill at each balance date, comparing the purchase price with the book value of the investee company as shown in its Balance Sheet. 'Book value' was defined as the sum of share capital and reserves, excluding the current year's profit except to the extent that transfers had been made to reserves. The French system was similar, excepting that all current profits or losses were excluded. Nobes and Parker (2000) comment:

> These methods meant that the size of the difference varied from year to year and was a mixture of goodwill, undervaluation of assets and post-acquisition profits. Some companies split the difference into debit and credit portions. In any case there was some diversity of practice.

The authors, writing in 2000, note that both France and Germany had moved closer to UK and US practices, although the French still permitted a wide range of accounting procedures, including capitalization and amortization (most common), writing off goodwill to reserves and the creation of non-depreciable intangibles, such as brand names.

The European Commission, which is primarily responsible for accounting requirements in Europe, called for listed companies in the European Union to move towards the adoption of IFRS in 2005 (with some provisions for delay until 2007). Currently, the Fourth Directive still applies to private companies.

4.11 Japan

According to Nobes and Parker (2000: 263 and 266), non-consolidation purchased goodwill is able to be capitalized and written off over five years, on a tax deductible basis. Similarly, goodwill arising on consolidation was, up to 2000, normally amortized over five years, although occasionally shorter periods were used. However, from March 2000, Japan moved towards international practice in permitting amortization over twenty years.

4.12 Australia

AASB 1013, having been issued in 1988, was revised in June 1996. It prescribed the treatment of goodwill in Australian financial statements of entities subject to the Corporations Act until its provisions were overridden by the AIFRS adopted from 1 January 2005 as part of the international harmonization programme. Its provisions are very similar to those of AAS 18, which relates to those entities not subject to that statute. A number of these provisions have been quoted earlier, but are repeated here for convenience.

Definitions

i. Goodwill is defined, in para. 13.1, as: 'the future benefits from unidentifiable assets', being 'those assets which are not capable of being both individually identified and specifically recognized'.
ii. Identifiable assets are: 'those assets which are capable of being both individually identified and specifically recognized in the books of account' (not restricted to tangible assets).
iii. 'Recognized', in turn, is defined as: 'reported on, or incorporated in amounts reported on, the face of the profit and loss account or balance sheet (whether or not further disclosure of the item is made in the note thereto)'.

Distinction between internally generated and purchased goodwill

AASB 1013 then draws the normal distinction between goodwill that has been internally generated by an entity and goodwill that has been purchased, prescribing quite different accounting treatments for these two classes of goodwill.

AASB 1013 requires the amortization of purchased goodwill over an arbitrary period of no longer than twenty years from the date of acquisition. However, the unamortized balance of goodwill is required to be reviewed at each reporting date and recognized as an expense to the extent that it is no longer supported by probable future benefits. While the Standard does not use the word 'value', it is clear that the review required entails an evaluation of purchased goodwill. The Standard is not explicit as to

---

The Standard itself is in bold; the balance of the extract represents commentary upon the Standard.

4.   Internally Generated Goodwill

4.1   Goodwill which is internally generated by the entity must not be recognized by that entity.

4.1.1   Goodwill which is internally generated by an entity is not permitted by this Standard to be recognized as an asset by that entity. This is principally because of the difficulty, or impossibility, of identifying the events or transactions which contribute to the overall goodwill of the entity. Even if these were identifiable, the extent to which they generate future benefits and the value of such benefits are not usually capable of being measured reliably. Internally generated goodwill which is not recognized as an asset will either go completely unrecognized or will be recognized as an expense.

5   Purchased Goodwill

Accounting Treatment for Purchased Goodwill

5.1   Goodwill which is purchased by the entity must be recognized as a non-current asset at acquisition.

5.1.1   Consistent with the definition of assets as service potential or future economic benefits controlled by the entity as a result of past transactions or other past events, this Standard specifies that goodwill is an asset. In particular, goodwill comprises the future benefits from unidentifiable assets which, because of their nature, are not normally individually recognized. Examples of unidentifiable assets include market penetration, effective advertising, good labour relations and a superior operating team. Unidentifiable assets do not include assets of an intangible nature which are capable of being both individually identified and separately recognized, as may be the case with patents, licences, rights and copyrights.

5.1.2   A distinction is frequently drawn between goodwill which is purchased and goodwill which is internally generated. This Standard specifies that the concept of goodwill as an asset is the same regardless of whether it has been purchased in an exchange transaction or generated internally. However, purchased goodwill can be measured more reliably, on the basis of the amount paid for it, than can internally generated goodwill which is not usually capable of being measured reliably. Consequently, the accounting treatment for purchased goodwill differs from that specified for internally generated goodwill.

5.1.3 Goodwill is recognized as an asset only when it satisfies the following asset recognition criteria:

(a) it is probable that the future benefits embodied in the unidentifiable assets will eventuate; and

(b) it possesses a cost or other value that can be measured reliably.

5.1.4 This will be the case only when goodwill is purchased in connection with the acquisition of an entity, or part thereof, through acquisition of the assets therein or, in the case of an investment in a subsidiary, the acquisition of some or all of the shares in another entity. Such purchased goodwill reflects future benefits which are internally generated by the vendor prior to the date of acquisition and are expected to flow to the purchaser and future benefits which arise from the combination or inter-relationship of entities or groups of assets.

5.2 Purchased goodwill must be amortized so that it is recognized as an expense in the profit and loss account on a straight-line basis, over the period from the date of acquisition to the end of the period of time during which the benefits are expected to arise. This period must not exceed twenty years from the date of acquisition.

5.2.1 In accordance with paragraph 5.4, the unamortized balance of goodwill must be reviewed as at each reporting date and recognized in the profit and loss account as an expense to the extent that future benefits are no longer probable.

whether the review is to exclude the contaminating influence of internally generated goodwill.

No indication is given in the Standard as to how the evaluation of purchased goodwill is to be carried out. This is hardly surprising, given that internally generated goodwill is stated to be not usually capable of being measured reliably, and the Standard acknowledges that the concept of goodwill does not differ whether purchased or internally generated. The Standard also does not deal with the practical difficulty of distinguishing between purchased and internally generated goodwill after a period has elapsed since the acquisition of goodwill, as discussed previously.

The purpose of the Standard is stated in para. 3.1 as being to:

(a) specify the manner of accounting for goodwill and discount on the acquisition of an entity, or part thereof; and

(b) require disclosure of information relating to goodwill so that users of financial reports are provided with information about the financial position and performance of the entity.

The discussion in Chapters 3 and 4 has highlighted the anomalies that exist even in standards that were operative relatively recently, such as AASB 1013. The contradictory treatment of the two categories of goodwill, despite the acknowledgment of the Standard that they are similar in concept, must confuse a reader of financial statements. The write-off of purchased goodwill over a maximum, arbitrarily determined period of twenty years is a second source of potential confusion; certainly, most laymen would find it difficult to understand why, in certain circumstances, an asset, the value of which is manifestly increasing, is being written down in the accounts. However, it must be acknowledged that it is not easy to '[disclose] information relating to goodwill so that users of financial reports are provided with information about the financial position and performance of the entity' in a historical cost environment.

As noted, AASB 1013 has now been replaced by the relevant AIFRS following Australia's virtually total adoption of IFRS. This has resolved some, but by no means all, of the anomalies following a shift to an impairment model of accounting for purchased goodwill.

4.13 International Accounting Standards

The comparable International Accounting Standard during the currency of AASB 1013 was IAS 22 'Business Combinations'. Because it deals with goodwill in the context of an acquisition, it does not specifically mention internally generated goodwill, but it does require goodwill to be carried at cost less amounts written off by way of both amortization and impairment (para. 43).

The normal maximum amortization period was twenty years. This was justified by the claim that a payment for goodwill is made in anticipation of future economic benefits, arising either from synergy or from assets that would otherwise not qualify for recognition (para. 42). This makes estimates inherently more unreliable the longer the estimated life – hence the presumption that the life of goodwill will not exceed twenty years.

While there was no allowance for goodwill to be considered to have an indefinite life, the twenty year limit was treated as rebuttable, under specific conditions, where the goodwill could be related to a specific asset or group of assets that had an economic life of more than twenty years, and it was reasonable to expect the life of the goodwill to coincide with that of the specific assets. In these special circumstances, however, an annual impairment review was mandatory; however, similar provisions existed that required the amortization method and period relating to all goodwill to be reviewed annually.

On 31 March 2004, the IASB issued three new Standards, dealing with Business Combinations (IFRS 3), Impairment of Assets (IAS 36) and Intangible Assets (IAS 38). These came into force on 1 January 2005 and are effective for financial years ending on or after that date. The provisions of these Standards are discussed in the following chapter.

4.14 Current developments

As is readily apparent from this chapter, fashions in the treatment of purchased goodwill have come and gone over the last 100 years. No treatment has proved effective or resilient in the long run. Each has had inherent contradictions that eventually led to its abandonment. The replacement has lasted only until the cycle repeated itself.

Perhaps the most obvious flaw in the amortization model which dominated the latter part of the twentieth century was the enforced amortization of purchased goodwill at a time when it could be strongly argued that its actual value was being maintained or even increased. When this contradiction was magnified by the large sums that were being paid for goodwill, there was overwhelming pressure for yet another paradigm shift.

The next chapter will examine the currently fashionable treatment – impairment. At the end of Chapter 3, it was emphasized that the historical exclusion from the Balance Sheet of internally generated goodwill was still generally accepted. Impairment review is thus currently only adopted, or in the course of adoption, for purchased goodwill.

5 Impairment

The current conventional wisdom

The process of testing for impairment takes us deep into valuation issues which have long been anathema to accountants, principally because of the unavoidable elements of subjectivity.

(K. Wild, as cited in Brown and Chrispin 1998)

5.1 Introduction

Chapter 3 reviewed methods of accounting for internally generated goodwill, and the current principles and standards underpinning them. It was clear that there has been little or no move to vary the accepted orthodoxy that internally generated goodwill should not be recognized in financial statements; for example, the revised IAS 38 states unambiguously 'internally generated goodwill shall not be recognized as an asset' (para. 48), and the Standards adopted recently in the UK and US contain similar provisions. For the sake of completeness, it should be noted that IAS 38 also prohibits the recognition of certain IIAs such as 'internally generated brands, mastheads, publishing titles, customer lists and items similar in substance' (para. 63). This contradicted Australian practice, at least prior to 1 January 2005, and has proved one of the most controversial steps (at least for Australian company managers) in the transition towards harmonization with International Standards.

In contrast, there has been a very strong movement aimed at varying the amortization regime, usually with a maximum period, which was the paradigm applicable to accounting for purchased goodwill in the latter part of the twentieth century. Led by the UK and the US, and with the IASB not far behind, there was a shift during the 1990s towards an 'impairment' concept which, in the context of goodwill, finally received the IASB imprimatur in March 2004.

Impairment is defined in the 1998 UK Standard, FRS 10, as 'a reduction in the recoverable amount of ... goodwill below its carrying value' (para. 63). The 2001 US Standard, SFAS 142, defines impairment as 'the condition that exists when the carrying amount of goodwill exceeds its implied fair value' (para. 18), noting that the fair value of goodwill can only be determined as a residual. The new International Standard, IAS 36, defines an impairment loss as 'the amount by which the carrying amount of an asset. . . . exceeds its recoverable amount' (para. 6).

AASB 10 'Recoverable Amount of Non-Current Assets' requires a company to write-down the carrying amount of non-current assets to their recoverable amount when the former is less than the latter (para. 5.1). 'Recoverable amount', in this context, is defined as 'in relation to an asset, the net amount that is expected to be recovered through the cash inflows and outflows arising from its continued use and subsequent disposal' (para. 9.1).

On the face of it, this does not appear to differ greatly from the new impairment assessment procedures but, in practice, there are a number of differences. AASB 10 did not prescribe procedures for ascertaining 'recoverable amount', whereas the comparable procedures are detailed in the impairment standards. For example, AASB 10 referred to cash inflows and outflows, while giving an apparent option (para. 7.3) as to whether it was required to discount those cash flows to their present value. This was partly mitigated by the need to disclose the discount rate used, if any, among the assumptions made in computing the recoverable amount. Prior to 1 July 2000, this disclosure was not required; the original version of AASB 10 was issued in 1987.

It will be seen that the determination of income-generating units is a key feature of current impairment standards, which give considerable guidance as to how these are to be determined. The previous standard is far looser, requiring only that, where the cash flows relate to 'a group of assets working together', the recoverable amount test must be applied to the carrying amount of that group of assets (para. 5.2). Such flexibility has created problems in other settings (such as the public sector), as described by Johnstone and Gaffikin (1996: 50–65).

On 1 July 1998, the previous statutory provision that required non-current assets to be shown in the accounts at an amount not exceeding their reasonable replacement value to the company as a going concern was repealed. This was a very different test from the 'recoverable amount' provisions of AASB 10, which had been introduced, as mentioned previously, in 1987, and the conflict had caused considerable confusion. Since 1 July, 1998, however, the provisions of the Standard have applied unambiguously. For completion, it should be noted that, in terms of the *Corporations Act 2001* (Section 296(1)), Australian companies listed on the ASX are required to comply with Australian Accounting Standards.

Jan McCahey, a PricewaterhouseCoopers partner with considerable regulatory experience, made an interesting comment that pinpointed the practical difference between the two concepts. She described the recoverable amount test as 'a sort of wait-and-see test', commenting 'a lot of us apply tougher tests than this in practice, but it does give us the opportunity to "wait and see" and manage down the value of the asset into earnings' (quoted in Ravlic 2001). One can only surmise what criteria have been applied in 'managing down' asset values.

The recent standards vary in detail, but concur in that, if the value of (purchased) goodwill is not impaired, there is no need to amortize it. The UK, the US and the International Standards all include detailed recommendations as to procedures to be followed to ascertain whether impairment has taken place.

5.2 The UK

a. FRS 10 and FRS 11

The first country to adopt an impairment standard was the UK, where two financial reporting standards that took effect in respect of companies ending their financial years in December 1998 are definitive. These are FRS 10 'Goodwill and Intangible Assets' and FRS 11 'Impairment of Fixed Assets and Goodwill'. The firm of Deloitte Touche Tohmatsu issued a contemporaneous publication (Brown and Chrispin 1998), which offers an excellent summary and commentary on these Standards, and has been extremely useful in preparing this brief analysis, supplemented by reference to a general reference work published under the aegis of Ernst & Young (Wilson et al. 2001: especially chapters 11 and 13).

FRS 10 maintains the prohibition in the previous Standard against recognizing internally generated goodwill; however, whereas purchased goodwill could previously either be written off against reserves immediately or capitalized and amortized over a period, FRS 10 abolished the acceptability of the former practice (despite the fact that it was traditionally more popular). The treatment prescribed for goodwill is very similar to that prescribed for IIAs. Consequently, apart from more precise definition of assets appearing in the Balance Sheet, there is now little incentive to seek to classify intangible assets as identifiable rather than as goodwill.

There is a presumption in FRS 10 that the life of intangible assets, including goodwill, is limited and, in the absence of other evidence, a maximum amortization period of twenty years is to apply. If goodwill is amortized, the period chosen and the reason for this choice must be disclosed. However, FRS 10 does allow for the possibility that the life of such assets may be longer or, indeed, unlimited. If the company maintains that this is the case, it must disclose in its accounts the reasons for rebutting the twenty year presumption and carry out impairment reviews annually; the procedure for such reviews is set out in FRS 11. Unless such a review takes place, the twenty year amortization rule applies.

FRS 10 requires amortization to reflect the expected pattern of depletion of goodwill, and strongly recommends the straight line basis of amortization, although without explaining why this method would be expected (on average) to be the most accurate in achieving its aim. This is one of a number of fiats in Standards not supported by evidential based reasoning. The Standard does provide that, in calculating the amortization rate, there is to be no allowance for residual value, thus ensuring complete amortization over the chosen period in the absence of impairment reviews.

Intriguingly, FRS 10 permitted all past goodwill written off against reserves to remain so written off, but established an option allowing goodwill previously written off in this way to be capitalized under the new rules, with amortization attributable to years prior to the capitalization to be reflected as a prior period adjustment. It also permitted goodwill acquired after the introduction of the Standard to be capitalized while the result of prior acquisitions could remain written off.

One marked contrast between the current UK and US procedures is that the UK still permits pooling of interests, although in very limited circumstances. For example, as a dual listed company, reporting its results through the ASX and the London Stock Exchange, the world's largest mining company, BHP Billiton, has been allowed to use pooling accounting, thus avoiding the need to bring purchased goodwill to account. Note 39 to the company's 2006 financial statements discloses that purchased goodwill, under US Generally Accepted Accounting Principles (GAAP), would have been calculated at US$2.151 million.

It should be noted that, on 10 May 2006, the UK Accounting Standards Board issued a press notice seeking views on the future application of reporting requirements to UK companies, tentatively proposing that all UK listed companies would be required to apply full IFRS. At the time of writing, this project was still in progress.

b. The impairment provision of FRS 11

Impairment is measured by comparing the carrying value of an asset or group of assets with its recoverable amount, i.e. the higher of its value in use or immediate resale. The latter is easier to calculate, if parameters are available; the former is defined as the present value of the future cash flows obtainable from the continued use and ultimate sale of the asset or group of assets.

FRS 11 encourages an impairment review on the basis of smaller units, rather than allowing the aggregative entity position; it indicates that certain unique intangible assets, such as brands and mastheads, create independent income streams and lend themselves to separate monitoring. The income-generating units (IGUs) used as the basis for the calculation should be grouped into the smallest groups for which impairment could be material. Presumably, this stipulation is made in the interests of conservatism; the larger the IGU, the more likely it is that an impairment loss can be avoided because it will be offset by an improvement in value elsewhere in the IGU. Central assets (e.g. head office) and working capital may have to be apportioned across IGUs on a logical and systematic basis; alternatively, a separate impairment review could be carried out taking into account the combined value of the total IGUs and the central assets. Why conservatism is a virtue to be sought is not discussed.

Goodwill is allocated to IGUs in the same way as assets and liabilities of the entity; where several IGUs are acquired in one investment, they may be combined to assess the recoverability of goodwill. Detailed provisions are furnished in FRS 11 for the valuation of assets in use, including guidance as to the projected growth rate, how to deal with projected capital expenditure and the appropriate pre- or post-tax discount rate to be applied. For example, assets are judged to be impaired if they no longer earn a market rate of return.

Thomas, in several publications, observed that the process of allocation is itself fraught with theoretical difficulty. In 1975, he pointed out that financial accounting allocations 'generally suffer from a logical defect of incorrigibility that renders them arbitrary'. 'Incorrigible', in this context, is a term 'used by logicians, and here signifies that these calculations and allocations can neither be verified nor refuted and that, in consequence, any one is just as good as any other'.

Thomas' notion of incorrigibility is based on similar grounds to his analysis of the allocation problem, which was mentioned in Chapter 3.12 above. He contends that allocations are generally incorrigible whenever individual costs are allocated to two or more cost centres, because it is the interaction of the multiple elements of an entity that produces its output. His analysis is complex, but demonstrates the high degree of subjectivity that necessarily attaches to the allocation process, whether between financial years or between so-called cost centres, and that the process does not sufficiently take the interaction process between those cost centres to account. His views were confirmed in an article that was published as part of the 'Festschrift' issue of *Abacus* in December 1982.

Reflecting the requirements of UK Companies' legislation, FRS 10 prohibits the capitalization of internally generated goodwill. The provisions of FRS 11:50 in this regard are worth quoting in full, as they indicate the level of complexity that is imposed by this requirement:

> Where an acquired business is merged with an existing business and results in an income-generating unit that contains both purchased and (unrecognized) internally generated goodwill:

a. the value of the internally generated goodwill of the existing business should be estimated and added to the carrying amount of the income-generating unit for the purpose of performing impairment reviews;
b. any impairment arising on merging the businesses should be allocated solely to the purchased goodwill within the newly acquired business;
c. subsequent impairments should be allocated pro rata between the goodwill of the acquired business and that of the existing business;

d. the impairment allocated to the existing business should be allocated first to the (notional) internally generated goodwill; and

e. only the impairments allocated to purchased goodwill (and, if necessary, to any recognized intangible or tangible assets) should be recognized in the financial statements.

The provisions of FRS 11:50 are a classic illustration of how accountants continue to struggle with the valuation and goodwill concepts. For example, 11:50(a) requires a valuation of the existing enterprise (or IGU) including its internally generated goodwill. This valuation is used subsequently (e.g. 11:50(c)) and presumably is reliable enough for this purpose; nevertheless, the valuation can never be used to recognize the value of internally generated goodwill, but merely to act as a basis for a number of arbitrary assumptions (11:50(b), (c) and (d)). The complexity, problematic and 'incorrigible' nature of the impairment process is increased, while its relevance is decreased. Of what use is it to a reader of the financial statements to know how much purchased goodwill is deemed to have decreased in particular areas without a knowledge of the total goodwill attaching to the business (or IGU, as the case may be), especially if the allocations and apportionments underlying the calculations are arbitrary? Audit verification of these calculations is fraught with difficulty in practice.

Revaluation of goodwill is not permitted; impairment is a one way test. However, FRS 10 does permit an impairment write-off to be reinstated only in the very limited case in which an external event caused the recognition of an impairment loss in a previous period, and subsequent external events clearly reverse the effects of that event in a way that was not foreseen at the time. If impairment takes place because of lack of profitability, which is subsequently restored by management action, the restoration is deemed to be due to internally generated goodwill and may thus not be used to reinstate the goodwill written off. On the other hand, if, for example, the effects of an external event had been incorrectly forecast (e.g. adverse publicity relating to a consumer claim that proved to have less effect than forecast), reinstatement is permitted. It is difficult to see how this distinction matters from the point of view of a reader of the financial statements.

On the whole, illogicalities such as those pointed out and the complexities of applying the UK procedure, particularly in relation to the relatively small IGUs, the difficulties of apportionment and the necessity for continuous valuations are likely to influence many UK companies to live with the amortization regime that is still the basic accounting treatment under FRS 10. This would merely involve taking advantage of the 'rebuttable presumption' that the life of goodwill is limited to twenty years or less; only if the durability of purchased goodwill beyond this period can be demonstrated and is capable of continued measurement does the impairment regime become applicable.

Ken Wild, the National Director, Assurance and Advisory Services, of Deloitte Touche Tohmatsu, notes 'the process of testing for impairment takes us deep into valuation issues which have long been anathema to accountants, principally because of the unavoidable elements of subjectivity' (Brown and Chrispin 1998).

The procedure for valuation laid down in FRS 11 involves the discounting of future estimated cash flows at an appropriate rate. An Ernst & Young manual comments:

> The selection of a suitable discount rate is a case in point: as a small alteration in the discount rate used can have an enormous effect on the value in use, there is inevitably scope for genuine differences of opinion to occur in practice. In fact, there is so little guidance in the Standards on selection of a future discount rate, that it raises the possibility that an impairment provision could, to some extent at least, be regarded as optional.
>
> Wilson et al. (2001: 1069)

This comment does not even take into account the inherent unreliability of the estimates of the cash flows to which the discount rate is applied, which is also dealt with by a number of the comments on the IASB exposure draft ED 3 'Business Combinations' (see Section 5.4 below) and, in particular, the valuations required to determine goodwill impairment. (Obtained from the IASC website http://www.iasc.org.uk – commentaries on ED 3). For example, the Confederation of British Industry commented: 'There are conceptual and practical problems with impairment testing, notably the mingling of internally generated goodwill and the costly and subjective nature of some impairment testing', and the China Accounting Standards Committee had a similar comment: 'After initial recognition, we don't believe it is always appropriate that goodwill should be accounted for at cost less impairment losses, because in many cases [the] impairment test result is not very reliable'.

The Conseil National de la Comptabilité concurred with impairment proposals, but conditionally:

> ... Provided a rigorous and workable impairment test could be devised, testing goodwill for impairment rather than amortizing it systematically over an arbitrary defined useful life would provide users with a more useful and relevant information (sic). We strongly insist on the pragmatic and practical aspect of the impairment test.

Another European view was provided by the French Society of Financial Analysts:

> The replacement of goodwill amortization by an impairment test which, by considering both acquired and internally generated goodwill together, would, in practice, lead to no impairment being recognized. This

implicit recognition of internally generated goodwill is in contradiction with current IAS practice in this regard.

On the other hand, the AASB and CPA Australia, in their submissions, do not make any adverse criticism of the valuation aspects of the impairment proposals. Presumably, also, auditing verification issues were not seen as too problematic.

5.3 The US

a. SFAS 142

It will be remembered that, following the issue of APB 17 in 1970, goodwill was to be treated like any other long life asset. It had to be originally accounted for at cost, and amortized over its estimated useful life, with an arbitrary maximum of forty years, although this period was to be subject to continuous review. Partial or total diminutions in value were to be recognized in the financial statements by appropriate write-offs against profits.

The US followed the UK in moving to impairment, but with greater emphasis on abandoning the previous provisions. SFAS 142, which applied to fiscal years commencing after 15 December 2001, is also a very complex Statement. The following summary of the procedures required for its implementation draws heavily on an 'Implementation Guide to FASB Statements 141 and 142' issued in 2002 by Deloitte & Touche LLP.

b. Procedure for implementing SFAS 142

The procedure required by SFAS 142 at the end of each financial year is as follows:

i.   Identify reporting units (this is the level at which goodwill is tested for impairment [comparable to IGUs above]). This is done initially by identifying operating segments of the company, being components which earn revenue and incur expenses, whose operating results are regularly reviewed by the chief operating decision maker in order to make decisions regarding resource allocation and performance, and for which discrete financial information is available. Operating segments having similar characteristics are aggregated to identify the reporting unit.

ii. Assets and liabilities are assigned to each reporting unit, being those which relate to the operations of that unit and which will be considered in determining the fair value of the reporting unit as a whole.

iii. All goodwill recognized in an entity's statement of position at the inception of SFAS 142 is to be assigned to one or more reporting units. Goodwill arising on new acquisitions is to be assigned to reporting units in a reasonable manner.

iv.   At the inception of SFAS 142, annually thereafter, and on an interim basis as warranted, it is necessary to determine the fair value of each reporting unit to assess whether the fair value is less than the carrying value of the reporting unit. If this is the case, it is necessary to allocate the fair value to the assets and liabilities of the reporting unit, as if that unit had been acquired at the fair value determined for the reporting unit. Goodwill resulting from the fair value allocation process is then compared with the carrying value of goodwill applicable to that reporting unit to determine if and by how much goodwill has been impaired.

v.   On the other hand, if the fair value of the reporting unit exceeds its carrying value, no further testing is required and the value of goodwill is treated as not having been impaired.

vi.   The value of IIAs not subject to amortization is required to be tested independently each year (or as otherwise required) to ensure lack of impairment.

vii.   Once written down for impairment, no future recovery of goodwill can be recognized.

c. Features of special interest

In moving from an amortization regime to an impairment regime, SFAS 142 accepts that valuation is needed, breaking the longstanding tradition (particularly in the US) of rigid adherence to the historical cost principle. This introduces a number of features of special interest, as it seeks to come to terms with an area that accountants have traditionally found uncomfortable. For example, it requires formal consideration of how to deal with valuation procedures, internally generated goodwill and, as noted above, the function of the auditors under the new regime.

It is apparent from the operation of SFAS 142, which calls for the annual valuations of reporting units, that the distinction between purchased and internally generated goodwill has become blurred. While it is not permitted to recognize internally generated goodwill initially, the value of internally generated goodwill is automatically taken into account in determining any subsequent impairment in the value of the business unit. In all subsequent valuations, the value of purchased goodwill is compared with the total goodwill of the business unit, both purchased and internally generated, to assess impairment. This contrasts with the current UK Standard (see Section 5.2 above), which endeavours to maintain the historic distinction between the two.

It is acknowledged that some entities will need to rely on third party specialist valuers to determine some or all of the fair value measurements. In addition, the entities and their auditors are required to determine the level of evidential matter necessary to support fair value measurements. This is, effectively, a substantiation of Chambers' view that realizable values are objectively measurable (in context, these are little different from fair values, as defined by most standards setting bodies), although it should be stressed that Chambers was strongly opposed to showing goodwill as an asset on the Balance Sheet (see Chapter 7.5).

When measuring the fair value of a reporting unit, SFAS 142 (para. 23) expressed the view that 'quoted market prices in active markets are the best evidence of fair value and shall be used as the basis for the measurement, if available'. However, it would be possible 'that the market price of an individual equity security (and thus the market capitalization of the reporting unit with publicly traded equity securities) may not be representative of the fair value of the reporting unit as a whole' (Deloitte & Touche LLP 2002: 21). The Securities and Exchange Commission (SEC) staff, in correspondence with the FASB staff dated 16 August 2001, indicated that they believed that such divergence would be rare and, in such cases, emphasized the need for documentation supporting deviation from market price and the basis for concluding that the market price was incorrect. The need for the independent auditors to confirm the validity of the data employed and the consequent justification of this deviation was emphasized. Deloittes indicate that there has been some moderation in the belief that these occurrences would be rare, but that this moderation has not affected the need to document the reason for the view taken.

One reason why market prices may not represent fair value in this case has already been discussed. Quoted market prices relate to the value of a minority parcel, and do not recognize any premium for control – a consideration clearly relevant to 'the fair value of the reporting asset as a whole'. The control premium can be material. Lonergan (2004: 87) indicates that 30 per cent is a typical control premium, while McMonnies (1988: 5.3) states that the average amount of the takeover premium has been found to be in the region of 15–20 per cent. The reasons why market capitalization has nevertheless been selected as a base for the MCS are set out in Chapter 6.3.

One matter of definition that has not attracted much attention is the SFAS definition of 'fair value', viz. 'the amount at which an asset (or liability) could be bought (or incurred) or sold (or settled) in a current transaction between willing parties, that is, other than in a forced or liquidation sale'. Harms and Gibbs (2001: 6) point out that this definition has a number of distinguishing features from the traditional 'fair market value' definition used in the US. It does not require that buyer and seller both have reasonable knowledge of the relevant facts – possibly because the valuation procedure requires the use of management forecasts that intrinsically rely on management-specific knowledge.

This definition has, in turn, been further amended by the definition of fair value in SFAS 157, which was issued in September 2006 and has been discussed at length in Chapter 2.2. Another significant difference is that the valuation process illustrated acknowledges the existence of potential synergy benefits, which are generally considered to be properly excluded when establishing 'fair market value'. The role of control premiums in establishing valuation procedures has not been fully defined or expressly included in SFAS 142.

Although valuation is now an accepted procedure in carrying out the test for goodwill impairment, there are still stringent precautions against such valuations leading to an increase in carrying value; they are only to be used to measure impairment of carrying values. This has long been the case. Consider the following extract from the 1969–70 Eggleston Committee Report (para. 11), which shows that the Australian authors of a major committee report of thirty-five years ago would no doubt have approved this approach:

> Logically, there should be no difference between cases in which the assets are undervalued and those in which they are overvalued, though it has sometimes been said that it is misleading to show assets at an amount higher than their true value (sic). *It has certainly never been regarded as untrue or unfair to show assets at a figure below their true value* (emphasis added).

Initially, a reporting unit is defined as an operating segment or one level above an operating segment. It is permitted to aggregate components of operating segments to determine the reporting unit (e.g. if the components have similar economic characteristics) (SFAS 142, para. 30), and the fairly broad guidelines as to when such aggregation is appropriate will probably ensure that, in many cases, the reporting unit will be the group as a whole. This would certainly be the case for corporate entities and groups with only one operating segment, the divisions of which have similar economic characteristics; for more complex corporate groups, time and observation of practice will confirm whether this prediction is correct. An FASB Exposure Draft entitled 'Fair Value Measurement' contained an exhaustive discussion on this topic, but SFAS 157: Fair Value Measurement, issued in September 2006, does not itself define 'reporting unit' although it uses the phrase.

Harms and Gibbs (2001) show that materially different results in the allocation of purchased goodwill between business units could result from the use of varying, but reasonable, bases. The amount of goodwill initially allocated to each such unit could vary considerably, depending on whether the allocation was based on the net tangible assets, the estimated fair value, the implied goodwill (the difference between estimated fair value and the identifiable net assets assigned to the reporting unit) or the total net assets applicable to each unit acquired (Harms and Gibbs 2001: 14). This adds further emphasis to the relevance of Thomas' 'incorrigibility' in this situation.

5.4 IASB/Australia

The IASB undertook a major project in relation to updating its Standards relating to Business Combinations (IFRS 3), Impairment of Assets (IAS 36) and Intangible Assets (IAS 38), following the issue of an Exposure Draft (ED 3). As noted in Chapter 4.13, the final versions of these Standards were issued on 31 March 2004, thus meeting the deadline that the IASB had imposed.

Australia, through the AASB, issued an exposure draft (ED 109) that was similar to ED 3, except that it invited comment on the transitional procedures from the old Australian Standards and whether the proposed IASB Standards would serve the interests of the Australian economy. In practice, however, in April 2004, the AASB announced that it would accept the revised IASB Standards listed above in their entirety, to take effect from 1 January 2005 and relate to companies having financial year-ends on or after that date. This chapter of the book will accordingly treat the new Australian and International provisions together; paragraph references apply to either the Australian or the International Standards.

At the time of an acquisition, goodwill should be recognized at cost, 'being the excess of the cost of the business combination over the acquiror's interest in the net fair value of the identifiable assets, liabilities and contingent liabilities. ... ' (IFRS 3, para. 51). In its June 2003 Bulletin, the IASB noted that, 'as part of a broader consideration of fair value measurement issues, the FASB agreed to amend the fair value hierarchy', and noted that the IASB agreed with the FASB that 'market prices, when available, are considered to be best evidence of fair value'.

Goodwill is clearly defined as being 'a payment made by the acquiror in anticipation of future economic benefits from assets that are not capable of being individually identified and separately recognized' (IFRS 3, para. 52). It is 'measured as the residual cost of the business combination after recognizing the acquiree's identifiable assets, liabilities and contingent liabilities' (IFRS 3, para. 53).

After initial recognition, the acquirer shall measure goodwill at cost less any accumulated impairment losses. Tests for impairment losses are to be made annually or more frequently if there is an indication of impairment. Recoverable amount is defined, as in the UK Standard, as the higher of net selling price or value in use (IAS 36, para. 6), and an impairment loss must be recognized whenever the recoverable amount is less than the carrying, or book, value.

Initially, the IAS exposure draft provided that an impairment loss for goodwill could be reversed, if the specific event that caused the recognition of the impairment loss reversed, to the amount that would have been recognized as the carrying value had no such loss occurred. This provision has now been modified in the final Standard; reversal is no longer permitted under any circumstances (IAS 36, paras 124–25).

IAS 36 requires that, for the purpose of impairment testing, goodwill is allocated to 'each of the acquiror's cash-generating units or groups of cash-generating units' that is expected to benefit from the synergies of the combination, irrespective of whether other assets or liabilities of the acquiree are assigned to those units or groups of units. Units are chosen to represent the lowest level at which goodwill is monitored, and shall not be larger than an accounting segment (IAS 36, para. 80). This provision, which recognizes the fact that the synergistic benefits of an acquisition may be felt in areas other than the unit that forms the subject of the acquisition, reinforces the views expressed by Ma and Hopkins (1988) (see Chapter 3.12). By inference, the method prescribed for the determination of recoverable amount takes into account goodwill generated internally since the acquisition, as well as the realization of synergistic benefits. However, IAS 36 steadfastly maintains, in justifying why impairment losses for goodwill cannot be reversed,

> [The Standard] prohibits the recognition of internally generated goodwill. Any increase in the recoverable amount of goodwill in the periods following an impairment loss for that goodwill is likely to be an increase in internally generated goodwill, rather than a reversal of the impairment loss recognized for the acquired goodwill.
>
> IAS 36 (para. 125)

This contradiction is one of the major factors that is likely to cause the impairment paradigm to share the fate of its predecessors.

The IASB uses the concept of a cash-generating unit, defined (IAS 36, para. 6) as 'the smallest identifiable group of assets that generates cash inflows that are largely independent of the cash flows from other assets or group of assets', as the yardstick for measuring impairment. Impairment has been defined in Section 5.1 above. In some cases, the carrying value with which the recoverable amount is to be compared will be the original cost of goodwill reduced by amortization recorded prior to the date the new provisions come into force.

The IAS 36 concept of a cash-generating unit (similar to the previously noted IGUs), as defined above, differs from the US definition (see Section 5.3b above), which tests goodwill at the reporting unit level. The latter is arrived at by aggregating operating segments having similar characteristics. The proposed IASC concept seems to be set at the lower operating segment level, which clearly reduces the opportunity to offset impairment in one segment against increase in goodwill values in another; in doing so, it is closer to the UK concept (see Section 5.2b above).

If harmonization is regarded as being desirable, it is regrettable to see differences such as this already developing in Accounting Standards. The smaller the unit selected, the more conservative the approach to recognizing goodwill impairment will be. It is clearly a victory for the defenders of traditional historical cost accounting if the effects of potential offsets are minimized or even prohibited. If this philosophy prevails, the usefulness of the new impairment proposals in making the Balance Sheet 'valuable' to interested parties is likely to be itself impaired.

It is apparent that the International Standards have been influenced by both the UK and US models. However, they are closer to the US model in two significant aspects. First, they utilize a pure impairment model, unlike the UK model, which has, as its basic presumption, that the life of goodwill is limited to a presumptive maximum period of twenty years and which only allows the impairment alternative to be adopted if the company maintains that the amortization model is inappropriate. Second, by inference, a diminution in the value of purchased goodwill may be set off, or compensated, by internally generated goodwill since acquisition.

5.5 Differences between previous and new Australian Standards

The AASB has highlighted a number of significant differences between the previous Standards and the newly adopted AIFRS. These are detailed in the 'pending accounting standards' documents, obtainable from the AASB website (http://www.aasb.com.au) and summarized herein, particularly as they relate to goodwill.

a. Differences between AASB 136 'Impairments of Assets' (the new Standard) and AASB 1010 'Recoverable Amount of Non-Current Assets' (the old Standard)

AASB 136 'Impairment of Assets', unlike AASB 1010, provides specific indications as to when an asset's value may be impaired. These include an unusual decline in the value of an asset and technological change that might render the asset obsolete. A more subtle indicator is a rise in interest rates, necessitating a review of the discount rates used in previous impairment calculations of recoverable amount. Of particular relevance to the proposed MCS is the statement in the new Standard that a review is indicated whenever 'the carrying amount of the net assets of the entity is more than its market capitalization' (para. 12). The entity is also required to review carrying values having regard to its internal plans, if these have an adverse effect on the asset or make it obsolete.

AASB 136 extends the previously quoted definition of a cash-generating unit in para. 6 by describing it as one in which 'an active market exists for the output produced by an asset or group of assets, even if some or all of the output is used internally' (para. 70). This definition is very different from the 'class of non-current assets', which was the 'group' used to assess impairment under AASB 1010. Under the old Standard, goodwill could be reviewed in aggregate (see also AASB 1013, para. 5.4, which required the unamortized balance of goodwill to be reviewed at each reporting date and expensed to the extent that future benefits were no longer probable). Under the new Standard, the goodwill content of each cash-generating unit is reviewed, with offsets not permitted.

One of the provisions of AASB 1010 that aroused considerable criticism is that it did not require future cash flows to be discounted to present value in determining net recoverable amount; AASB 136 is quite explicit that discounting is necessary (para. 31(b)), and has a number of provisions stipulating how that discount rate is to be chosen (e.g. paras 55 and 57). Surprisingly, the Standard specifies the use of a pre-tax discount rate. A post-tax rate would be more appropriate, in that it takes better account of non-tax-deductible capital expenditures and the fact that tax payments are made at precise dates, rather than being spread over the year.

The new Standard provides (para. 104) that, having evaluated a cash-generating unit, any impairment is first to be applied against the goodwill content of its carrying value. As AASB 1010 did not envisage cash-generating units, there is no corresponding provision.

Finally, AASB 136 demands very detailed disclosures in respect of cash-generating units containing a goodwill element that is significant in relation to the total carrying amount of an entity's goodwill (para. 134). Not only must the goodwill element be disclosed, but also considerable detail as to how management has determined 'value in use' or 'fair value less cost to sell'. These details include key assumptions and how they are supported, periods over which cash flows have been forecast, growth rates forecast (with reasons if these are higher than would normally be expected) and discount rates applied. The effect of changes in key assumptions on recoverable amount is also required to be disclosed.

b. Differences between the new AASB 1038 'Intangible Assets' and AASB 1013

The most significant difference is that AASB 1038 (para. 88) does not have a rebuttable presumption that the life of an intangible asset is limited; an entity is required to determine whether intangible assets have a finite or infinite life. As noted previously, AASB 1013 effectively created a presumption that the life of goodwill was limited to twenty years (para. 5.2) and required amortization over its expected life.

In practice, amounts previously categorized as goodwill are now being analysed more extensively into IIAs. Many of these, such as contractual customer relationships, are being amortized, rather than subjected to an impairment review. The period of amortization is derived from the nature of the asset and is nearly always far shorter than twenty years.

c. AASB 3 and initial recognition of goodwill

The new Standard for business combinations requires that, in an acquisition resulting in goodwill, the acquirer must disclose the factors giving rise to goodwill, including any intangible asset, the fair value of which could not be measured reliably (para. 67(h)).

The disclosures in respect of purchased goodwill are also much more extensive than those of AASB 1013. It is now required (para. 75) to reconcile the opening and closing amounts shown for goodwill, showing movements in great detail, including goodwill purchased, goodwill de-recognized on disposal of a business, impairment losses recognized and changes in goodwill arising from subsequent recognition of deferred tax assets.

5.6 Impending problems

As the 'impairment approach' has gathered momentum, following its adoption in the US and the UK and its endorsement by the IASB, it is worth examining potential problems.

All prescribed impairment calculation methods to date rely on predictions of future earnings and cash flows to determine recoverable value in use. History has shown, and accounting and audit standards have traditionally recognized, that such predictions are inherently unreliable and that actual results are 'unlikely to occur as forecast'. For example, a study published in 1989 (Goodwin 1989) analysed all listings on the ASX between July 1982 and June 1986 to determine the accuracy of forecasts made in prospectuses. Prospectus forecasts are normally subject to a due diligence review process that is far more rigorous than that which would apply to normal management forecasts underpinning value-in-use estimates.

Goodwin found a wide degree of error in examining the specific forecasts made by the fifty-one companies in the sample. While there was no evidence of bias in the results (approximately as many companies overestimated future profits as those who made underestimates), only 10 per cent of companies achieved an absolute prediction error of less than 10 per cent. Other interesting findings were that a total of sixteen companies overestimated their future profits by more than 50 per cent; of these, eight were optimistic by 250 per cent or more, with four of these being incorrect by more than 1,000 per cent. Goodwin does not attempt to establish why the forecasts were wrong. The reasons could range from the use of unrealistic assumptions to the occurrence of events, having a dramatic effect on the enterprise concerned, which could not reasonably have been forecast. For present purposes, the distinction is immaterial in that conclusions based on the accuracy of those forecasts will turn out to have been wrong.

A relatively recent article by two South African researchers (Mbuthia and Ward 2003), which analysed forecasts by 506 companies listing on the Johannesburg Stock Exchange between 1980 and 1998, found a mean overestimate of profits of 14.29 per cent; perhaps more significantly, estimate error ranged from an underestimate of 284 per cent to an overestimate of 511 per cent. Mbuthia and Ward (2003) also furnish a comparative table showing the results of similar studies. There is little consistency in the results of these studies, which show average forecasting errors ranging from an underestimate of 92 per cent (a 1992 New Zealand Study) to an overestimate of 112 per cent (a 1972 UK Study).

The only Australian study cited by Mbuthia and Ward was a 1999 paper by Brown, Clarke, How and Lim. No reference was furnished by them for this study, which found a mean earnings forecast underestimate of 7.95 per cent over 431 companies between 1980 and 1996. As noted, however, the mean error is not particularly relevant; for purposes of impairment, it is more relevant to have regard to the fact that, inevitably, the studies show that some companies make major errors in forecasting results, even under the rigorous legal obligations imposed in preparing a prospectus. It is reasonable to conclude that forecasts in impairment calculations will be at least as inaccurate.

Even accepting that all companies made genuine attempts to forecast their profits, it seems inevitable that errors of this magnitude will eventually destroy the valuations underpinning the impairment regime. The examples of Enron, HIH, WorldCom and Fannie Mae have shown that it only needs a few high profile cases to discredit an accounting regime. It is inevitable that some impairment calculations will be based on overoptimistic figures and, especially if the companies concerned subsequently experience financial difficulties, there will be an outcry against the procedures that allowed goodwill to remain on the Balance Sheet as a substantial asset. The actions of directors of marginal companies are likely to bring the process into disrepute, even if it works as envisaged for the great majority of listed companies.

Under an impairment regime, the role of auditors will be very difficult. The proposed MCS calls for goodwill to be recognized in the accounts, albeit in a separate statement, on a 'mark to market' basis with easily verifiable *external* commercial referents. In contrast, auditors struggling with issues of valuation and prospective financial information will, in practice, be largely dependent on their clients' views in areas likely to be difficult and controversial in assessing the truth and fairness of the view presented by the financial statements. In Australia, auditors are instructed that, in reporting on prospective information, they are to use cautionary phrases such as:

> The actual results are likely to be different from the prospective financial information since anticipated events frequently do not occur as expected and the variation could be material. Likewise, when the prospective financial information is expressed as a range, there can be no assurance that actual results will fall within that range. ... Prospective financial information has been prepared using a set of assumptions that include hypothetical assumptions about future events and management's actions that are not necessarily expected to occur.
>
> AUS 804 'The Audit of Prospective Financial Information' (para. 32)

It is difficult to reconcile this degree of caution with the wording of the normal audit report attached to financial statements:

> In our opinion, the financial report of [X Limited] is in accordance with:
> (a) the Corporations Act 2001, including:
>   (i) giving a true and fair view of the financial position of X Limited and consolidated entity as at [30 June 2007] and of their performance for the year ended on that date. ...

The problem regarding the uncertainty of forecasts will be exacerbated, because the auditors will be subjected to intense criticism if their judgment is shown to be wrong, and this is most likely to occur in the case of marginal companies where representations made by management will be difficult to evaluate.

While the question of accurate forecasting of prospective earnings is clearly an issue, there are other areas where impairment is vulnerable. It can even now be confidently predicted that companies will seek to make the valuation units as large as possible, to enable declines in one area to be offset by improvements in another.

The question as to whether internally generated goodwill should be allowed to offset declines in the value of purchased goodwill (even on the premise that the two can be distinguished after a few accounting periods have elapsed) is yet to be fully and explicitly clarified. In the US and IASB Standards, such an offset will be permitted, even if only by implication. Once this is established, the inconsistency of treatment between the two forms of goodwill will once more become evident, although in a slightly different form. Theorists will question why it should be permissible to recognize internally generated goodwill as an offset when purchased goodwill declines in value, but not in any other circumstance. After all, if it can be measured for that purpose, why should it not be capable of being measured for other accounts-related purposes?

Differences in valuation technique and bases will also have to be examined in detail. It has been noted that the 'fair value' definitions used do not, for example, expressly address the role of synergy in determining earnings predictions and values. In practice, synergy plays a role, whether in evaluating earnings of an existing enterprise in its present form or in considering the possible proceeds of a sale. However, traditional valuation methods tend to exclude considerations of synergy, which is not built into the 'willing buyer' 'willing seller' definition of fair value.

Especially where earnings are forecast over a lengthy period, as will often be the case when substantial business units are being valued, the discount rate chosen will be of great importance. Comparatively small variations in this rate can have large effects on discounted values, and it is not unlikely that management will seek to use discount rates that are unrealistically low in order to support unrealistic valuations, thereby avoiding write-downs.

Arguably today, most theorists would agree that it is better to be realistic than conservative. However, current proposals for the accounting treatment of goodwill, even under an impairment regime, have been based heavily towards conservatism. To give two examples, valuations can only be used to determine impairment and not to revalue goodwill; similarly, once the value of goodwill has been written down following an impairment review, the US and International Standards do not permit reinstatement, while the UK only does so in very limited circumstances. These conservative proposals, while understandable in the light of concerns about the reliability of valuations, will not answer critics (see Chapter 1.2) who are calling for increased and meaningful Balance Sheet recognition of the intangible items that often make up so much of a company's market capitalization (see Chapter 7 and Appendix 1).

I have referred previously to the anomalies inherent in the requirement to value goodwill on a reporting unit basis, rather than on an enterprise basis. Investors may be validly interested in falls in the value of a particular unit, but it seems counterproductive to deny them information regarding rises in the value of other such units; in the end result, it is likely to be the value of the enterprise as a whole that is of prime interest to readers of the accounts. In addition, the prohibition against restoring a value after it has been written down is difficult to understand. Assume, for example, that a period of high interest rates reduces the value of all reporting units because of its effect on the discount rates applied in the valuation. A subsequent decline in interest rates could not be recognized by a revaluation, even if predictions for the units concerned remained constant, or even improved substantially.

The fact that these issues are so foreseeable, even at the initiation of the impairment regime, makes it likely that this is just another chapter in the 'recycling of ideas', to be followed by its eventual rejection as yet another flawed paradigm once its defects are exposed in the light of actual experience.

The new impairment regime does address one inconsistency that was apparent under the amortization regime and attracted considerable criticism, particularly from the business community, viz. the requirement to charge amortization against profits when it was apparent that the value of goodwill had been maintained or improved. However, this has only been achieved at the cost of introducing a subjective valuation element into previously sacrosanct areas of historical cost accounting. The restricted provisions described above illustrate how difficult a step this has been for the accounting profession. At best, the new regime represents a partial solution, in that it does address one major problem that has reflected adversely on the credibility and usefulness of accounts prepared under amortization principles. At worst, the recommended procedures are subjective, complex, overconservative and not universally accepted.

Chapter 7.3 sets out the advantages of the proposed MCS, which addresses a number of the issues not addressed under impairment proposals, and seeks to provide a simpler and more complete solution to the problem of accounting for goodwill.

6 The Market Capitalization Statement (the MCS)

It is not the practice to disclose the value that the market places on an entity's issued capital. Accordingly there is nothing to concentrate the minds of readers of corporate reports on the difference between that figure and the figure shown in the balance sheet for shareholders' funds. We feel that there could be definite advantages in being able easily to make the comparison and to seek explanations of the difference.

(P. N. McMonnies, 1988)

6.1 Goodwill is an increasingly important constituent of the value of listed companies

It has become increasingly apparent, when market capitalization is computed, that goodwill is a large and growing component of that figure. Chapter 1.2 mentioned the part played by writers such as Lev and Tobin in drawing attention to this development, as well as a contemporary Australian Department of Industry study. In June 2001, the Business Competitiveness Division of the Australian Government Department of Industry, Science and Resources published a paper entitled 'Invisible Value – the case for increasing and reporting intellectual capital'. The foreword to the paper notes that the National Innovation Council, in February 2000, had included a recommendation 'to enhance recognition of the significance of intellectual capital and other intangible assets' (page 7). That paper cites several studies (unfortunately, the citations do not provide full reference details) at paragraph 31 *et seq.*, providing examples of the increasing relative importance of intangible assets in determining the capital market's assessment of the value of a company, although not the values of its separate assets. Some of these are:

i.   an analysis of 390 corporate takeovers in the US from 1991–93 (a period considerably predating the late 1990s–early 2000 high-tech boom and bust) showed that the average price paid by purchasing companies to acquire a company was 4.4 times the value of assets recorded in their Balance Sheets;

ii. the average market-to-book ratio of the Standard & Poor's 500 companies (many of which are not in high-tech industries) reached 6.25 in 1999;

iii. a study by the Centre for European Policy Studies in 1997 examined the market-to-book ratios for thousands of European and US companies between 1990 and 1995. Over this period, the European average ratio rose from 149 per cent to 202 per cent, while the corresponding US increase was from 194 per cent to 296 per cent;

iv. between 1973 and 1993, the median ratio of market value to book value of American public companies doubled;

v.   an analysis in *Business Week* (July 1997) found that 7 per cent of the US $148.5 billion market capitalization of Microsoft was accounted for by the book value of the traditional assets recorded on its Balance Sheet; intangible assets accounted for the remaining 93 per cent of its market value.

An analysis of the *Fortune 500* companies showed that, in 1975, 60 per cent of their market capitalization was represented by tangible assets but, twenty years later, that percentage was only 25 per cent. The trend has continued since 1995 (Ernst & Young website, accessed via http://www.ey.com/Global/content.nsf/UKCF_._SFS_._Intellectual_property). Lev (2001) also cites a number of relevant studies that reinforce this conclusion. The articles cited include Chang (1998), Barth et al. (undated) and Hall (1999, 2000).

An article co-authored by Feng Gu and Lev (2001) examines a methodology for establishing the value of intangible assets. The article does not purport to identify specific intangible assets, but rather to determine a value for 'knowledge capital', a generic term to cover all intangibles. The value of knowledge capital is determined independently, and not as a residual, and the technique, while worthy of study, falls outside the scope of this book. Table 2 attached to the article is, however, relevant in that it compares the ratio of median market value to median book value of the five leading stocks in twenty-two non-financial industries at 31 August 2000. Of these, only Airlines had a ratio of less than 1 (0.96). The highest was Computer Hardware with a ratio of 17.53.

The table has been rearranged to show the industries selected in the order of market value/book value Table 6.1. An additional column has been added to show the percentage of goodwill to total market value.

31 August 2000 is a date not long after the US stock market had begun its decline after reaching record levels in April/May 2000. At that date, goodwill (or, more correctly, the excess of market value over the net book value of the company as disclosed in the accounts of the companies concerned) made up more than half the market value in eighteen of the twenty-two categories, including a number of 'old economy' categories such as food/beverages, retail and newspapers. In no less than nine categories, that figure constituted more than 80 per cent of the aggregate market capitalization of the five largest companies in the industry. Potential control premiums, if

Table 6.1 Analysis of the percentage of market capitalization consisting of goodwill in twenty-two categories of US listed companies (August 2000)

Industry	Market value US$'bn	Market value/ Book value	% of Goodwill to market value
1. Computer hardware	202.719	17.53	94.3
2. Biotech	13.940	16.29	93.8
3. Computer software	48.465	15.15	93.4
4. Semi-conductors	89.911	12.57	92.0
5. Pharmaceuticals	116.073	12.16	91.8
6. Food/beverages	27.007	9.13	89.0
7. Speciality retail	17.154	8.01	87.5
8. Telecom equipment	96.184	7.73	87.0
9. Home products	29.257	6.57	84.8
10. Retail	18.486	3.75	73.3
11. Electrical	6.081	3.63	72.5
12. Telecom	118.288	3.47	71.2
13. Oil	55.150	3.30	69.7
14. Industrial	16.922	3.30	69.7
15. Newspapers	6.594	3.18	68.6
16. Media	82.396	2.72	63.2
17. Chemical	7.746	2.18	54.1
18. Electric utilities	19.418	2.09	52.1
19. Motor vehicles	9.205	1.87	46.5
20. Aerospace and defence	11.407	1.77	43.5
21. Forest products	10.322	1.48	32.4
22. Airlines	5.496	0.96	(4.2)

added to market capitalization as determined above, would further materially increase the percentage of goodwill to market value.

Appendix 1 contains an analysis of several Australian 'dot.com' companies listed on the ASX as well as six companies included among the top thirty by market capitalization. Intuitively, one would expect the market capitalization of a 'dot.com' company to consist largely of goodwill. However, the figures in Table 6.2 indicate that this is true of some of our largest 'old economy' companies 1 News Corporation, then Australia's largest corporation by market capitalization, recognizes its mastheads in its Balance Sheet at valuation), so that the goodwill percentages shown are closer to true goodwill.

Thus, for six of Australia's largest companies, covering a wide range of business activities, the goodwill content of market capitalization averaged 67 per cent over the period analysed. Even at 30 June 2002, following the steep decline in market prices from their earlier peak, the goodwill content averaged 59 per cent of market capitalization, with three of the six companies recording a figure of 80 per cent or more.

As explained previously, the Accounting Standards in Australia and elsewhere concern themselves virtually exclusively with purchased goodwill rather than internally generated goodwill. Table 6.3 is constructed on the simplifying assumption that purchased goodwill (as recorded in the Balance Sheets of the

Table 6.2 Percentage of market capitalization consisting of goodwill – six leading Australian listed companies

Company	1999 30/6	31/12	2000 30/6	31/12	2001 30/6	31/12	2002 30/6	Average over seven dates
News Corporation	47	52	67	45	47	36	27	**46**
Telstra	91	89	87	84	83	82	80	**85**
Wesfarmers	69	67	68	73	82	85	82	**75**
Westfield Holdings	90	89	89	90	90	85	83	**88**
Amcor	58	51	63	56	59	60	45	**56**
QBE	53	62	63	62	63	44	34	**54**
Average* at each date	**68**	**68**	**73**	**68**	**71**	**65**	**59**	**67**

* These averages are arithmetical; they have not been weighted to take account of the relative market capitalizations of the companies concerned.

companies in question) is fairly valued. It follows that the excess of the market capitalization over the total book values of the net tangible assets and purchased goodwill is a rough measure of the implied internally generated goodwill. Table 6.3 then sets out the average percentage of market capitalization that can be attributed to internally generated and purchased goodwill respectively. Even allowing for the approximate nature of the data, the lesson from the table is clear.

Table 6.3 Analysis of goodwill portion of market capitalization between internally generated and purchased goodwill

Company	Internally generated goodwill 1999 30/6	31/12	2000 30/6	31/12	2001 30/6	31/12	2002 30/6	Average over seven dates %	Purchased Goodwill %
News Corporation	46	51	67	44	46	35	25	**45**	1
Telstra	91	89	87	84	81	80	76	**84**	1
Wesfarmers	65	62	64	69	78	70	65	**68**	7
Westfield Holdings	90	89	89	90	90	85	83	**88**	0
Amcor	43	33	39	29	59	34	28	**38**	18
QBE	52	62	61	59	62	41	31	**53**	1
Average* at each date	**65**	**64**	**68**	**63**	**69**	**58**	**51**	**62**	5
% of market capitalization due to purchased goodwill	3	4	5	5	2	7	8	5	5

* These averages are arithmetical; they have not been weighted to take account of the relative market capitalizations of the companies concerned.

On average, purchased goodwill for the companies chosen (admittedly, a very small number) made up, on average, some 5 per cent of the total 67 per cent of market capitalization attributable to goodwill in total. The balance of 62 per cent was made up of internally generated goodwill; against that background, it is worth repeating at this stage that:

i.   Accounting Standards expressly exclude internally generated goodwill from recognition in the financial statements;
ii. almost a century of controversy and discussion has surrounded the accounting treatment of purchased goodwill, without the development of any real consensus, let alone a satisfactory consensus.

As noted above, during the period surveyed, it was not uncommon for Australian companies to include IIAs on their balance sheets. These were accordingly included in net identifiable assets, so that the MCS goodwill figures shown (as defined in Chapter 1.6 above) excluded these assets (except to the extent that the market considered they were undervalued). One such company is News Corporation, the company with the largest market capitalization, which includes an asset 'Publishing rights, titles and television licences' on its Balance Sheet, at cost. The market capitalization of News Corporation attributed the following relative values to these assets (at their book values) and 'MCS goodwill' (Table 6.4).

It is clear that the market attributed substantial value both to these assets and to residual, or MCS, goodwill (assuming that the purchased IIAs were considered fairly valued in the Balance Sheet). However, News Corporation noted in its 'USA GAAP' Balance Sheet at 30 June 1999:

As a creator and distributor of branded information and entertainment copyrights, the Company has a significant and growing amount of intangible assets, including goodwill, free and cable television networks and stations, film and television networks and stations, film and television

Table 6.4 Comparison of goodwill and IIA proportions of News Corporation market capitalization

Year ended 30 June	IIAs per Balance Sheet $'M	Market capitalization $'M	Ratio of book value of IIAs to market capitalization (%)	Ratio of MCS goodwill to market capitalization (%)
1999	19,598	46,178	42	47
2000	26,884	90,031	30	67
2001	31,051	79,653	39	47
2002	35,348	46,521	76	27

libraries, sports franchises, entertainment franchises and other copyright products and trademarks. In accordance with generally accepted accounting principles, the Company does not record the fair value of these internally generated intangible assets.

This emphasizes that, in the case of complex companies such as News Corporation, MCS goodwill functions as a 'master valuation account' under present accounting conventions. Intangible assets made up a far less significant portion of the assets of the other five companies examined. Westfield and Amcor had no such assets (apart from an immaterial $9 million reflected by Amcor in 2002), and Wesfarmers' only identifiable intangible asset was trade names, reflected at $42 million throughout the period.

Telstra reflected patents, trademarks and licences throughout the period, at values ranging between $421 million and $772 million, while in 2001 and 2002 brand names and customer bases were added to the list of intangible assets. The highest figure for total intangible assets (other than goodwill) was $1,464 million in 2001, which only amounted to some 2 per cent of market capitalization. However, the Balance Sheet value of QBE's IIAs (which included insurance licences, infrastructure and Lloyds syndicate capacity) ranged from 7 per cent to 11 per cent of its total capitalization from 2000 to 2002.

With the adoption of the new International Accounting Standards, it will no longer be possible to recognize such IIAs in the Balance Sheet if they are internally generated, while purchased intangible assets will fall under a similar impairment regime to that of goodwill (except that, in certain narrowly defined circumstances, revaluation of such assets will be permitted).

The data in Tables 6.3 and 6.4 invite the comment that the current amortization versus impairment debate, and much of the goodwill controversy over past years, has been concerned with what is, in relative terms, a minor matter. Although the number of companies is far too small to be conclusive, it is indicative. The entire volume of Accounting Statements, UIG Abstracts (the UIG, or Urgent Issues Group, is an Australian body that was formed with the power to issue authoritative and speedy pronouncements on controversial accounting issues) and Statements of Accounting Concepts dealing with Balance Sheet issues is directed to proper accounting for factors dealing with some 38 per cent of these companies' average market capitalization, including purchased goodwill representing 5 per cent of that 38 per cent. Similarly, the goodwill debate has been focused on purchased goodwill, which is a relatively minor constituent of goodwill as a whole (5 per cent out of 67 per cent for those companies). The six companies analysed are among Australia's largest, and are far removed from the 'dot.com bubble', where the market capitalization of companies relied, almost by definition, on non-purchased goodwill. The Accounting Standards expressly exclude a factor responsible for 62 per cent of market capitalization from their scope.

6.2 Information regarding goodwill should be in the Annual Report

The information above has shown that the Annual Report contains accounts prepared in accordance with rules that expressly provide that accounting is not concerned with a factor which makes up a major component (often the major component) of market capitalization. This is especially illogical, because the Annual Report is accepted as the major source of information for shareholders and others who wish to analyse a company. It is supplemented and updated by other information releases, but it remains the most extensive document routinely produced by the company during the year that is readily accessible to shareholders and the public. For example, an Australian study by Anderson in 1981, which polled institutional investors, showed that, out of 188 such investors, 109 rated the Annual Report of maximum (21) or great (88) importance, while only thirty-four rated it of slight (30) or no (4) importance (Anderson 1981: 262).

A comparable study in the US (SRI International 1987: 35) assessed the importance of the Annual Report to investors and professional analysts, in various categories. The percentages of those who listed the Annual Report as among their most used information sources, in each category, were as shown in Table 6.5.

Figures such as those illustrated in Table 6.5 indicate a wide reliance on the Annual Report and are an incentive for making it as useful and relevant as possible.

It is generally accepted that providing a shareholder or other reader of the Annual Report with means of access to information is not an adequate replacement for providing the information itself. For example, the Accounting Standards differentiate between recognition (i.e. explicit recognition by inclusion in the financial statements themselves) and mere inclusion in the notes attached to those statements. While a shareholder could, no doubt, calculate the value of a company by reference to its issued capital and market price, it is clearly easier if this information is provided in the Annual Report, as McMonnies observed:

> It is not the practice to disclose the value that the market places on an entity's issued capital. Accordingly there is nothing to concentrate the minds of readers of corporate reports on the difference between that figure

Table 6.5 Usefulness of the Annual Report as an information source

Individual investors		Professionals	
All investors	59.3%	All professionals	84.6%
Buy and hold investors	60.4%	Sell side analysts	82.0%
Opportunity driven investors	56.6%	Buy side analysts	82.0%
Semi-professionals	64.2%	Brokers	89.0%

Source: SRI International (1987)

and the figure shown in the balance sheet for shareholders' funds. We feel that there could be definite advantages in being able easily to make the comparison and to seek explanations of the difference.

McMonnies (1988: para. 4.9)

Information regarding a company's share price at its balance date is not readily accessible, and it is the market capitalization at that date that is most relevant for financial analysis purposes. A company's market capitalization and the extent to which it is represented by goodwill is an essential element in assessing the state of affairs of a listed company. The movements in the value of goodwill from year to year provide a reader of the financial statements with a guide as to how the market assesses the company under review, which is very important in evaluating its state of affairs and its future prospects. Goodwill is heavily dependent on the economy and the market in general, but it is also a function of internally generated information supplied to shareholders and the market. Given the fact that public companies use their shares to make acquisitions, their market status is critical in assessing their ability to grow. Conversely, an undervalued company may be a tempting takeover target, especially in periods when leveraged buyouts are common.

Proper accounting for goodwill is a major task for the accounting profession, and the work of Lev and the other examples listed and quoted herein confirm that it is inappropriate and dangerous to abrogate their responsibilities in this regard. This principle is developed by Clarke, Dean and Oliver (2003: 326):

> Attempts to take away the supposed *gap* between what accountants and auditors do and what they are expected to be doing by the public at large is apposite. We are told what accountants do and how they do it is not questionable, it is more the case that everybody other than members of the profession and regulators has unreasonable, misguided expectations – there is an *expectation gap* – a gap, that is, between what the consumers unreasonably expect from accounting and auditing and what they get.
>
> That is true enough. One would think that a better way of fixing the image would be to improve the products. ... What is inexplicable is the promotion of the idea that the way to repair the damaged image of accounting and auditing is to have consumers understand that accounting data are not serviceable, that statements of financial performance and financial position are limited in their usefulness, and fairness ... that is, to explain that there is not so much an expectation gap as what amounts to a *credibility gap*.

The proposed MCS seeks to provide disclosure of serviceable data in a manner that will assist in reducing the credibility gap.

6.3 Market capitalization

Listing of companies on the ASX and other stock exchanges provides a day by day objective 'valuation' of such companies by way of their market capitalization, obtained by a simple formulation:

> Market capitalization = number of issued shares (including any shares held in escrow for ASX purposes) multiplied by the closing price of an individual share on the day in question.

The semi-strong form of the efficient market hypothesis indicates that the market (and hence the market capitalization) already allows for the potential effect on market capitalization of publicly available knowledge such as the potential exercise of options and the existence of compound financial instruments with conversion rights. This largely explains why market capitalization is so simply defined. *The Financial Taxonomy* by Lynn Wheeler (http://public.planetmirror.com/pub/lynn/fintax.htm#t3813) defines the term as 'the total dollar value of all outstanding shares. Computed as shares times current market price. It is a measure of corporate size'.

Other definitions of the term are equally simple and are similar. The glossary on the Irish Stock Exchange website (http://www.ise.ie.) defines it as 'the number of shares in issue multiplied by the current market share price', while the glossary of the Financial Times Stock Exchange, or 'Footsie', website (http://www.havenworks.wm/acronyms/a-z/f/ftse) defines market capitalization as 'Value at current market prices of a company's equity share capital. It equates to the share price times the number of shares outstanding'. The glossary of share market terms attached to the ASX website (http://www.asx.com.au) adds little: 'The total number of shares on issue multiplied by their market price. This can be applied to work out the market value of the company or of the value of all companies listed on the Exchange'.

Although all these definitions use the word 'value', the 'value' given by the formula is an arithmetic value, rather than a true value of the net worth of the company. This aspect is discussed in the following paragraphs.

Clarke, Dean and Oliver (2003: 278) comment, in relation to market prices:

> Markets are never perfect. Information is never complete. But the market prices of items are as objective in evaluation of their contemporary money's worth, of their current contribution to the wealth of their owners, as can be found. ... Share prices might reasonably be expected to capture not only their companies' current financial position and an understanding of how it arose, but also impound all the expectations and fears for the future that the information might evoke. A rational economic perspective would suggest that.

The rules of the ASX are specifically designed to ensure an informed market, with requirements for timely and continuous disclosure of information relevant to investors. As noted earlier, the semi-strong form of the efficient market hypothesis states that the market can quickly absorb and adjust for public information. This reinforces the suitability of market capitalization for the purpose chosen, in that the measure is likely to be both objective and efficient. Standard setters in the US and the IASC have embraced market prices as the most realistic *prima facie* indicators of fair value.

SFAS 157 'Fair Value Measurements', which is effective for financial years commencing after November 2007, establishes a hierarchy of values for 'fair value' determination. Level 1 is the most reliable determinant of value, and the summary of SFAS 157, posted on http://www.fasb.org/st/summary/stsum157.shtml, states:

> This Statement affirms the requirement of other FASB Statements that the fair value of a position in a financial instrument (including a block) that trades in an active market should be measured as the product of the quoted price for the individual instrument times the quantity held (within Level 1 of the fair value hierarchy). The quoted price should not be adjusted because of the size of the position relative to trading volume (blockage factor).

Of particular interest is that the quoted price is deemed to be reliable at Level 1, despite any 'blockage factor'. The IASB has currently issued a discussion paper on the issue of 'Fair Value Measurements'. At para. 47, the IASB notes that it favours the hierarchical system used in SFAS 157, but calls for further comment. The final date for comments was 2 April 2007.

AASB 1015 (para. 12.1.7) examines the question of determining the fair value of marketable securities in the context of offering such securities as part or all of the purchase consideration, and concludes that 'the fair value of those securities is normally their market price as at the acquisition date'. In this context, however, AASB 1015 notes that, 'in some instances the notional price at which they could be placed in the market is a better indication of fair value'. This may occur, for example, when in order to place a significant number of shares in a company, it may be necessary to offer a discount to market value, although, as noted above, SFAS 147 specifically notes that this 'blockage' factor is not to be taken into account. It will be interesting to see which of these views is eventually relied upon in any relevant IFRS.

There are other reasons why, in any individual case, the market capitalization formula given above may not provide a 'fair' value for the company as a whole. Perhaps most significantly:

i. the price of an individual listed share ignores any 'control premium' that may be payable if an offer is made for the whole of the issued capital or a majority interest therein;
ii. the price on any single day may be affected by atypical market issues, or may be subject to some degree of market manipulation;
iii. for some listed companies, the shares are 'thinly traded', and the volume of trades may be too small to provide a reliable price for this purpose.

While it is true that the formula does not expressly provide for a control premium, if the market considers that a takeover bid is likely or imminent, this will be recognized to some extent in the market price of the share in question. Clarke and Dean (2007) make this point strongly: 'Whether there is control would have an impact on the respective prices the shareholding would fetch in the market. The market might reasonably be expected to unravel that'.

Moreover, the company value derived is a value relevant to the great majority in number, if not necessarily in value, of shareholders; if they sell their shares on the market, in the absence of a general takeover offer, the price quoted corresponds with that which they will receive on the day in question. Because the market price is externally determined, it is likely to be more reliable than an internal assessment of 'what the company is worth', especially given the continuous disclosure requirements aimed at ensuring a properly informed market.

Using market price consistently also ensures that the basis of ascertaining market capitalization is constant from year to year. Although conservatism, of itself, is not a virtue in accounting, using actual market value rather than increasing that value to provide for a putative takeover premium helps to ensure that the value obtained is not likely to be unrealistically high.

Most importantly, market capitalization calculated on this basis is simple, objective and able to be both precisely calculated and externally verified. Valuations commissioned by the board of directors would be open to the charge of subjectivity and could create problems for the valuers in that they would almost inevitably rely on forecasts not available to the general public; this would apply whether the valuations were carried out by independent experts or by internal company staff. This could be excused, perhaps, if forecasts were inherently reliable but, as AUS 804 'The Audit of Prospective Financial Information' (para. 32) points out, they are not:

> The actual results are likely to be different from the prospective financial information since anticipated events frequently do not occur as expected and the variation could be material. Likewise, when the prospective financial information is expressed as a range. ... there can be no assurance that actual results will fall within that range. ... Prospective financial information has been prepared using a set of assumptions that include hypothetical assumptions about future events

and management's actions that are not necessarily expected to occur. (This paragraph has been quoted previously, in the context of audit responsibility for reporting on forecasts – see Chapter 5.6 above.)

With regard to the second matter listed above, viz. the possibility of market manipulation or atypical market issues affecting the price on any single day, it would be possible to minimize this risk by using an average of the closing market prices for a period of, say, three to five days before and after the end of the financial year. Generally speaking, the risk is lower when the shares in an individual company are heavily traded; this is further explored in the extract from McMonnies (1988) quoted below and previously in Chambers (1966) and subsequent works. Similarly, in the case of thinly traded stocks, the price used could be defined to include sufficient trades to establish a reliable basis for the determination of market capitalization, rather than just using the closing price at balance date.

Because market capitalization is able to be objectively and easily calculated, this book has used the phrasing 'Market Capitalization Statement' rather than 'Market Value Statement'. In doing so, it is recognized that market capitalization fills the function of a valuation in enabling the calculation of goodwill as a residual.

The idea of providing market capitalization data to assist readers of the Annual Report is not new. McMonnies (1988: 5.3) commented: 'We believe that the total wealth of an entity and the changes in it from period to period are what should be of major importance to managers and to investors', and went on to say, at para. 5.21, 'we suggest that it would be helpful if managements disclosed the market capitalization figure as a guide to the approximate value of the unidentifiable or unmeasurable net "assets" from which a company benefits'. The MCS, as presented here, extends this idea.

McMonnies' comments on market capitalization are relevant, and are quoted extensively in view of the importance of this concept in presenting the MCS.

6.13   The value of a company which is quoted on a recognized and liquid stock exchange is most precisely measured during a merger or takeover negotiation, whether hostile or friendly ... In the case of sales of public companies, it can be assumed that the transaction is entered into by two knowledgeable sets of parties, so that the value arrived at is a fair price.

6.14   The value of the shares of public companies at other times will in general be subject to much less scrutiny. The actively traded alpha stocks are almost certainly kept at a value which is close to the true figure. ... (For those not familiar with the expressions, 'alpha', 'beta' and 'gamma' were terms applied at the time of the 'Big Bang' to stocks and shares on the basis of the quantities in which they were traded on the exchange. 'Alpha' signified those with the largest turnover, 'gamma' those with the smallest.)

6.15   Beta and gamma stocks, by definition, receive less attention than alpha stocks. There are fewer traders making the market and fewer shareholders are interested in what they are doing. It is therefore possible that, in the absence of any merger activity, the price at which a beta stock trades may be further away from its 'true' value than an alpha would be.

6.16   At the same time, so far as we are aware, there is only one case on record in which the premium on a successful bid for a company quoted on the London exchange was negative. It would seem to follow that the price for which shares are currently quoted on the exchange gives an estimate of the value of the entity which is consistently at or below the true value. The quoted price will be closest to that value during merger negotiations, and below it the rest of the time. The amount by which it is below will be relatively small for alpha stocks, and higher for the less actively traded.

6.17   The market capitalization, computed by taking the current share price and multiplying by the number of issued shares, is therefore a conservative estimate of the true value of the business. The error is likely to be in the region of 15–20% on the average share, as this has been found to be the average amount of the takeover premium.

6.18   This error is very significantly less than the errors which would be likely to arise if the historical cost book figure were to be used. Such book figures in balance sheets are not intended to have a relationship to market capital values.

It is posited that the error is likely to be significantly less than that which would be obtained by utilizing directors' valuations of the company, which are likely to be based on subjective views of prospective data. A valuation by a third party expert at the end of each year would have the advantage of independence, but would be far more costly and complex. It would also have to rely on subjective evaluation of future projections and suitable discount rates, which could place the expert in a very difficult position if actual future events proved the valuation to have been in error. It is these considerations that have led to the recommendation to use 'market capitalization' and to eschew the term 'value' in the MCS.

6.4 Traditional treatments of goodwill provide unserviceable data

Chapter 1 introduced the concept of the MCS, which would permit the readers of Annual Reports to obtain reliable information regarding goodwill, without the distortions and inconsistencies imposed by the professionally approved methods of accounting for goodwill that have been adopted to date.

The preceding chapters have put the case that it is impossible to obtain reliable, logically consistent and undistorted information of this kind within the rigid framework imposed by the historical cost based system of accounting. This is because the goodwill of an entity is developed by many transactions and interactions that do not have an identifiable cost that can be isolated and charged directly to goodwill. This is recognized explicitly in AASB 1013 (para. 4.1.1), which states:

> Goodwill which is internally generated by an entity is not permitted by this Standard to be recognized as an asset by that entity. This is principally because of the difficulty, or impossibility, of identifying the events or transactions which contribute to the overall goodwill of the entity. Even if these were identifiable, the extent to which they generate future benefits and the value of such benefits are not usually capable of being measured reliably. *Internally generated goodwill which is not recognized as an asset will either go completely unrecognized or will be recognized as an expense* (emphasis added).

Although AASB 1013 is no longer applicable, the new AIFRS do nothing to change this.

It is comparatively easy to define the cost of purchased goodwill and recognize a specific figure in the accounts of an entity. However, experience has shown that there is no treatment of this figure, once established, that has met with universal approval; more than a century of impassioned debate has failed to produce an accounting standard that would resolve the inherent inconsistencies inescapable within the historical cost framework.

Not least among these inconsistencies is the fact that, although the cost of purchased goodwill is easy to establish, its separate identity is, in practice, soon lost as the acquired entity becomes merged into the operations of the acquirer. The debate during the exposure draft period, prior to the recent introduction of the impairment standards, has highlighted the validity of the point made by Ma and Hopkins (1988). Except in the comparatively rare case when the business acquired has maintained an entirely separate identity within the acquiring group, it is difficult, if not impossible, to isolate purchased goodwill sufficiently, as a component of total goodwill, to calculate whether its value has been impaired or not.

Given the acknowledgment in AASB 1013 (para. 5.1.3) that 'the concept of goodwill as an asset is the same regardless of whether it has been purchased in an exchange transaction or generated internally', there seems little purpose in devising elaborate procedures to isolate purchased goodwill in order to calculate whether any impairment in its value has occurred while specifically excluding consideration of any offsetting appreciation in the value of internally generated goodwill. The distinction may be of technical interest to accountants straining to preserve the integrity of the historical cost principle; it is of no importance to a reader seeking to extract meaning from financial statements.

Not only has the Balance Sheet been affected; reported results have become ambiguous. The confusion that still exists, despite all the goodwill accounting standards, is illustrated by the following comment which appeared in *BRW* as recently as 10 June 2004 (p. 41). In relation to listed company Flight Centre (a company in the ASX top 100, with a market capitalization of $1.7 billion), analyst Sophie Mitchell, of ABN-Amro, is quoted as saying:

> ... the company experienced a sharp downturn in its share price in late February because of the way it presented its interim results. 'The way [the results] were reported sent out mixed messages'. The company reported earnings of $34.1 million after tax in the six months to December 31 last year, a 10% increase on the previous corresponding half. The shares immediately fell by 12% to $19.70.

Mitchell says:

> The company reported on a post-goodwill basis, so it looked like they were growing at only 10%, and [the market] is used to double that for Flight Centre. If you added back the goodwill, then growth was about 20%, which was fine. I think for want of a better word, the [price] has not recovered from this misunderstanding.

6.5 Is goodwill an asset? – the controversy revisited

This hotly debated topic is, in many ways, rendered irrelevant by the proposed MCS. There are many recent writers such as Walter Schuetze who maintain that goodwill should not be recognized at all in financial statements:

> I use my sister as a guidepost when I think about accounting issues. ... she recently bought out one of her competitors and paid about $100,000 in excess of the fair value of the identifiable net assets acquired. The competitor agreed not to compete against my sister's business for five years. I told her that the $100,000 represented the cost of the non-compete agreement and purchased goodwill, which, under generally accepted accounting principles, should be reported as assets. She laughed at me. Try to pay salaries, rent, the electricity, or dividends with those assets, she says. That kind of accounting may be okay for Wall Street but not for Main Street in Comfort, Texas.
>
> Schuetze (2001a: 20)

Elsewhere, Schuetze (2004) described goodwill as a 'blob'.

This follows the view of Chambers (1974: 212), who contends that goodwill is not an asset of a business, for the following reasons:

i. it is non-severable, whereas severability is an integral part of his definition of an asset ('any severable means in the possession of an entity');

ii. it cannot be reliably measured. He distinguishes between valuation
(described as being personal and entirely subjective) and measurement,
which is universal and objective;

iii. it vests in the owner, rather than in the business entity;

iv. if goodwill were calculated perfectly accurately, and were included as an
asset, the risk adjusted rate of return on all business assets would be
equal (i.e. such a calculation and inclusion would disguise the fact that
businesses do earn differing rates of return on their net assets).

These reasons are open to criticism, particularly in the context of listed
companies.

i. Goodwill may in fact be severable in relation to many different business
units within the overall group or company structure.

ii. As discussed previously, severability is a limited criterion for asset
recognition. In certain cases, an entity may be able to derive financial
benefits from an asset, even though unable to alienate it, e.g. by leasing it.

iii. The usefulness and accuracy of valuations based on future projections
has been questioned. However, in practice, valuations of public companies are done routinely; these valuations can be used to calculate goodwill in a generally acceptable manner. Market capitalization is another
measure that would enable goodwill to be measured with a reasonable,
practical degree of accuracy (although, as discussed, it does not incor-
porate a premium for control, unlike most formal valuations).

iv. Goodwill, if it results from the sale of some or all of its business by the
corporate entity, vests in the entity rather than the shareholders; it is
only in the case of a takeover that the shareholders realize the direct
benefit of the goodwill realization.

v. Chambers' comment regarding the rate of return was discussed in Chapter
3.4. As defined, it is correct but tautologous. In practice, it is unlikely
that goodwill calculations could be made across the board in such a way
as to equate return on assets employed.

Others such as Catlett and Olson (1968) have also argued for the exclusion
of goodwill from financial statements (see Chapter 4.8 above). Their reasons
for doing so have been summarized previously.

On the other hand, if the definition in SAC 4 (para. 2.5) is followed,
goodwill would qualify to be recognized as an asset when it is probable that
future benefits embodied in the asset will eventuate. This conforms to the
position in virtually all current Accounting Standards, which accept that
(purchased) goodwill does qualify as an asset for recognition purposes.

IAS 38 (paras 37–38) emphasizes that it is the difficulty in ascertaining
the cost of internally generated goodwill that prevents it from meeting the

criteria for asset recognition, rather than the inherent nature of such good-will. As has been seen from the numerous definitions quoted earlier, how-ever, there is general agreement, at least, on the following propositions:

i. goodwill cannot be determined, in total, without a valuation of the entire enterprise;
ii. whatever the factors making up goodwill in any individual case, goodwill can be valued by the following formula:

Goodwill = Total entity value − Fair value of net identifiable assets;

iii. there is no qualitative difference between purchased and internally gen-erated goodwill.

The MCS proceeds from these three propositions to develop a simple and logically coherent method of accounting for goodwill.

6.6 The MCS – a modification of the double account

The concept of expanding the financial statements beyond the traditional Balance Sheet and Profit and Loss Account is by no means new. The UK's *1975 Corporate Report* proposed a Value Added Statement. In Australia, a Statement of Source and Application of Funds formed part of the financial accounts from 1991 until 30 June 1998; after that date, it was replaced by the Statement of Cash Flows (see AASB 1026). McMonnies (1988: paras 7.23 and 7.27) recommended the supplementation of the Balance Sheet and Profit and Loss Account with a Statement of Changes in Financial Wealth and a Distributions Statement. These additional recommendations were contained in a discussion document issued by the Research Committee of The Institute of Chartered Accountants of Scotland, entitled *Making Cor-porate Reports Valuable*. Significantly for the ideas developed below, it also recommended that financial statements should report the market capitali-zation of an enterprise.

Morgenstern (1963: 82) drew attention to the fact that asset values in a conventional Balance Sheet were all expressed in a similar way and appeared to have the same degree of precision. In fact, certain assets, such as cash, may be stated precisely, while the value of other assets, such as inventory and, in particular, goodwill, can only be established subject to a degree of estimation error. He proposed that at least two values (the carry-ing value and a 'most likely' value) be furnished for all assets other than cash, using a columnar form of Balance Sheet. Morgenstern was primarily concerned with 'value' as a factor in making economic decisions, and assessed the usefulness of the Balance Sheet on that basis.

The concept of a separate MCS to be relied upon here is drawn from the format used in the 'double account' system used, *inter alia*, by railway and other utility companies in the UK in the latter part of the nineteenth century, and UK municipal corporations until the early 1990s. Coombs and Tayib (1998) note that it was as late as 1993 that the Capital Accounting Working Group was set up. It led to the requirement that local authorities in the UK replace their system of debt charge accounting for capital assets, 'based broadly on the double account system and the basis of how the asset was financed', with a more modern system charging service managers with an asset rent.

The double account system is still used in India. An examination paper issued by the Institute of Chartered Accountants in India in November 2003 tested students on their knowledge of the system as applied to an electricity company which replaced its plant with one of larger capacity (obtained from the internet at the site http://www.icai.org/students/rtp_pc2_accounts_part1.doc). Walker, Clarke and Dean (2000: 134) point out that variants of the double account concept have been proposed for diverse purposes such as reporting on infrastructure during periods of high inflation, for electricity and mining companies in Australia and for public sector accounting in both Australia and the UK. As noted, municipal corporations and utilities have also used the concept in the UK.

Edwards (1985: 19) notes that the distinguishing characteristic of the double account system is the sub-division of the conventional Balance Sheet into the following two accounting statements:

1. The Capital Account, which sets out the capital raised from issuing shares and debentures and the amounts spent on 'fixed' or 'capital' assets, that is, assets of a permanent nature acquired to carry on the business.
2. The General Balance Sheet, which sets out the 'floating' assets and liabilities that are in a continuous state of change as the result of trading transactions.

He observes that the double account emerged in response to shareholder demands for better information, seeking improvements in reporting practices that had been fairly rudimentary. Following the railway financial mania in the 1840s, the early UK railway companies responded to a crisis in shareholder confidence both by providing more information using the double account and by changing the basis of reporting, from cash based accounting to the accrual concept.

The original double account system included, via the capital account, a separate statement of how the capital raised was spent on infrastructure. The balance remaining unspent was carried down to the 'floating capital' section of the Balance Sheet and served as a link. In the MCS, the link between the Balance Sheet and the MCS is provided by the amount expended on purchased goodwill and other intangible assets; the MCS then shows how much of market capitalization consists of 'MCS goodwill', of which purchased goodwill and intangible assets are components. The primary function of the capital portion of the original double account was a stewardship one – it served to demonstrate whether or not funds raised by way of capital had been invested in fixed assets, and thus tended to reflect a permanent historical record of infrastructure spending. The MCS, on the other hand, reflects a number of constantly changing amounts, and it is the fluctuations that give the statement its significance: 'The present study makes use of the concept underlying the double account system in the sense of requiring the identification, on a separate account, of expenditure different in kind from the remainder so that its significance can be assessed by shareholders'. (This quotation and much of the paragraph preceding it is drawn from comments made by an examiner in an initial review of the thesis on which this book is based.)

The modification of the double account concept is proposed as a simple and practical way to address the redefined problem set out in Chapter 1.3, viz. to provide improved information relating to goodwill in the financial statements contained in the Annual Report.

6.7 The structure of the MCS

The structure of the MCS is simple; preliminary examples have been furnished in Chapter 1. Its simplicity is a virtue, in that the salient points are more easily appreciated. No less an authority than Popper commented (1934/1961, as cited in Chambers 1995: para. 859): 'Simple statements, if knowledge is an object, are to be prized more highly than less simple ones because they tell us more; because their empirical content is greater and because they are better testable'.

This is supported by Ross (1966, as cited in Chambers 1995: para. 793): 'What we need is a relatively few significant figures, properly calculated and clearly stated ... a general overall view is all that can be expected from a balance sheet and income statement ... additional detail that does not affect the general picture ... is undesirable'. Chambers, too, has argued for the 'reform of accounting ideas and practices by recourse to the essential simplicity of commercial intercourse' (1999: 121). As recently as 2001, Schuetze (2001a: 18) commented: 'Ordinary people, chief executive officers, line operating managers, members of boards of directors, investors and creditors and regulators, who are not accountants, should be able to look at financial statements and reports and understand the information portrayed and conveyed'.

I have used the expanded MCS, incorporating IIAs, as the preferred version in this chapter. The MCS would form a supplement to the conventional Balance Sheet, or Statement of Financial Position. The only change initially envisaged to the Statement of Financial Position, as presently conventionally presented, is that any amounts expended in the purchase of goodwill and other intangible assets should be *explicitly* deducted from the figure currently shown as Owners' Equity (i.e. Share Capital and Reserves). It follows that the Statement of Financial Performance will not be charged with any amortization of purchased goodwill and IIAs. This would bring the financial statements, at least as far as goodwill is concerned, in line with the position advocated by Chambers, Schuetze, Catlett and Olson and a number of earlier advocates mentioned in previous chapters (Table 6.6).

6.8 The MCS forms a link between conventional financial statements and accounting for intellectual capital

Guthrie, Petty and Johanson (2001: 365) have commented:

> Particularly for companies in non-traditional industries, book values of assets tend historically to correlate poorly with market capitalisation. This renders an understanding of how value is represented problematic from the perspective of an ordinary accounting calculus, and has the potential to further erode the currency of accounting as a function that supports informed decision making by external stakeholders. Important also is the recognition that internal stakeholders in public and private sector organisations require diverse types of information, extending beyond that delivered by traditional accounting practice. Partly in response to this realisation, a discourse and visualisation of intellectual capital has emerged and has been accompanied by a push to establish new metrics and other ways that can be used to record and report the value attributable to intellectual capital within an organisation.

The analysis herein shows that the lack of correlation between book values and market capitalization is not limited to companies in non-traditional areas.

If Knight's (1940) analysis is accepted (see Chapter 2.4 above), the ability of an enterprise to manage uncertainty is the major factor underlying the generation of profits, which, in this context, can be equated to super-profits, as a 'normal' return to capital is assumed. The factors creating this ability can be correlated with intellectual capital, so that an understanding of intellectual capital and the ability to create goodwill are closely linked.

The MCS, by focusing on MCS goodwill and intangible assets in a meaningful way, provides a link between conventional financial statements and current developments in accounting for intellectual capital, in terms of both explaining the constituents of intellectual capital and quantifying them. Appendix 2 explores some of these developments, which could lead to an expansion of the MCS as presented here or support the presentation of additional meaningful data in the Annual Report.

Table 6.6 Complete illustration of MCS with explanatory notes The current Equity portion of the Balance Sheet would read as follows: (using illustrative figures)

	Current Year $'000	Previous Year $'000	Notes
Contributed equity	1	40,000	38,000
Reserves	1	10,000	10,000
Retained profits	1	20,000	15,000
	1	70,000	63,000
Less: Cost of goodwill and other intangible assets purchased	2,3,13	20,000	18,000
Net tangible assets	4	50,000	45,000

The accompanying MCS would be structured as follows:

Market capitalization statement

Number of issued shares		150,000	140,000
Market price per share ($)		50¢	60¢
Market capitalization	5	75,000	84,000
Comprising:			
IIAs, at valuation	6,7,8		
Patents		3,000	4,000
Contracts with suppliers		5,000	5,000
Licences		2,000	1,500
Technology		4,000	6,000
Total IIAs		14,000	16,000
MCS goodwill	9	11,000	23,000
Total intangible assets	10	25,000	39,000
Net tangible assets	4	50,000	45,000
Market capitalization	5	75,000	84,000
Ratio of MCS goodwill to market capitalization	11	15%	27%
Ratio of total intangible assets to market capitalization	11	33%	46%
Details of cost of goodwill and other intangible assets purchased:			
Patents		2,000	3,000
Contracts with suppliers		4,000	4,000
Technology		4,000	6,000
Total IIAs purchased		10,000	13,000
Goodwill	12	10,000	5,000
	13	20,000	18,000

Explanatory notes:
1. As per conventional Balance Sheet.
2. The aggregate amount of all purchased goodwill and other (i.e. identifiable) intangible assets. This would be calculated as at present with fair values for IIAs determined at the point of purchase and goodwill as a residual.

3. In the year of introduction of the MCS, it would be necessary to write back the net book value of all goodwill and other intangibles at the commencement of the year. Purchases during the year would be transferred to the MCS at cost.

4. The tangible assets and liabilities making up net tangible assets would be shown in the same manner as at present, and in accordance with current accounting standards and recommendations. The amount of net tangible assets appears both in the Balance Sheet and the MCS. (But see Chapter 7)

5. The "market capitalization" of the company at year-end would be determined simply by multiplying the number of issued shares at balance date by the closing price of the share on that date. This would include all listed shares, as well as shares not listed temporarily (e.g. shares held in escrow at the time). It would not include preference shares or shares having no right to participate in a distribution of surplus assets.

6. The valuation techniques utilized for IIAs will be that currently used to establish the "fair value" of such assets on the acquisition of another entity, **but applied to the whole economic entity, not just to the purchased entity.** This is not the place for a treatise on those valuation techniques, but it is envisaged that the principles laid down in SFAS 157 be employed. Most notably, notes supporting the valuations should indicate, as a minimum:

   (i) the level within the hierarchy used for each asset or group of assets, distinguishing between quoted prices in active markets for identical assets or liabilities (Level 1, which would be likely to be extremely rare), significant other observable prices or inputs (Level 2) and significant unobservable inputs (Level 3);

   (ii) for Level 3 measurements, the valuation techniques used to measure fair value and disclosure of any changes in those techniques from the prior period.

7. For simplicity, it is highly recommended that only one value need be shown in respect of any single intangible asset (e.g. licences, favourable contracts etc). This would permit a decline in the value of portion of such an asset to be offset by an appreciation in the value of a similar asset.

8. As each valuation is carried out independently on an annual basis, it follows that a decline on the value of an asset in one year would not preclude that asset being given a higher value in a subsequent year if circumstances changed to support that higher value.

9. MCS goodwill represents the difference between the market capitalization and the aggregate of the book value of net tangible assets and the fair value of IIAs. It may thus correctly be described as the unidentifiable intangible portion of market capitalization.

10. Total intangible assets cannot be compared with the cost of goodwill and other intangible items purchased, because it will normally include a significant amount of self generated value. However, if the present value of all intangible assets is less than the cost of those purchased, there would be a presumption that the value of intangibles had not been maintained.

11. These are given as examples of useful ratios which could be included in the MCS. Fluctuations in these ratios from year to year are likely to be informative to readers.

12. Although MCS goodwill is not directly comparable with purchased goodwill, if it is less than that figure it would be a strong indication that the value of purchased goodwill had not been maintained.

13. This total agrees with the comparable figure deducted from Equity in the Balance Sheet. The individual figures are not directly comparable with their counterparts in the MCS, because the latter include internally generated items in each category as well as purchased items.

6.9 Identifiable intangible assets

Australia was a pioneer (and stood virtually alone for a long time) in recognizing IIAs on the Balance Sheet. AASB 138 (para. 8) permitted the possibility of valuation of certain intangible assets, in cases where an active market exists. This requires that the items traded are homogeneous, that willing buyers and sellers can normally be found at any time and prices are generally available. The Standard also states (para. 78) that such markets 'cannot exist for brands, newspaper mastheads, music and film publishing rights, patents or trademarks, because each such asset is unique'. In spite of this comment, there were assets that did not meet the AASB criteria, but that management nonetheless considered capable of valuation. For example, companies such as Publishing and Broadcasting Limited and News Limited routinely claimed in their financial statements to value their mastheads to ensure that the book value is not impaired, which implies that these assets can be valued. Similarly, Australian companies have included and revalued assets such as internally generated mastheads and brands, although the practice has not been adopted frequently.

Chapter 2.3 discussed the constituents of goodwill, and noted that, with the adoption of AASB 38 'Intangible Assets' in Australia in 2005, there had been a fundamental change in the way in which identifiable assets were viewed for accounting purposes. This book is concerned with accounting for goodwill rather than IIAs. Nevertheless, it is concerning to see the developments in the latter field repeat the cycle of errors and inconsistencies that have manifested themselves in goodwill accounting in the past.

Not surprisingly, these new problems arise from the inconsistent procedures adopted in accounting for internally generated IIAs and their purchased counterparts. No accounting standard currently recommends that the former are brought into account. The required procedure for the latter, in terms of AASB 3 'Business Combinations' (para. 36), is to recognize the acquiree's identifiable assets at their fair values at acquisition date. Paragraph 37 states that, in the case of an intangible asset, recognition is only to take place if its fair value can be measured reliably. However, para. 35 of the Standard confirmed that 'the fair value of intangible assets *acquired in business combinations* (emphasis added) can normally be measured with sufficient reliability to be recognized separately from goodwill'.

It is impossible to maintain logically that the identifiable assets of an acquiree are capable of sufficiently accurate valuation without simultaneously accepting that the above is true of the IIAs of the acquirer, so that one of the major obstacles to recognizing internally developed intangibles would seem to have been removed. The distinction found in SFAS 157, which establishes a fair value hierarchy, is sensible, because many valuations of IIAs would rely on unobservable inputs and thus only qualify for Level 3 (the lowest level) of reliability. SFAS 157 requires that the level of reliability be disclosed – another sensible requirement.

Nevertheless, the valuation cat is out of the bag. Even if the valuations of individual IIAs are viewed with some scepticism, specification of those IIAs in the MCS will serve to emphasize which IIAs management considers to be the most important constituents of value. In addition, fluctuations in the value of those items from year to year will prove of interest to investors; indeed, the movements in value are likely to be as informative as the absolute values.

It would serve little purpose to repeat the arguments for consistency of treatment between purchased and internally IIAs that have been put forward in the case of goodwill, but it is clear that they are little different. The inconsistencies will become more obvious and relevant as more and more purchased IIAs appear on financial statements.

The intellectual justification for amortizing purchased IIAs is found in the writings of Leake, and represents a reversion to the view he expressed (see Chapter 4.2 above) that the purchaser has already paid away some portion of his future profit, and that this portion should be amortized out of the profits generated by the purchased entity so as not to overstate the consolidated post-acquisition profit. The contrary arguments have been set out in detail in previous chapters.

Valuation of intangible assets is a reasonably costly process, and there may well be questions raised as to whether the expense is justified. It should be stressed that these valuations are now required in order to account for all acquisitions, and the major accounting firms have all developed specialist teams to carry them out. The techniques are becoming far more widely used and known, and can be expected to become as routine as those employed in the valuations carried out in conjunction with independent expert reports commissioned in takeovers and related party transactions. IIA valuations will be far cheaper as a detailed, carefully phrased public report is not required. It can also be expected that, in most cases, once the applicable techniques (including the gathering of the necessary data) are established with regard to the initial valuations for a given enterprise, the task will be simplified in following years. Costs could also be limited by the adoption of a few sensible rules, e.g. it should not be necessary to value any individual intangible asset the value of which constitutes less than, say, 5 per cent to 10 per cent of the difference between market capitalization and net tangible assets for the company concerned.

There can be little doubt that the information provided will be valuable to readers of the Annual Report. As discussed previously, almost all of the Accounting Standards address items that are relatively less important as far as contribution to market capitalization are concerned. In the Appendices, a number of examples are furnished that illustrate the benefits of a simplified form of MCS that does not address intangible assets other than goodwill. The value of the information that could be gained from that exercise indicates that extending the analysis is likely to be worthwhile. This is potentially a very interesting field for academic research.

Under IFRS, not all purchased IIAs will be amortized. Some (such as the value of a favourable fixed term contract) will usually be amortized over the remaining life of that contract, as will patents and other assets with a clearly determined life. Some assets, such as non-patented but valuable technology, are now commonly treated on an impairment basis, recognition being given to the fact that expenditure maintaining the technology in future years will commonly be expensed, so that amortization would represent a duplicated charge to the Profit and Loss Account. As proof of the tendency of accountants to recycle problems and solutions, this treatment effectively parallels the 'type A' and 'type B' requirements of ARB 24, which was first introduced in 1944 (see Chapter 4.8a).

6.1 Summary of the advantages of the MCS

The examples furnished in Appendix 1 highlight a number of advantages in the use of an MCS, although those examples also used a simplified version that did not attempt to distinguish between goodwill and IIAs. These advantages are summarized below; they should be read in conjunction with Appendix 1.

a. Information not currently available at all from Annual Reports

i. The MCS provides an objective statement of the market capitalization of the company at its balance date.
ii. It shows the proportion of market capitalization composed of goodwill, alerting the reader to the fact that market sentiment, rather than net asset value, is often the dominant force in establishing the market capitalization at balance date.
iii. Fluctuations from year to year in the value of market capitalization, total goodwill and internally generated goodwill are highlighted; very significantly, increases in MCS goodwill are given the same prominence as decreases.
iv. By eliminating goodwill from the conventionally prepared Balance Sheet, the MCS enables that document to reflect unambiguously the carrying value of net tangible assets (albeit currently defined in terms of existing Accounting Standards). The Appendix 1 examples are framed in terms of net identifiable assets rather than net tangible assets.
v. It is possible to ascertain how much of the Shareholders' Equity has been expended by the company on the direct purchase of goodwill and IIAs; this is interesting information in a number of cases examined in the illustrative examples. In particular, in cases in which the value of 'net identifiable assets' is lower than that of 'contributed equity', the MCS will assist those readers who wish to establish whether capital has been maintained, by taking MCS goodwill and IIAs to account. Those such as Schuetze who maintain that expenditure on goodwill does not result

in an asset will be able to judge whether capital has been maintained following the express removal of purchased goodwill and IIAs from the Balance Sheet.

vi. It provides a measure of the total goodwill of the company, unlike proposals that demand a valuation of individual reporting units, while prohibiting the offsetting of increases and decreases in the values of those units. Total goodwill disclosure is likely to be of more value to the investor than partial and incomplete disclosure of goodwill relating to individual reporting units, often determined subjectively with an eye to convenience rather than accuracy.

b. Internally generated goodwill

i. The MCS focuses attention on goodwill, even when no goodwill has been purchased.

ii. The MCS solves the intractable problem of accounting for internally generated goodwill. Because it is prepared expressly on a valuation basis and outside the historical cost limit imposed by the conventional framework, it avoids the paradox inherent in virtually all treatments currently and historically recommended in Accounting Standards, viz. that even though there is no conceptual difference between purchased and internally generated goodwill, internally generated goodwill cannot be recognized because it is impossible to establish its cost reliably.

iii. By aggregating purchased and internally generated goodwill, it recognizes the fact that the two are, in practice, usually inextricably merged as a commercial imperative, the point theoretically demonstrated by Ma and Hopkins in 1988.

iv. Treatment of internally generated goodwill is intellectually consistent with the treatment of purchased goodwill – both are eliminated from the 'conventionally prepared accounts'. However, unlike many previous suggestions, which achieve consistency only by eliminating all consideration of any type of goodwill, the recommended treatment provides the disclosure of significant information regarding both purchased and internally generated goodwill, as well as IIAs.

v. The MCS does not use market values as a surrogate measure of 'cost' for internally generated goodwill. The use of a separate statement of this nature does not in any way purport to reflect internally generated goodwill as a representation of the cost of the unidentifiable assets controlled by the enterprise at that point in time.

c. Purchased goodwill

i. The points made above regarding the intellectual consistency of treatment and the elimination of the artificial separation between the two types of goodwill are equally valid from the point of view of accounting for purchased goodwill. Furthermore, it avoids the allocation problem and recognizes that the goodwill inputs are 'hopelessly entangled, blurred together' (see Chapter 3.12 above, quotation from Thomas 1969).

ii.   The MCS treatment accords with a long line of historically accepted accounting treatments whereby purchased goodwill was eliminated against reserves on purchase. While this appealed to conservative accountants, and those who did not consider goodwill an asset, theorists such as Catlett and Olson have justified the practice on additional grounds (Chapter 4.8 above).

iii. The arbitrary and always contestable prescription of maximum amortization periods is avoided, as is the almost impossible task of selecting a 'correct' period over which purchased goodwill is to be amortized. On the other hand, it would be reasonable to amortize certain assets in the MCS, once these have been valued. For example, patents could be reasonably amortized by the straight line method over their legal life, provided the value was not clearly impaired over that period.

iv.   The need for the current absurd situation (e.g. in ASX returns) in which profits are quoted both before and after goodwill amortization is eliminated.

v.   Large one-time charges against profits arising from one-time write-offs relating to purchased goodwill are avoided, as are random fluctuations arising from changes in the period selected for amortization.

vi.   Potential acquisitions involving significant expenditure on goodwill will not become undesirable merely by virtue of the fact that amortization will result in substantial charges against reported profits.

vii. The 'businessman's argument' that there is no sense in amortizing goodwill when its value is patently above cost is defused.

viii. Cases in which the market valuation of goodwill is less than its cost are clearly identified; a number of cases have been illustrated in which market value of goodwill is less than its book value even after amortization.

ix.   The recent 'impairment' standards require valuation of purchased goodwill of a number of business units independently, not a valuation of the goodwill of the enterprise in total. In practice, this is difficult; the necessity for it is avoided under the MCS. At best, the new proposals will enable management to provide its view as to whether or not the value of these individual items of purchased goodwill has been maintained.

x.   The valuations of reporting units are necessarily subjective in that they involve projections of future results, the selection of an appropriate discount rate and other variables. The MCS uses an objective measure in market capitalization. It is also preferable to the new proposals because it is based on an aggregate, rather than on individual reporting units. The information value of the new Standard is sharply reduced because it does not permit upward valuations of individual business units, while insisting on applying impairment provisions to unsuccessful business units. It is thus not possible to form an aggregate view based on the financial statements.

xi.   The complexity of the procedures called for under impairment proposals is likely to influence accountants to retain the current amortization parameters whenever doing so is a reasonable alternative and permitted by local Standards (e.g. in the UK).

d. And in conclusion

The MCS is extremely easy to understand, even by a relatively unsophisticated reader. It provides additional information on the state of a company's affairs that is important if readers of an Annual Report are to improve their understanding beyond the limited historical cost based data currently furnished.

But, it is by no means perfect. The problems inherent in historical cost accounting for tangible assets, as interpreted by current Accounting Standards, mean that the MCS goodwill figure is still largely a 'master valuation account'. There are some significant ways in which the MCS could be augmented and refined:

i.   provision of supplementary information to explain MCS goodwill and whether it is likely to increase in the future. Appendix 2 discusses a number of current developments relating to data that would be useful in relation to the MCS;

ii. inclusion of information regarding the dates on which goodwill was purchased to assist in assessing whether goodwill is likely to have been maintained;

iii. the provision of details regarding the valuation of IIAs, which would explain variations in those items from year to year.

These areas could profitably serve as questions for detailed research, as to both their general value in enhancing information and the precise information that would prove most valuable to readers in conjunction with the MCS. This would enable a proper assessment to be made as to whether the MCS was cost effective.

As a further, and more radical, step, the MCS could be implemented, not as an adjunct to historical cost based accounts, but in the context of a cohesive exit price based system, such as Professor Chambers' CoCoA, which would have the additional benefit of removing many of the problems and distortions that have been noted previously. This is explored in Chapter 7.

7   The MCS and CoCoA

... the defects of the conventional system are so demonstrable that a change which removes many of them is overdue.

(R. J. Chambers)

7.1 Introduction

The MCS, as described in Chapter 6, is subject to a valid criticism that was foreshadowed in Chapter 1.6 and creates the need for the 'MCS goodwill' to be defined, in the note forming part of the illustrated examples, as 'the difference between market capitalization and the aggregate of the book value of net tangible assets and the fair value of IIAs'. This defines goodwill specifically for purposes of the MCS, instead of using a more widely accepted definition from the literature or one found in an Accounting Standard.

In Chapter 2.2, the concept of calculating goodwill as a residual for accounting purposes is explored. Goodwill is calculated, both conventionally and in the MCS, as the difference between the total value of the enterprise and the 'comparison value', being the carrying value of the other items appearing on the Balance Sheet.

Goodwill has a logically consistent value only if the comparison value is the 'fair value' of all the remaining assets and liabilities. If the comparison value is historical cost adjusted to some extent in accordance with prevailing accounting principles, this is no longer the case. Goodwill becomes a 'master valuation account' – as defined by Canning (1929) and previously quoted: '... a catch-all into which is thrown both an unenumerated series of items that have the *economic*, though not necessarily the *legal*, properties of assets, and an undistributed list of undervaluations of those items listed as assets. It is the valuation account par excellence'.

Canning went on to say that, under these circumstances, goodwill could not be regarded as an asset. As set out previously, transfer of goodwill from the conventional Balance Sheet to the MCS does much to answer this criticism. Nevertheless, it would be a considerable accounting and logical advance if goodwill could be transformed from a master valuation account to a meaningful residual. This aspect is now examined.

7.2 The MCS and CoCoA

During research for this book and the thesis that preceded it, I was exposed to the works and Library of Professor Ray Chambers. In his *Accounting, Evaluation and Economic Behavior* (1966/1974), he set out the foundation of an accounting system that became known as CoCoA. The key features of CoCoA have been summarized in many places, including in an article by Chambers 'Continuously Contemporary Accounting: Misunderstandings and Misrepresentations':

> Those features are the use of resale prices (or dated money equivalents) for non monetary assets, and the use of price variation and capital maintenance adjustments in the calculation of periodical increases, to take account of the effects of changes in asset prices and changes in the general purchasing price of money.
>
> Chambers (1976: 295)

As far as liabilities were concerned, 'The monetary measurement of ... a liability at a point in time is its current cash equivalent at that time' (Chambers 1966/1974: 120), which was defined as the sum obtained '... by discounting the sum payable in the future to a present sum using the rate of interest payable for the immediate use of the money necessary to enable immediate settlement to be made' (Chambers 1966/1974: 107).

This appears to be contrasted in Chambers' December 1976 *Abacus* article (p. 304), which appears to recommend that liabilities be brought to account at their full contractual amount, rather than discounted value:

> For a going concern in the ordinary course of business, as long as a debt is outstanding its amount is the amount payable out of its assets. Its amount is the money equivalent or cash equivalent of the debt at the date of the statement in which it appears. No creditor would tolerate it being written down to some lower figure; and any potential creditor who was told, when about to lend, that the firm is owed less than in fact it owed would be entitled, on discovery, to claim misrepresentation.

This statement is made in refutation of a contention that 'where the enterprise has the opportunity to redeem a liability before maturity at a price other than the contractual amount owed, it would seem logical to conclude that this value would constitute the liability's current cash equivalent or exit value'.

Chambers' earlier formulation, recommending that the carrying value of a liability be brought to account at its appropriately discounted value, appears more logical. A recent article by Gray (2003: 250–61, also noting other writers with similar views) reinforces this conclusion in calling for full fair value accounting to be applied to both assets and liabilities of commercial banks in order not to distort the performance of such banks as a result of interest rate fluctuations. Gray notes that Chambers' endorsement of the use of 'the amount payable out of its assets' was made in the context of a more general theory of accounting than the limited context of accounting for a commercial bank. However, in circumstances in which it would be commercially possible to liquidate a debt at a figure lower than its face value, there would seem little justification in an asymmetrical treatment of assets and liabilities were a principle of fair, or net realizable, value accounting to be adopted.

Schuetze (2001b) has recommended that the fair value of liabilities be defined as: 'the least amount of cash that the counterparty would accept in an immediate and complete liquidation of his/her/its claim against the reporting enterprise'. In practice, this definition would imply that liabilities should be discounted to present value, as appropriate.

AASB 1004 'Revenue' (para. 5.1.2) expressly endorses the use of discounting in establishing fair value, although in the context of determining the fair value of consideration offered in a transaction:

> For example, the entity may provide interest-free credit to the buyer or accept a note receivable bearing a below-market interest rate from the buyer as consideration for the sale of goods. When in substance the arrangement is a financing transaction, the fair value of the consideration is determined by discounting all future receipts using the implicit rate of interest.

A further important constituent of the proposed CoCoA system was the Capital Maintenance Adjustment, which is:

> ... the amount necessary to restate wealth at the period's commencement in terms of the general purchasing power of the currency at the end of the period. It is a scale adjustment to account for the price variation in the general purchasing power dimension of the monetary unit of measure.
>
> Clarke and Dean (1992)

In order to simplify the discussion, the examples illustrated effectively assume a 'no-inflation' world, or that accounting continues its present practice of using a monetary unit of measure without expressly taking effect of inflationary changes in the value of that unit. The full version of Chambers' CoCoA provides an extra degree of refinement.

7.3 Use of resale prices in 'Making Corporate Reports Valuable'

'Making Corporate Reports Valuable' (McMonnies 1988) is a major contribution to the development of a value based, rather than a cost based system of financial reporting. In this discussion document, issued by the Research Committee of the Institute of Chartered Accountants in Scotland in 1988, the authors comment (references are to paragraph numbers):

> 1.2 ... all financial reports ought to reflect economic reality. As a corollary, if financial reports do not reflect economic reality, they are deficient.
> 1.3 We then thought about the reasons for financial reports, which highlighted the importance of communication.
> 1.14 ... there is no consistent conceptual basis underlying the production of (the profit and loss account and the balance sheet). Indeed, some of the concepts used appear to defy normal understanding of financial affairs.
> 1.17 ... we would endeavour to restructure the corporate report in order to liberate it from the form which has become conventional and into which the present failings had become built.

They conclude, in para. 6.3: 'We believe that the total wealth of an entity and the changes in it from period to period are what should be of major importance to managements and the investors'. In order to achieve this, they postulate an Assets and Liabilities Statement that would take the place of the current Balance Sheet and (para. 7.12) 'would show the assets and liabilities of the entity at the end of the accounting period, *each stated at its net realizable value*' (emphasis added).

In coming to the conclusion that the needs of investors and other readers of the Annual Report were best served by the use of net realizable values for assets and liabilities, the authors of the discussion paper expressly acknowledged and endorsed the conceptual work of Chambers, as well as that of Sterling.

A paper by Fraser on net realizable value (NRV) accounting, which is attached to the Scottish Institute discussion paper, comments that 'although NRV accounting has been the subject of considerable, and formidable, academic support it has received little in the way of professional acceptance'. Fraser concludes 'that there is not a compelling case for the adoption of NRV as the primary measurement base for financial statements', although 'the theoretical debate does provide some significant arguments in favour of the system'.

Fraser notes that NRV accounting is very effective as an indicator of adaptability and liquidity, and that it gives 'a measure of the financial means at the disposal of an entity, ... a major element in Chambers' argument'. NRV is also noted as being effective in dealing with additivity and allocation, dilemmas raised in the literature about conventional accounting.

On the other hand, Fraser considers that these advantages are outweighed by the fact that NRV lacks relevance for a continuing business. Values produced for fixed assets 'are likely to be meaningless and in some cases obviously absurd, having no bearing or no relationship to the use value of the asset'. In addition, the income statement is claimed to be misleading because depreciation is replaced by changes in realizable value.

The controversy regarding the use of replacement cost accounting, or other alternatives to the historical cost basis, as against NRV is clearly outside the scope of this book, as is a full consideration of Fraser's comments, and will not be pursued further. (One detailed examination of a number of possible alternatives is found in 'Measurement in Financial Accounting', a 1998 accounting theory monograph by the Australian Accounting Research Foundation.) What is relevant, in context, is that a system of accounting very similar to CoCoA was deemed sufficiently reliable to use as a basis for 'Making Corporate Reports Valuable' by the authors of the study. One major difference is that CoCoA also catered for changes in the general level of prices, and this feature can be combined with the use of the MCS. Among its many advantages is that the use of such a system enables a logically consistent method of accounting for goodwill to be developed in conjunction with the MCS. Section 7.5 below shows how the MCS answers Chambers' objections to the inclusion of goodwill in financial statements, thus enabling it to be integrated seamlessly into CoCoA.

In the general connection of the relevance of the historical cost basis and its possible replacement, SAC 3, para. 19 is relevant.

> ... distinction needs to be drawn between faithful representation of transactions and events and effective representation of them. For example, it is possible to report the historical cost of an asset in a manner that conveys to the user that no attempt is being made to ascribe a current value to it; that it is a dated cost and nothing more. An assessment as to whether the historical cost is the most effective basis of measurement would flow from considerations of the objective of general purpose financial reporting and from the concept of relevance, rather than from considerations of reliability, unless current values were inherently unreliable.

This lends some support to the assertion that current values are to be preferred to historical cost in reporting, because of their greater relevance. Of course, this would require that current values were not 'inherently unreliable'. The concept of reliability has been discussed in Chapter 3.9.

'Value' is a less precise concept than 'cost'. However, there is a compelling case that it is better to be reasonably right than precisely wrong, as historical cost based accounting so often is. Kirkegard has asked 'Can we live with accounting being inaccurate and balance sheets being uncertain in the information society of the future? The answer is that we shall have to. It cannot be avoided' (1994: 8). In support, Kirkegard cites Popper (1934/ 1961): '... both precision and certainty are false ideals ... it is always undesirable to make an effort to increase precision for its own sake. ... One should never try to be more precise than the problem situation demands'.

Much earlier, Paton (1918: 31) had made a similar point: '... accounting deals primarily, not with absolute certainties, but with estimates. Every valuation is an estimate. All inventories are estimates. Depreciation is purely a question of estimates and yet no one argues that accrued depreciation should be omitted from the accounting records'.

It is outside the scope of this book to consider definitively whether sufficient data exist to enable net realizable values to be computed across the board for all major assets and liabilities. However, it may be mentioned that many financial assets and liabilities (listed shares, bonds, debentures, etc.) have well developed markets that would permit their values to be determined with Level 1 reliability. In the writer's commercial experience, auctioneers and other similar parties routinely furnish reasonable estimates to liquidators, administrators and valuers of securities as to the values of assets owned by companies. When Current Cost Accounting was proposed, detailed manuals were developed to assist in obtaining estimates of market prices (generally replacement prices of assets).

The valuation procedures imposed by the impairment method of accounting for goodwill call for valuations of assets and liabilities. Should this be required for all listed companies, that very requirement is likely to cause the development of specialist valuers, both within and outside the ranks of the auditing profession. Furthermore, the detailed valuation procedures prescribed in the various Standards dealing with impairment will be tested in use in the forthcoming period, and will provide practical guidance as to the problems involved (such as the selection of the most appropriate and practical units to which valuation procedures are to be applied).

7.4 Use of CoCoA solves the 'master valuation account' problem

If a coherent system of reporting using the MCS is being considered, reports based on CoCoA principles have immediate and obvious relevance, precisely because all Balance Sheet assets and liabilities are stated on a common basis, viz. current resale prices, so that basic arithmetical rules will not be violated. The market capitalization of a company is based upon the current market price of its shares, and the fact that net identifiable assets, under CoCoA, would be stated on a consistent and comparable basis has the effect that the difference between those two values (goodwill) becomes a logically consistent and coherent residual, which measures the difference between two similarly computed figures.

A legitimate criticism of conventionally prepared Balance Sheets is that the total figures are meaningless, in that they aggregate numbers prepared on different bases. Using CoCoA and the MCS would ensure that this theoretical issue was defused and the interrelationship between the Balance Sheet and the MCS was seamless.

Under conventional accounting, as presently employed, bringing goodwill to account necessarily incorporates an implicit adjustment of all Balance Sheet over- and undervaluations. Using CoCoA, goodwill can be precisely defined as the excess of market capitalization over the carrying value of net identifiable assets, where assets and liabilities are carried at resale prices. Once owners' equity (and, correspondingly, net tangible assets) are carried in the Balance Sheet on this basis, goodwill as defined in the MCS is very close to its generally accepted definition in Australia. In AASB 1013, the comparison value is the 'fair value', i.e. the amount for which an asset could be exchanged between a knowledgeable, willing buyer and a knowledgeable, willing seller in an arm's length transaction. As demonstrated (see Chapter 6.3), the MCS measures this value for a listed company, with the exception that it excludes any potential takeover premium or premium for control or unless the market price used in the computation is artificially distorted.

There is some debate as to whether costs of realization of the assets concerned should be a factor in the calculation. AASB 1013 does not specify a price net of acquisition costs, perhaps because the definition furnished is in the context of an overall acquisition of assets or a business entity, when acquisition costs could be expected to be brought to account as part of the purchase price. The new AASB 136 (paras 5(a) and 6) does deal with this point, explicitly confirming that selling costs must be taken into account in determining 'recoverable amount'. Chambers (1974: 252) and Chambers and Dean (1986: Vol. V) note: 'Holdings of listed shares are readily priced by reference to stock exchange quotations (i.e. "buyer"). Allowance *may* be made for commissions payable on sale, to obtain the *net* money equivalent of the investment' (emphasis added). At the conclusion of this article, Chambers (p. 262) provided a footnote illustrating a CoCoA Balance Sheet with the comment: 'All assets are shown at the best available approximations to their money equivalents at the respective balance dates'.

It is perhaps surprising that neither AASB 1013 nor Chambers makes this point perfectly clear; logic would dictate that, in calculating the money equivalent or fair value of individual assets or liabilities, it would be appropriate to deduct the costs of resale where these are material and specific (e.g. legal and agents' costs of realizing property assets, broker's commission on listed investments or any other marginal costs clearly identifiable with the selling process). AASB 136, para. 18, which became effective on 1 January 2005, is unambiguous – 'recoverable amount' is defined as 'the higher of an asset's or cash generating unit's fair value *less costs to sell* and value in use' (emphasis added). On the other hand, it would be difficult, if not impossible, to calculate the broker's commission, or other direct selling cost, when calculating total market capitalization; in practice, no formulation of market capitalization examined made provision for such a cost.

7.5 Chambers' position on goodwill in the MCS context

Chambers (1966/1974) strongly recommended that goodwill should not be carried in the Balance Sheet, because it did not meet his definition of an asset. Chapter 6.5 above contains a critical evaluation of Chambers' view in this regard in the context of current accounting theory as related to Australian listed companies. However, as this chapter of the book relates to Professor Chambers' CoCoA, an integrated system with its own rules, it is relevant to examine the MCS treatment again in this context. It is suggested that the MCS treatment meets all Chambers' objections in this regard.

a. Goodwill is not a severable asset

'... the property of severability was stipulated as a defining characteristic of assets' (Chambers 1966/1974: 209). The MCS does not treat goodwill as an asset; in fact, purchased goodwill is specifically excluded from the Balance Sheet, by deduction from shareholders' equity, and internally generated goodwill is also not carried as a Balance Sheet asset. The preparation of a separate MCS, in which goodwill is clearly identified as a differential, or residual amount, actually emphasizes the point that goodwill is not an asset like other Balance Sheet assets, but an amount requiring special treatment. Similarly, by aggregating identifiable net assets and goodwill to arrive at market capitalization, it acknowledges the fact that goodwill is not severable.

b. Goodwill cannot be measured

In the MCS format within CoCoA, goodwill can be measured precisely. Market capitalization itself is an objectively determinable amount; virtually every accountant, given the same parameters, would calculate the market capitalization of a listed company using the same base data and would arrive at the same figure.

The total number of issued shares in a company is an absolute figure; the market price of a share is also a clear example of a measurement:

> Prices are measurements. They measure at a time and place the numbers of monetary units which may be substituted for the non monetary changes to which they are assigned. As prices are determined in the market, they are objective measurements; whether one buys or not, market prices are objective measurements.
>
> Chambers (1966/1974: 91)

It is the essence of Chambers' approach that the shareholders' equity (or net identifiable assets) is a measurable amount, because each item in the Balance Sheet is a measurable amount. It follows that goodwill, as defined in the MCS, being the difference between two measurable amounts, is itself measurable.

c. *The* **reductio ad absurdum**

As noted in Chapter 3.4 above, Chambers points out that, if goodwill is reflected in the Balance Sheet, and goodwill is defined as the present value of expected super-profits, this calculation will have the effect of ensuring that, for all comparable companies, the rate of return on shareholders' equity will be equal, so that 'all opportunities would seem to be alike and the potential constituents could not choose between them' (Chambers 1966/1974: 91).

The presentation of the MCS as a separate statement effectively defuses this criticism, as shareholders' equity (whether or not presented on CoCoA principles) is clearly separately identified in the Balance Sheet and excludes goodwill. Rates of return calculations would proceed exactly as they do at present, without the interpolation of goodwill as a neutralizing or complicating factor. Indeed, such calculations would be simplified, as there would be no need to make a specific adjustment for goodwill included on the Balance Sheet issued.

d. *Goodwill of a going concern runs to the constituents, not to the firm*

Chambers comments (1966/1974: 211) that, even if cash has been paid for goodwill: '... the indicated treatment of it is to reduce the amount of the residual equities from the prices paid to the current cash equivalent of the new firm's component assets less its liabilities'.

The treatment of purchased goodwill exactly matches Chambers' recommended treatment by eliminating it from the Balance Sheet, and also confirms his argument that the mere payment of cash in acquiring goodwill does not of itself increase the adaptability of the firm. Those shareholders and analysts who wish to take an 'uncontaminated' view of the Balance Sheet in this respect will find their task facilitated by the MCS with CoCoA.

Market capitalization itself may be viewed as a calculation of the total value of the constituents' interest in the firm as well as an indication of the value of the firm itself. On this reading, the MCS also contravenes none of Chambers' principles.

7.6 The MCS is an important addition to a 'CoCoA' Balance Sheet

The factors brought out by the MCS are also important in assessing the adaptability of the firm. For a listed company, its shares are one form (and a very important form) of currency. The higher the rating given to the company by the stock market, the greater the value of that currency and the greater the degree of adaptability the company will have.

The examples given in Appendix 1 all confirm this contention in varying degrees, and show how important it is to have regard to the information given in the MCS (and the consequent changes to conventionally prepared financial statements) to get an adequate total view of a company's financial position. For convenience, the relevant portion of the Balance Sheet, prepared under MCS principles, and the MCS of Keycorp Ltd (KYC), a company limited on the ASX, are repeated in Table 7.1. This furnishes one illustrative example of the need to consider these factors rather than merely having regard to the net assets, as conventionally reflected in the Balance Sheet. The tangible assets and liabilities of KYC are all either immaterial or monetary; reflected under CoCoA principles, their carrying values would not have differed materially from those that produced the 'net identifiable assets' shown in Table 7.1. The MCS used is the 'simplified' version illustrated in Chapter 1, as details regarding IIAs were not available.

The comments made in the Appendix when reviewing KYC will not be repeated in detail here. It will suffice to point out a few cogent reasons why the MCS is needed as a supplement to financial accounts prepared under CoCoA principles:

i. From 31 December 1999 to 30 June 2002, goodwill constituted between 94 per cent and 149 per cent of KYC's market capitalization.
ii. In the last three periods, the net identifiable assets were AUS$7.346 million, AUS$17.081 million (negative) and AUS$34.138 million (negative) respectively. A conventional Balance Sheet would not reveal these figures. They are important in themselves, but viewing them in isolation is profoundly misleading. The MCS shows a market capitalization at those dates of AUS$175.484 million, AUS$158.415 million and AUS$69.408 million respectively, which gives a different, balanced and informative view of the state of affairs of KYC.
iii. The MCS tracks the rise in market capitalization from AUS$132.665 million at 30 June 1999 to AUS$703.378 million at 31 December 2000. During this time, net identifiable assets rose from AUS$35.634 million to AUS$40.010 million, a rise of less than AUS$5 million. The rise and fall of the adaptive capability of KYC cannot be assessed adequately from an examination of its net identifiable assets alone.
iv. The subsequent fall in market capitalization of AUS$634 million from AUS$703 million to AUS$69 million was accompanied by a fall in net identifiable assets of only AUS$74 million, which is significant but far less than the former decline.

In companies such as KYC, goodwill is of the essence of the company. Any presentation that directly excludes it is inadequate. As noted above, the analysis was constructed using a simplified form of MCS, which provided only for a comparison of purchased and internally generated goodwill. The data available did not permit an analysis of the 'goodwill' figure to allow for IIAs, as recommended. Even then, the information revealed is far in excess of that available in the conventional Annual Report.

Table 7.1 Illustrative example — KYC (all figures in $'000, except as noted)

Period ended	1999		2000		2001		2002
	30 Jun	31 Dec	30 Jun	31 Dec	30 Jun	31 Dec	30 Jun
Conventional Financial Statement							
Share capital and reserves	45,725	28,354	27,267	459,338	422,887	403,352	109,462
Goodwill per accounts							
Cost	11,193	11,193	13,004	423,442	445,617	445,617	443,734
Less:Amortized/written off	1,102	1,397	1,746	4,114	15,384	25,184	300,134
Book value	10,091	9,796	11,258	419,328	430,233	420,433	143,600
MCS presentation							
Balance sheet							
Share capital and reserves*	46,827	29,751	39,013	463,452	418,271	428,536	409,596
Less:Cost of purchased goodwill	11,193	11,193	13,004	423,442	445,617	445,617	443,734
Net identifiable assets	35,634	18,558	26,009	40,010	7,346	(17,081)	(34,138)
Market Capitalization Statement							
Number of issued shares (000)	35,567	35,912	35,962	75,967	75,967	81,657	81,657
Market price per share ($)	3.73	8.190	9.370	9.259	2.310	1.940	0.850
Market capitalization	132,665	294,119	336,964	703,378	175,484	158,415	69,408
Comprising:							
Purchased goodwill, at cost	11,193	11,193	13,004	423,442	445,617	445,617	443,734
Internally generated goodwill	85,838	264,368	307,951	239,926	262,787	270,121	340,188
MCS goodwill	97,031	275,561	320,955	663,368	182,830 (L)	175,496 (L)	103,546 (L)
Net identifiable assets	35,634	18,558	16,009	40,010	7,346	(17,081)	(34,138)
Market capitalization	132,665	294,119	336,964	703,378	175,484	158,415	69,408
Ratio of MCS goodwill to market capitalization (%)	73	94	95	94	104	111	149

* adjusted for goodwill amortization.

7.7 Chambers and the double account

It has been demonstrated herein that a modified version of the double account has the potential to resolve the goodwill dilemma. In 1976, Chambers came very close to suggesting a procedure similar to that recommended herein:

> In the double-account system once generally used by utilities, resale costs were represented separately from financial operations on current account. There are good reasons for recourse to the same device in respect of purchased goodwill, mine developments costs, highly specialized plant and other 'costly' items.
>
> Chambers (1976: 145)

He illustrates this principle with an example in which 'sunk costs' is expressly deducted from 'contributed funds'. One of the major advantages he adduces for such a proposal is that 'the risk due to reduced "disposable-asset-backing" would be made evident, and the higher rate of return on net assets (i.e. as disclosed in the balance sheet itself) would correspond with that risk'.

The transfer of goodwill to the MCS would have the Balance Sheet reflect net tangible assets just as in Chambers' example, and the return on these assets would be clearly evidenced in the Profit and Loss Account, without distorting factors such as arbitrary goodwill amortization. As has been shown in the examples cited, the fluctuations in goodwill highlighted in the MCS also reveal significant information of value to investors.

7.8 Conclusion

The use of the MCS to account for goodwill and to provide additional and valuable information to readers of an Annual Report is consistent with the principles enunciated by Chambers in developing CoCoA, although extending it using a modified double account system.

The express elimination of goodwill from the Balance Sheet itself directly accords with the principles that Chambers espoused. Furnishing additional information in the form of the MCS would seem, at very worst, a supplement to CoCoA financial statements, which, in many cases, increases the relevance and usefulness of those accounts. CoCoA of itself does not reveal or explain the value of the firm, treated as a whole; it concentrates on the individual identifiable assets and liabilities within the firm. The MCS, by highlighting the market capitalization of the firm, goes far to bridge that gap.

Paradoxically, the disclosure of net assets on a net realizable value basis might assist in narrowing the gap between market capitalization and the Balance Sheet value of net identifiable assets. Chambers himself, in a 1965 article entitled 'Information and the Securities Market' (reproduced in Chambers and Dean 1986: Vol. 1, 137–64) drew attention to the substantial premiums paid by takeover bidders, compared with the pre-offer price (p. 153). He ascribes much of the premium to the fact that shareholders of the target company were not furnished with adequate information. The proposed MCS structure, by providing a direct comparison between market capitalization and realistically valued net assets, would provide shareholders with data enabling a clearer assessment as to whether the MCS goodwill and IIA valuations were realistic, conservative or likely to be too high. It is at least theoretically possible that the existence of a better informed body of investors and analysts would lower the likelihood that a potential offeror could mount a takeover bid based on inadequate valuations of assets in the Balance Sheet; equally, it is possible that an investor would be less likely to sell his shares at less than their proper value even in the ordinary course of events when no takeover bid had been made.

In the same article, Chambers examined four possible objections to an accounting paradigm shift such as that contemplated by the introduction of an MCS. While his examination was carried out in the context of net realizable value accounting, the potential objections are equally possible in the context of the MCS.

The first is 'that the difficulties of discovering the rules and carrying them out are so great that no acceptable solution will emerge'. The MCS, as demonstrated here, is a very simple document, as are the rules under which it is constructed. It utilizes no new concepts, given that valuations of IIAs are now accepted in a normal business context, and its formulation is unambiguous.

The second possible objection is the cost incurred in the presentation of the data. The experience gained during the production of this book, involving in all some sixty companies (including approximately forty whose results have not been included) over an average of six balance dates, indicates that all aspects of the MCS other than the valuations of IIAs in the MCS can be prepared in under half an hour for a typical ASX listed company. All the information is either readily available from outside sources (such as the appropriate market price), taken directly from the conventionally prepared Statement of Financial Position or contained in audit working papers or the company's records, as in the case of amounts historically spent on goodwill and details of goodwill amortization. Clearly, valuations of IIAs, in cases where IIAs are significant, will be a costly and complex issue for some companies. It will be a task for detailed academic research to establish whether the potential gain, in those cases, is worth the cost involved. It is at least arguable that the more significant the IIAs are, the more important and informative it will be to include them in the MCS.

The third potential ground for objection is that its use would highlight fluctuations rather than 'smoothing' profits and averaging out fluctuations. Chambers regards such smoothing as one of the 'most vicious' principles;

correctly, because the fact that goodwill and profits do fluctuate is something the investor needs to know. Such fluctuations are 'indicative of the risks he will want to take account in bidding for or holding securities'. However, artificial profit (or goodwill) smoothing makes a risky business appear to be much less risky. In contrast, the MCS eliminates random fluctuations in profits due to arbitrary variations in the period of goodwill amortization and large one-off charges to profits when goodwill is wholly written off.

Finally, it could be contended that 'new methods should only be adopted when they have been tried out in practice and found to be as effective as they are claimed to be'. The examples of the suggested new method given in this book are, of course, few in number, but it is hoped that they are convincing enough to promote further research and development of the MCS format and principles. However, it is appropriate to quote Chambers' own words in rebuttal of this point, albeit in a different context: ' ... in any case, the defects of the conventional system are so demonstrable that a change which removes many of them is overdue' (p. 164; the context was the defects of historical cost based data as against the recommended use of current valuations in Balance Sheets.)

When research for the thesis that preceded this book commenced some six years ago, it was evident that the 'struggle toward some unforeseen truth' would not be successful if it merely retraced the paths trodden by all the writers and theorists who have endeavoured to find a logical, coherent and useful way of accounting for goodwill. The importance of the struggle became clear with the realization that, in the latter half of the twentieth century, goodwill was the major constituent of the market capitalization of many publicly listed companies; however, accounting standards, so detailed and complex in areas of relatively minor importance, could not cope with goodwill.

It was universally conceded that internally generated goodwill could not be 'recognized' at all, despite the fact that it was indistinguishable from purchased goodwill, with which it often merged. While it was easy, indeed unavoidable, to recognize purchased goodwill, arcane and heated debates raged as to what could be done with it, once recognized. The problem of accounting for goodwill could not be solved within the definition of the problem.

Rather than asking how best to deal with (purchased) goodwill in the conventional context, the traditional problem considered in the literature and the Accounting Standards, the problem was accordingly redefined as follows.

Recognizing that information regarding the goodwill attributable to a listed entity is useful to a person making and evaluating decisions relating to that entity, how can the current level of information relating to goodwill in the financial statements contained in the Annual Report of that entity be improved?

This volume has proposed the use of market capitalization at balance date, via a new financial statement, the MCS, to improve the current level of information relating to goodwill in the Annual Report. No identical method was discovered during the course of the research.

To use a hackneyed expression, the solution proposed by the MCS is 'outside the square'. It enables better data to be presented by moving outside the boundaries of the traditional Balance Sheet, both in presenting an additional financial statement and in making market based information the basis of that statement. This technique enables goodwill data and, to a large extent, data regarding IIAs to be freed from the traditional limits imposed by the historical cost system. Furthermore, it opens the way for supporting and explanatory data to be offered as a supplement to the MCS, while providing opportunities for analyses that are unavailable on the basis of traditionally presented data.

The derivation of the MCS from the nineteenth century double account is, to the best of the writer's knowledge, unique, as is the use of purchased goodwill as a link between the Balance Sheet and the MCS.

The advantages of the MCS have been set out in great detail in the conclusion to Chapter 6, and will not be repeated here, except to note that the removal of goodwill from the traditional financial statements is shown to improve those statements materially. However, it is not claimed that the MCS represents a complete solution to the problem of accounting for goodwill. Its limitations (especially under a historical cost based system) have been examined. These would be minimized under CoCoA or a similar resale price based system. The question of developing reliable IIA valuations, or adjusting to the inherent inaccuracy of such valuations, is also clearly an area for future study.

Appendix 1

How the MCS improves the accounting perspective on goodwill – illustrative examples

> The degree of success with which the accounting process fulfils its purpose depends to a large extent on the effectiveness of the financial statements in transmitting useful information.
>
> (J. N. Owen 1958: 66, as cited in Chambers 1995: 34)

Number and types of companies analysed

The companies chosen for detailed analysis fell into two groups:

i. a group of fourteen 'dot.com' companies, identified via their connection with internet operations. With one or two exceptions, these companies represented either companies originally listed during the speculative boom that commenced in 1999 or 'back door' listings resulting from the conversion of dormant listed companies over the same period (Appendix 1a);
ii. a group of six of Australia's largest listed companies, covering a diverse selection of activities (Appendix 1b).

Use of a simplified MCS

The analysis in this Appendix used publicly available data taken from the Annual Reports of the companies concerned. This meant that very little information was available regarding the values of IIAs. As a consequence, the simplified form of MCS, as in Chapter 1.5, is used throughout this Appendix, which differs from the illustrative MCS described in Chapter 6 in a number of important respects.

a. The MCS itself deals only with goodwill, rather than with IIAs. Few of the companies analysed reflected IIAs in their Balance Sheets but, when they did, no adjustment was made in respect thereof.
b. The link between the Balance Sheet and MCS was consequently effected by only deducting purchased goodwill from Equity. The MCS goodwill figure was calculated in these examples as the difference between net *identifiable* assets (as identified in the published Balance Sheet) and the

market capitalization of the company. In the MCS illustrated in the body of this work, MCS goodwill becomes the difference between the company's market capitalization and the aggregate of the value of tangible assets and the fair value of IIAs.

c. In the Appendix, internally generated goodwill is shown as the difference between MCS goodwill and purchased goodwill. In the recommended MCS, this distinction is not maintained.

d. In the example in Table A1.1, which illustrates the MCS used in Appendix 1, assume that financial statements are prepared on a historical cost basis in accordance with currently generally accepted accounting principles. Assume also that:

- the company has decided to recognize goodwill via an MCS for the first time, (comparative figures are ascertainable for the previous year);
- during the year, the company has purchased an enterprise, resulting in purchased goodwill, determined in accordance with traditional methods, of $1 million;
- the book value of net identifiable assets (including IIAs) at the year-end is $9 million;
- the market capitalization of the company is $12.5 million at the year-end; all other figures used are illustrative.
- Table A1.1
- For the purpose of this statement, 'MCS goodwill' is defined and calculated as the difference between market capitalization and the

Table A1.1 Illustration of the MCS used in Appendix 1

	Current year	**Previous year**
Shareholder's equity	10,000	7,000
Less:Cost of purchased goodwill*	(1,000)	–
Book value of net identifiable assets	9,000	7,000

*This amount would be specifically disclosed, as above

NEW MARKET CAPITALIZATION STATEMENT (MCS)	**Current year**	**Previous year**
Number of issued shares ('000)	50,000	50,000
Market price per share ($)	0.25	0.15
Market capitalization	12,500	7,500
Comprising:		
Purchased goodwill, at cost**	1,000	–
Internally generated goodwill	2,500	500
MCS goodwill	3,500	500
Net identifiable assets**	9,000	7,000
Market capitalization	12,500	7,500
Ratio of MCS goodwill to market capitalization (%)	28%	7%

**Per Statement of Financial Position

book value of the company's net identifiable assets (including identifiable intangible assets).

Sources of data for material in the Appendix

a. *Balance Sheet data* – details of the dollar value of share capital and reserves, the cost and amortization of goodwill, net identifiable assets and the number of issued shares at each balance date were extracted from the electronic copies of Balance Sheets (in the case of final balance dates) and ASX 'Appendix 4B Half Yearly Reports' (in the case of interim dates). (These figures were obtained from the Aspect Financial/ Aspect Huntley website. It is appropriate to acknowledge a special debt to this site, which made it possible to collect the data required in a reasonable time and state of completeness.)

Note: The Appendix 4B report does not require companies to show details of cost and aggregate amortization of goodwill separately from those relating to other intangible assets (refer item 4.15 of the form), although other details are given, such as amortization of goodwill during the period (items 2.1 to 2.3). It was accordingly occasionally necessary to estimate these items at interim balance dates, using information in the Appendix 4B report itself and the previous and subsequent year-end Balance Sheets.

b. Stock market prices at interim and final balance dates were obtained from Huntleys' Annual Stockmarket Summaries.
c. The description of each company's activities was also drawn from the Aspect Financial website.

Appendix 1a

The MCS and fourteen Australian 'dot.com' companies

The practical application and simplicity of the MCS are initially illustrated by reference to a range of companies drawn from Australian 'dot.com' companies over a period of time that saw considerable fluctuation in both goodwill and market capitalization. The experiences of these companies provided an ideal basis to examine the effect of the proposed MCS and the information it would furnish to readers of an Annual Report. Dot.com companies were primarily designed to exploit opportunities created by the Internet. Most of them were listed on the ASX during the year ended 30 June 2000, either by way of a prospectus and new capital raising or via a 'backdoor listing' (i.e. use of an existing dormant listed entity).

Method of selection

The Appendix tracks the details reflected in the MCS over at least six balance dates (although one company, ASP, which was only listed in April 2000 but had been in operation for some prior years, was included). The period selected was 30 June 1999 to 30 June 2002, which provided a maximum of seven balance dates, given that analysis was possible at the dates of both interim and final financial statements. The dates chosen were:

30 June 1999	31 December 1999
30 June 2000	31 December 2000
30 June 2001	31 December 2001
30 June 2002	

The Aspect Financial (now Aspect Huntley) (accessed via http://www.aspecthuntley.com.au or, using the University of Sydney internet access, via http://www.aspectfinancial.com.au/af/dathome?xtm_licensee = dat) site was consulted, and the site was interrogated to list all ASX listed companies listing 'internet' among their activities. This produced an initial listing of seventy-eight companies.

A number of companies in the original list were eliminated from analysis on the grounds that they were delisted during the period, taken over, changed the nature of their activities so as to make the data at the various balance dates not comparable or were listed too late during the period chosen to provide sufficient balance date data. The data analysis itself took place during the latter half of calendar 2002, by which stage the 'dot. com boom', which had commenced late in calendar 1999, was over. After these eliminations, thirty-nine companies remained.

Analysis of the results of the thirty-nine companies that had survived the initial cull showed that all the results of the analysed companies could be divided into the following categories at the selected balance dates:

- 'MCS goodwill' (i.e. the excess of market capitalization over the book value of net identifiable assets) exceeded the Cost of purchased goodwill (designated as a Category C result);
- MCS goodwill exceeded the Amortized value of goodwill, but was lower than its cost (a Category A result);
- MCS goodwill was positive, but was Less than the amortized, or book, value of purchased goodwill (a Category L result);
- MCS goodwill was Negative, i.e. the market capitalization of the company was less than the book value of net identifiable assets (a Category N result).

The fourteen 'dot.com' companies chosen for final inclusion in the Appendix and listed below provided illustrative examples of all of the above categories; it was found that extending the number of companies analysed became repetitive without adding compensating value to the analysis. Of the fourteen companies, ten had purchased goodwill and four had not, enabling an examination of the MCS under both circumstances. Given the behaviour of the market over the period analysed, the fluctuations of market capitalization showed broadly similar trends, although there were individual fluctuations in the case of particular companies that made the analysis of particular interest.

The companies chosen on this basis were:

- Adcorp Australia Ltd (AAU)
- Adultshop.com Ltd (ASC)
- Horizon Global Ltd (HZG)
- Publishing and Broadcasting Ltd (PBL)
- Tennyson Networks Ltd (TNY)
- Aspermont Ltd (ASP)
- UXC Ltd (UXC)
- Keycorp Ltd (KYC)
- Winepros Ltd (WPO)
- Multimedia Ltd (MUL)
- Ezenet Ltd (EZE)
- Easycall International Ltd (EZY)

- Melbourne IT Ltd (MLB)
- Fast Scout Ltd (FSL)

MCS goodwill in the context of a dot.com company

The MCS defines MCS goodwill as 'the difference between the market capitalization of the company and the Balance Sheet value of its net identifiable assets'. In the case of a dot.com company, a large proportion of the gap is clearly due largely to the market's evaluation of the technology owned by the company, but the technology cannot be viewed in isolation without the simultaneous evaluation of the company's ability to develop its technology, market it and use it to generate profits and cash flows. These factors are those traditionally included within the goodwill concept. It would be very difficult, prior to a sale of all the technology owned by a company to a third party that did not simultaneously acquire the vendor's staff and related business structure, to determine how much of 'MCS goodwill' was due to the pure value of the technology itself. For this reason, the terms 'MCS goodwill' and 'internally generated goodwill' are used throughout without specific reference to technology. As further justification of this position, the companies identified reflected purchased goodwill, which was clearly described as such in their Balance Sheets, rather than as technology or some other identifiable asset. Other intangible assets, which were identified and recorded in the Balance Sheet, were included in the analyses as part of 'net identifiable assets'. The discussion in Chapter 6.9 (relating to IIAs) is also relevant.

The 'dot.com' companies are especially suitable for analysis because:

i. a large proportion of their market capitalization was made up by MCS goodwill, so that an understanding of that component is vital in getting a realistic view of the state of affairs of the company at the year-end;

ii. almost all other assets and liabilities were cash, claims to or against cash or fixed assets purchased comparatively recently, so that book values were likely to be close to net realizable values;

iii. in the case of many of these companies, the period of analysis from 30 June 1999 to 30 June 2002 covered extraordinary fluctuations in total value and hence MCS goodwill values, so that all possible variations were able to be analysed within a reasonably restricted number of companies;

iv. the data was comparatively recent and was readily available.

As noted, the original list was reduced to fourteen companies, as this number was sufficient to provide illustrative examples of all of the following situations:

a. companies that had been consistently 'successful' during the period of analysis, in that the MCS goodwill exceeded expenditure on purchased goodwill, whether or not the goodwill had been purchased during the period. Annual or half-yearly results of this nature have been designated as a Category C result, because MCS goodwill exceeded the *cost* of goodwill. In the first five companies examined, all results during the period of analysis were Category C results;

b. the next five companies provide one or more instances, during the period, where:

   i.   MCS goodwill exceeded the Amortized, or book, value of goodwill, even though it was lower than the cost of goodwill purchased. These instances are marked by an (A) in the 'MCS goodwill' line of the MCS.

   ii. MCS goodwill was positive, but was Less than the amortized, or book, value of goodwill purchased. These instances are marked by an (L) in the 'MCS goodwill' line of the MCS.

Note: In both of the above cases, 'internally generated goodwill' appears in the MCS as a negative amount, which serves as an immediate notification to a reader of the accounts that the value of purchased goodwill has not been maintained.

   iii. MCS goodwill is Negative in total, i.e. the market capitalization of the company at that point in time was less than the book value of net identifiable assets. Cases in which this occurred are marked by an (N) in the 'MCS goodwill' line of the MCS.

c. The next three companies analysed had not purchased goodwill, so that all MCS goodwill is, by definition, internally generated. This leads to a simpler MCS than those illustrated in the previous examples.

d. The final company illustrated is an extreme example of a company whose market capitalization has been materially below its net identifiable asset value for the entire period of the analysis; the company in question, like the three preceding it, had not purchased goodwill.

The format followed for each company is to present the following figures as they appeared in the actual, conventionally prepared financial statements and interim reports available for the period of analysis:

i.   share capital and reserves (in total);

ii. goodwill, showing cost, the amounts amortized or written off and the book value (for those companies that had purchased goodwill).

In a small number of cases, goodwill figures had to be estimated, as they were not shown separately in ASX interim reports; goodwill is grouped with all other 'Intangible Assets' in the standard Balance Sheet format used over that period by the ASX.

The MCS is then set out, following the format in Appendix 1 at each reporting date. For each of the companies analysed, the MCS is then followed by comments that highlight the following aspects where they are significant in relation to that company:

i. the company's amortization policy over the period and its effect on the book value of purchased goodwill, compared with MCS goodwill;
ii. the portion of share capital and reserves that has been utilized to purchase goodwill (and which is no longer represented by net identifiable assets);
iii. the amount of goodwill charged against profits, thus reducing the company's ability to pay dividends out of those profits;
iv. the disclosure of MCS goodwill and the ratio that it bears to the market capitalization of the company;
v. the MCS' disclosure of fluctuations, in both the value of MCS goodwill itself and the ratio of goodwill to market capitalization over the various balance dates during the analysed period;
vi. where applicable, a discussion of (A), (L) and (N) results highlighted by the MCS.

Illustrative examples (Category C)

In all these examples, MCS goodwill exceeded its cost throughout the period analysed.

a. Adcorp Australia Ltd (AAU)

Principal activity – Advertising agency services specializing in human resources, education, real estate, auctioneering and pharmaceuticals; an employment internet recruitment site; website design, development and database support services; and supplier of web-based products for the employment market.

Listing details – AAU was listed in November 1999 (Table A1a.a)

b. Adultshop.com Ltd (ASC) – this company is smaller than AAU, but has shown many of the same characteristics.

Principal activity – The provision of online adult entertainment; the sale of adult products via the internet; the wholesaling of adult products; the sale of adult products through company owned stores, franchise stores and mail order; and the provision of adult telephone services.

Listing details – ASC was listed in November 1999 (Table A1a.b)

Table A1a.a Adcorp Australia Ltd (AAU)

Conventionally prepared financial statements (all figures in $'000, except as noted)

Period ended	1999	2000		2001		2002
	31 Dec	30 Jun	31 Dec	30 Jun	31 Dec	30 Jun
Share capital and reserves	13,675	14,341	15,203	16,174	17,718	19,886
Goodwill per accounts						
Cost	7,230	7,454	11,118	14,372	14,711	16,179
Less: Amortized/written off	72	390	652	1,475	1,929	2,640
Book value	7,158	7,064	10,466	12,897	12,782	13,539

Using Market Capitalization Statement

BALANCE SHEET

Share capital and reserves (see note)	13,747	14,731	15,855	17,649	19,647	22,526
Less: Cost of purchased goodwill	7,230	7,454	11,118	14,372	14,711	16,179
Net identifiable assets	6,517	7,277	4,737	3,277	4,936	6,347

Note: In this, and in all succeeding examples, share capital and reserves have been adjusted by writing back all goodwill amortized or written off.

MARKET CAPITALIZATION STATEMENT

Number of issued shares ('000)	55,016	55,016	55,288	56,008	56,017	57,164
Market price per share ($)	1.550	1.640	1.020	0.900	0.900	1.000
Market capitalization	85,275	90,226	56,394	50,407	50,415	57,164
Comprising:						
Purchased goodwill, at cost	7,230	7,454	11,118	14,372	14,711	16,179
Internally generated goodwill	71,528	75,495	40,539	32,758	30,768	34,638
MCS goodwill	78,758	82,949	51,657	47,130	45,479	50,817
Net identifiable assets	6,517	7,277	4,737	3,277	4,936	6,347
Market capitalization	85,275	90,226	56,394	50,407	50,415	57,164
Ratio of MCS goodwill to total market capitalization (%)	92	92	92	93	90	89

Note: For the purpose of this statement, 'MCS goodwill' is defined and calculated as the difference between market capitalization and the book value of the company's net identifiable assets.

Comments:
1. AAU is following a conventional policy of amortization in relation to purchased goodwill. The notes to the accounts indicate that goodwill is being amortized over twenty years. Although MCS goodwill has reduced in value since the 2000 financial year, its value has, at all times, been substantially greater than the amount expended on purchased goodwill.
2. The MCS treatment highlights that the majority of share capital and reserves has been utilized to purchase goodwill. This is less apparent from the conventional treatment.

3. By 30 June 2002, a total of $2.64 million had been charged against profits, thus reducing the amount available to pay dividends to shareholders and reported profits. Examination of the MCS shows that the value of MCS goodwill has, throughout the period, been more than three times the cost of purchased goodwill, which highlights the lack of logic in the amortization policy forced on AAU by current Accounting Standards.
4. A change to an accounting policy based on impairment principles, whereby purchased goodwill was not amortized so long as its value was less than total goodwill, would have been more 'realistic'. However, such a policy would not have revealed the considerable amount of internally generated goodwill that has been a feature of this company's performance since listing.
5. The MCS treatment highlights the significant fluctuations in MCS goodwill values from period to period. Unlike many comparable companies, AAU has retained substantial value throughout the period, but the MCS goodwill has fluctuated from $82.9 million (high) to $45.5 million (low) while net identifiable assets have only fluctuated between $7.3 million (high) and $3.3 million (low). This fluctuation would not be ascertainable in any way from a conventionally prepared Annual Report, yet it is arguable that it is one of the most significant features that readers would require to have brought to their attention.
6. AAU has been a successful company that has enjoyed market confidence. This is reflected by the fact that, throughout the period, some 90 per cent of its market value has been represented by MCS goodwill. Nevertheless, a shareholder examining this ratio would be made aware of the importance of favourable market sentiment in maintaining the value of a shareholding in AAU. This information is not available at all from conventionally prepared financial statements, which clarify, in considerable detail, the balances making up the remaining 10 per cent of market capitalization.

Table A1a.b Adultshop.com Ltd (ASC)

Conventionally prepared financial statements (all figures in $'000, except as noted)

Period ended	1999 31 Dec	2000 30 Jun	31 Dec	2001 30 Jun	31 Dec	2002 30 Jun
Share capital and reserves	15,163	29,836	25,003	26,907	27,179	32,648
Goodwill per accounts						
Cost	–	13,840	15,301	25,967	25,967	25,967
Less:Amortized/written off	–	9,165	9,970	10,781	12,367	13,953
Book value	–	4,675	5,331	15,186	13,600	12,014

Using Market Capitalization Statement

BALANCE SHEET

Share capital and reserves	15,163	39,001	34,973	37,688	39,546	46,601
Less: Cost of purchased goodwill	–	13,840	15,301	25,967	25,967	25,967
Net identifiable assets	15,163	25,161	19,672	11,721	13,579	20,634

MARKET CAPITALIZATION STATEMENT

Number of issued shares ('000)	181,047	237,510	242,621	305,321	305,321	305,321
Market price per share ($)	1.457	0.710	0.170	0.160	0.170	0.370
Market capitalization	263,785	168,632	41,246	48,851	51,905	112,969
Comprising:						
Purchased goodwill, at cost	–	13,840	15,301	25,967	25,967	25,967
Internally generated goodwill	248,622	129,631	6,293	11,163	12,359	66,368
MCS goodwill	248,622	143,471	21,594	37,130	38,326	92,335
Net identifiable assets	15,163	25,161	19,652	11,721	13,579	20,634
Market capitalization	263,785	168,632	41,246	48,851	51,905	112,969
Ratio of MCS goodwill to market capitalization (%)	94	85	52	76	74	82

Note: For the purpose of this statement, 'MCS goodwill' is defined and calculated as the difference between market capitalization and the book value of the company's net identifiable assets.

Comments:
1. ASC's stated goodwill amortization policy is to amortize goodwill over five years, which it appears to have followed since 30 June 2000; in the six-month period ended 30 June 2000, there was a substantial write-off of goodwill (which had just been acquired) in addition to normal amortization. It has another intangible asset, 'Website acquisition costs and copyright and mail order lists', which it amortizes over a two-year period.
2. Despite this fairly rigorous programme of amortization and write-offs, MCS goodwill has always exceeded purchased goodwill comfortably. Indeed, at 30 June 2000, when the amortization and write-off of goodwill totalled $9.165 million, internally generated goodwill totalled $129.6 million, or more than $120 million in excess of the amount written off. This example highlights the lack of logic in current impairment proposals, which require purchased goodwill to be written down in similar circumstances (assuming that a loss in the value of purchased goodwill can be identified). The market clearly considered at that date that goodwill as a whole (the only commercially meaningful figure) had been more than maintained. This is clearly indicated in the MCS.
3. The MCS highlights the fluctuation in value of the company. The Annual Report, of course, appears only at the financial year-end, not at interim dates; nevertheless, a shareholder would have found it interesting and relevant that the market capitalization of ASC had fallen from $168.6 million at 30 June 2000 to $48.9 million a year later; the rise in value from $48.9 million to $113 million in the year ended 30 June 2002 would have been equally interesting and relevant to readers.
4. The percentages of MCS goodwill to total market capitalization remained fairly constant and high at each financial year-end (85 per cent, 76 per cent, 82 per cent), indicating that favourable market sentiment is constantly a major driver of value for ASC. The MCS clarifies this; for example, from 30 June 2000 to 30 June 2001, the value of net identifiable assets fell $13.4 million, while total MCS goodwill (as assessed by the market) fell $106.3 million. In the following year, net identifiable assets rose $8.9 million, while MCS goodwill increased by $55.2 million.

c. Horizon Global Ltd (HZG)

Principal activity – Development of internet technology.

Listing details – HZG was originally a mining company, which purchased software technology in July 1999. From that date, its emphasis shifted away from mining; by August 2001, the company had formally transferred to the Industrial Board of the ASX, and announced that its main area of business was its 75 per cent investment in Horizon TV (Operations) Pty Ltd. Results are included from the six-month period ended 31 December 1999 (Table A1a.c).

d. Publishing and Broadcasting Ltd (PBL) – This is a major 'Packer' (Kerry Packer is regarded as being the wealthiest person in Australia – see BRW, May 2004) company – the scale is considerably greater than the previous companies examined. Although clearly not predominantly an 'internet' or 'dot.com' company, it was identified as such by virtue of its investment in Ecorp Ltd.

Principal activities – Television production and broadcasting; magazine publishing and distribution; gaming and entertainment; and investment in the internet, pay television and other media and entertainment sectors.

Listing details – PBL first listed in 1987 (Table A1a.d).

e. Tennyson Networks Ltd (TNY)

Principal activity – The further development and sales and marketing of a data/voice convergence platform that provides users with a sophisticated telephone system, computer networking and access to the internet.

Listing details – TNY was originally a mineral explorer. It launched its software related activities in May 1999. TNY was suspended from trading on the ASX between March and August 2001. The June 2001 market price is the last price before suspension (Table A1a.e).

Illustrative examples (categories A and L)

Whereas the results of the previous five companies analysed fall in Category C throughout the analysed period, the MCS of the following companies shows that, at least on one date, the total goodwill value, although positive, fell below the cost of purchased goodwill. In this case, there are two possibilities that, as noted above, are designated:

A where the total value of goodwill exceeds the Amortized or written down value of purchased goodwill, but is less than its cost;
L where the total value of goodwill is Less than the amortized value of goodwill, but not 'negative' ('negative' goodwill occurs when the market capitalization of the company is less than the book value of its net identifiable assets).

Table A1a.c Horizon Global Ltd (HZG)

Conventionally prepared financial statements (all figures in $'000, except as noted)

Period ended	1999	2000		2001		2002
	31 Dec	30 Jun	31 Dec	30 Jun	31 Dec	30 Jun
Share capital and reserves	1,092	2,009	2,032	2,474	2,345	811
Goodwill per accounts						
Cost	–	723	721	721	721	721
Less:Amortized/written off	–	–	–	–	18	721
Book value	–	723	721	721	703	–

Using Market Capitalization Statement

BALANCE SHEET

Share capital and reserves	1,092	2,009	2,032	2,474	2,543	1,532
Less: Cost of purchased goodwill	–	723	721	721	721	721
Net identifiable assets	1,092	1,286	1,311	1,753	1,822	811

MARKET CAPITALIZATION STATEMENT

Number of issued shares ('000)	33,469	39,469	39,469	40,419	40,419	40,419
Market price per share ($)	0.330	0.170	0.290	0.360	0.300	0.075
Market capitalization	11,045	6,710	11,446	14,551	12,126	3,031
Comprising:						
Purchased goodwill, at cost	–	723	721	721	721	721
Internally generated goodwill	9,953	4,701	9,414	12,077	9,583	1,499
MCS goodwill	9,953	5,424	10,135	12,798	10,304	2,220
Net identifiable assets	1,092	1,286	1,311	1,753	1,822	811
Market capitalization	11,045	6,710	11,446	14,551	12,126	3,031
Ratio of MCS goodwill to market capitalization (%)	90	81	89	88	85	73

Note: For the purpose of this statement, 'MCS goodwill' is defined and calculated as the difference between market capitalization and the book value of the company's net identifiable assets.

Comments:

1. HZG did not amortize goodwill at all until the 2002 financial year. It did not disclose this in its accounting policy notes; there is no accounting policy note regarding goodwill in any of the three years reviewed, despite the fact that goodwill is 'material' in relation to share capital and reserves. Goodwill was totally written off at 30 June 2002; an amortization policy of writing of goodwill off over twenty years appears to have been initiated in the first half of that year. This inconsistency in amortization policy highlights how arbitrary many such policies are; major variations can have major effects on reported profits. The introduction of an MCS would eliminate this inconsistency.

2. Even in 2002, the year of the complete goodwill write-off, MCS goodwill exceeded purchased goodwill. The chairman's report makes it clear that the company's

venture into technology had not been abandoned, although 'the commercializa-
tion of this technology has not occurred'. It appears that the market still attached
value to the technology in question.

3. The write-off did achieve one similar effect to the use of the MCS, in that it removed
goodwill from the conventional Balance Sheet, focusing attention on the fact that net
identifiable assets were now reduced to $811,000. This feature of the MCS is one of
its most valuable attributes; had HZG chosen to follow a twenty-year amortization
policy, the net identifiable (in this case net tangible) asset position would have been
obscured. The figures involved are not large in this case, but the principle is clear.

4. As a corollary, the MCS highlights the proportion of market capitalization of
HZG that is attributable to MCS goodwill (ranging from 90 per cent in December
1999 to 73 per cent in June 2002). It also highlights the fluctuations in overall
market capitalization and the value of MCS goodwill.

Table A1a.d Publishing and Broadcasting Ltd (PBL)

Conventionally prepared financial statements (all figures in $'000, except as noted)

Period ended	1999		2000		2001		2002
	30 Jun	31 Dec	30 Jun	31 Dec	30 Jun	31 Dec	30 Jun
Share capital and reserves	3,320	3,433	3,542	3,701	3,344	3,428	3,466
Goodwill per accounts							
Cost	63	79	79	80	80	80	80
Less:Amortized/written off	1	2	3	4	6	7	9
Book value	62	77	76	76	74	73	71

Using Market Capitalization Statement

BALANCE SHEET

Share capital and reserves	3,321	3,435	3,545	3,706	3,349	3,436	3,474
Less: Cost of purchased goodwill	63	79	79	80	80	80	80
Net identifiable assets	3,258	3,356	3,466	3,626	3,269	3,356	3,394

MARKET CAPITALIZATION STATEMENT

Number of issued shares ('000)	653	660	661	663	662	662	662
Market price per share ($)	9.97	11.63	12.85	13.047	9.008	9.80	9.05
Market capitalization	6,510	7,676	8,496	8,650	5,963	6,483	5,988
Comprising:							
Purchased goodwill, at cost	63	79	79	80	80	80	80
Internally generated goodwill	3,189	4,241	4,951	4,944	2,614	3,047	2,514
MCS goodwill	3,252	4,320	5,030	5,024	2,694	3,127	2,594
Net identifiable assets	3,258	3,356	3,466	3,626	3,269	3,356	3,394
Market capitalization	6,510	7,676	8,496	8,650	5,963	6,483	5,988
Ratio of MCS goodwill to market capitalization (%)	50	56	59	58	45	48	43

Note: For the purpose of this statement, 'MCS goodwill' is defined and calculated as the difference between market capitalization and the book value of the company's net identifiable assets.

Comments:

1. Clearly, purchased goodwill is not a material figure in the accounts of PBL; the company amortizes purchased goodwill over a twenty-year period, which is hardly necessary given the amount of internally generated goodwill, but the effect on profits and/or net assets is negligible.

2. PBL has material figures in its Balance Sheet for 'other intangible assets'. An amount of $239 million is described as 'casino management agreement'; it relates to the management of Crown Casino and is being amortized over the thirty-four-year period of the agreement. There is also an asset reflected as 'venue ticketing rights' (costing about $20 million).Its most substantial intangible asset is mastheads and licences. In the June 2002 financial statements, television licences were reflected at 'deemed cost' of $1.318 million, while magazine mastheads were shown at cost of $1.205 million, a total of $2.523 million. The accounting policy note with regard to these items in 2002 read as follows:

Licences and Mastheads

Licences and mastheads are carried at cost.

Television licences are renewable every 5 years under the provisions of the Broadcasting Services Act 1992.

Whilst certain of the television licences continue to be subject to Government legislation and regulation by the Australian Broadcasting Authority, the directors have no reason to believe the licences will not be renewed. The directors applied an earnings based approach to revalue PBL's television licences in 1997.

While the directors believe this approach provides a more appropriate carrying value, it does not fully reflect the values being assigned in today's market. PBL's policy is to regularly review the value of television licences and write down the value to a recoverable amount when required.

The directors regularly assess the carrying value of mastheads so as to ensure they are not carried at a value greater than their recoverable amount.

No amortization is provided against those assets as the directors believe that the life of the licences and mastheads to the consolidated entity is of such duration, and the residual value at the end of that life would be such that the amortization charge, if any, would not be material.

The casino licence premium is carried at cost of acquisition. It is being amortized on a straight-line basis over the remaining life of the licence at the time PBL acquired Crown Ltd, being 34 years.

3. It is highly likely that the figure designated in the MCS above as 'internally generated goodwill' is, in fact, a 'master valuation account' as defined by Canning (1929; see Chapter 2.2), which reflects, to at least some extent, the valuation of PBL's licences and mastheads at a higher figure than their book value. Of itself, the MCS will not solve this problem; it is discussed in Chapter 7.

4. The MCS highlights major changes in the market capitalization of PBL, such as that between 30 June 2000 and 30 June 2001, when it fell from $8.496 million to $5.963 million, a fall of $2.533 million, of which only $197,000 could be accounted for by a fall in net identifiable assets. The balance represents a market re-rating of PBL, although it is not possible to apportion the fall between a market review of the valuation of IIAs, on the one hand, and MCS goodwill on the other.

5. What is also apparent is that, throughout the period, the market has rated PBL at a value considerably in excess of its disclosed net identifiable asset value. The accounting policy quoted states that an up to date earnings based valuation of television licences would provide a more appropriate carrying value; interestingly,

a similar comment is not made in relation to mastheads. The carrying value of the latter is apparently only reviewed to ensure that it is not greater than the recoverable amount, although this necessarily implies an assessment of the recoverable amount attributable to mastheads.

Table A1a.e Tennyson Networks Ltd (TNY)

Conventionally prepared financial statements (all figures in $'000, except as noted)

Period ended	1999		2000		2001		2002
	30 Jun	31 Dec	30 Jun	31 Dec	30 Jun	31 Dec	30 Jun
Share capital and reserves	3,810	8,805	5,727	6,051	696	3,319	1,898
Goodwill per accounts							
Cost	703	703	703	703	703	703	703
Less:Amortized/written off	568	636	703	703	703	703	703
Book value	135	67	–	–	–	–	–

Using Market Capitalization Statement

BALANCE SHEET

Share capital and reserves	4,378	9,441	6,430	6,754	1,399	4,022	2,601
Less: Cost of purchased goodwill	703	703	703	703	703	703	703
Net identifiable assets	3,675	8,738	5,727	6,051	696	3,319	1,898

MARKET CAPITALIZATION STATEMENT

Number of issued shares ('000)	28,078	34,883	35,030	40,451	44,245	95,254	130,734
Market price per share ($)	0.950	1.460	1.060	0.750	0.400	0.050	0.038
Market capitalization	26,674	50,929	37,132	30,338	17,698	4,763	4,968
Comprising:							
Purchased goodwill, at cost	703	703	703	703	703	703	703
Internally generated goodwill	22,296	41,488	30,702	23,584	16,299	741	2,367
MCS goodwill	22,999	42,191	31,405	24,287	17,002	1,444	3,070
Net identifiable assets	3,675	8,738	5,727	6,051	696	3,319	1,898
Market capitalization	26,674	50,929	37,132	30,338	17,698	4,763	4,968
Ratio of MCS goodwill to market capitalization (%)	86	83	85	80	96	30	62

Note: For the purpose of this statement, 'MCS goodwill' is defined and calculated as the difference between market capitalization and the book value of the company's net identifiable assets.

Comments:

1. TNY is a long established company, which had been amortizing goodwill over a five-year period, terminating at 30 June 2000. Throughout the period analysed, MCS goodwill was well in excess of purchased goodwill. At its lowest point, 31 December 2001, it was more than double the cost of purchased goodwill (even though the latter had been completely amortized).
2. The fluctuations in MCS goodwill are not unlike that reflected in the analysis of ASC, with the lowest valuation in December 2001. The MCS serves to highlight these fluctuations in goodwill value.
3. As in previous examples, the MCS highlights the importance of goodwill in evaluating the state of affairs of TNY. In the first five periods examined, MCS goodwill constitutes between 80 per cent and 96 per cent of the market capitalization of the company. Even at 30 June 2002, after a considerable fall in the value of a TNY share, MCS goodwill accounts for 62 per cent of market capitalization.

Cases falling into the 'A' and 'L' categories are initially indicated by a negative figure under 'internally generated goodwill' in the MCS. The resultant 'MCS goodwill' figure has been designated '(A)' or '(L)' in the MCS.

f. Aspermont Ltd (ASP)

Principal activity – Publisher in the dual print and internet publishing environment. Primarily focused on resource and mining publications.

Listing details – ASP was listed in April 2000 (Table A1a.f).

g. UXC Ltd (UXC) previously Davnet Ltd

Principal activity – The supply, distribution and integration of data storage equipment and services.

Listing details – UXC listed in February 1997, but entered into the Davnet venture in September 1998. From that date, the company had a telecommunication focus.

Under its previous name, Davnet Ltd, UXC was one of the dot.com 'high fliers', as will be seen from its MCS statement. It acquired technology by which equipment could be individually installed in a commercial building, giving access to instantaneous transmission of internet data, voice and video to occupants of that building. Sadly, the operation never achieved commercial viability and, today, UXC, while still remaining active, has a vastly reduced scale of operations (Table A1a.g).

h. Keycorp Ltd (KYC)

Principal activities – Research, development, manufacture, marketing and sales of devices and systems to allow secure electronic payments at point-of-sale, through the internet and via smartcards and smartcard operating systems; installation, service and logistics for financial terminals; marketing and sales of transaction network solutions.

Listing details – KYC listed in 1987. It was involved in activities similar to those detailed above prior to the period under review (Table A1a.h).

i. Winepros Ltd (WPO)

Principal activity – Development of an international internet portal devoted to wine, based on recommendations by James Halliday, a well known wine critic.

Listing details – WPO was listed in December 1999 (Table A1a.i).

j. Multimedia Ltd (MUL)

Principal activity – Development and distribution of internet and e-commerce enabling tools such as web development portal building, and internet applications for three-dimensional technology; importation and resale of hardware and software.

Listing details – Originally listed as a mining company in 1987, but changed its classification on 1 December 1999 (Table A1a.j).

Illustrative examples (no purchased goodwill)

All previous examples have illustrated cases in which the carrying value of purchased goodwill has been compared with the value of MCS goodwill, ascertained via the market capitalization of the company. The MCS system is even simpler when there is no purchased goodwill, because it is not necessary to adjust the conventional accounts for the cost of goodwill or for amounts charged against profits for amortization or goodwill written off. The following examples illustrate that the MCS is still valuable.

k. Ezenet Ltd (EZE)

Principal activity – Setting up digital quality video services to the hotel/motel industry, including provision of movies to guests; marketing and distribution of television set-top internet boxes.

Listing details – EZE was listed on 7 December 1999 (Table A1a.k).

l. Easycall International Ltd (EZY)

Principal activity – Development of internet infrastructure network services and the operation of paging and messaging telecommunication services, as well as the operation of an education business.

Listing details – Effectively a 'back door' listing that became effective in February 1998. Until 7 April 2004, the shares were 'stapled' to shares in a subsidiary, Easycall Asia Ltd. On that date, shares in the latter company were delisted and destapled. Details furnished throughout the period are for Easycall International Ltd only (Table A1a.l).

Table A1a.f Aspermont Ltd (ASP)

Conventionally prepared financial statements (all figures in $'000, except as noted)

Period ended	2000		2001		2002
	30 Jun	31 Dec	30 Jun	31 Dec	30 Jun
Share capital and reserves	3,652	3,519	2,819	2,767	2,669
Goodwill per accounts					
Cost	2,438	2,438	2,438	2,438	2,438
Less:Amortized/written off	2,118	2,124	2,131	2,131	2,131
Book value	320	314	307	307	307

Using Market Capitalization Statement

BALANCE SHEET

Share capital and reserves	5,770	5,643	4,650	4,898	4,800
Less: Cost of purchased goodwill	2,438	2,438	2,438	2,438	2,438
Net identifiable assets	3,332	3,205	2,212	2,460	2,362

MARKET CAPITALIZATION STATEMENT

Number of issued shares ('000)	74,303	74,440	75,315	78,899	84,099
Market price per share ($)	0.120	0.105	0.054	0.082	0.067
Market capitalization	8,916	7,816	4,067	6,470	5,635
Comprising:					
Purchased goodwill, at cost	2,438	2,438	2,438	2,438	2,438
Internally generated goodwill	3,146	2,173	(583)	1,572	835
MCS goodwill	5,584	4,611	1,855 (A)	4,010	3,273
Net identifiable assets	3,332	3,205	2,212	2,460	2,362
Market capitalization	8,916	7,816	4,067	6,470	5,635
Ratio of MCS goodwill to market capitalization (%)	63	59	46	62	58

Note: For the purpose of this statement, 'MCS goodwill' is defined and calculated as the difference between market capitalization and the book value of the company's net identifiable assets.

Comments:

1. ASP has expressed its goodwill policy consistently over the three financial years, as follows:

    Goodwill and goodwill on consolidation are initially recorded at the amount by which the purchase price for a business exceeds the fair value attributed to its net assets at date of acquisition. Both goodwill and goodwill on consolidation are amortized on a straight line basis over a period of twenty years. The balances are reviewed annually, and any balance representing future benefits for which the realization is considered to be no longer probable are written off.

2. The company was first listed in April 2000. Prior to that, by 30 June 1999, purchased goodwill had been substantially written off or amortized to a nominal figure of $41,000. Goodwill of $279,000 was purchased in the 2000 financial year,

leaving a small goodwill figure of $320,000 to be amortized over twenty years. This policy was followed in the following financial year, but not in 2002, when there was no write-off, despite the stated policy.

3. The amount of goodwill to be written off over twenty years is not material ($16,000 per annum). The decision to abandon the amortization policy may have been partly due to this factor, and partly because the company does not amortize its other intangible asset, mastheads (purchased in the 2000 financial year for $1,936,000). The note recording this policy is interesting (taken from the 2002 financial statements of ASP):

Mastheads.

In the past, mastheads have been carried at cost and were not amortized as the directors were of the opinion that having regard to the duration of the life of the mastheads and their ultimate residual value amortization would not have been material.

While applicable accounting standards and other professional requirements require that assets such as mastheads be amortized over a period not exceeding twenty years, the directors have decided not to amortize mastheads for the following reasons:

a. On 21 February 2002, the company issued a prospectus to raise $2,200,000 by the issue of 11,000,000 new shares at an issue price of 20c each.

> *The issue under the prospectus was fully met and consequently the company's shares were quoted on the Australian Stock Exchange on 27 April 2000 and have remained quoted.*

b. The successful capital raising by the company and the subsequent listing of its shares on the Australian Stock Exchange has significantly increased the market capitalization of the company and provided an avenue for the sale of its shares.

c. Since the raising of new capital, the company has significantly enlarged its business through both increased revenues and the acquisition of related business assets.

d. The increased revenues are the result of improved circulation for publications and rises in advertising revenue; and

e. The company is regarded as a leader in the specialist and technical publishing world. As a result, the directors are of the opinion that the mastheads have increased in value but, in the light of the matters discussed above and having regard to the requirements of applicable accounting standards, they have determined to retain the mastheads at their existing carrying value and that no provisions for their amortization should be made at this time. The carrying amount is reviewed annually by the directors to ensure that it is not in excess of the recoverable amount. The recoverable amount is assessed based upon the present value of expected future cash flows.

The audit report does not comment on this policy and is unqualified.

AASB 1018 would not allow a similar view to be taken with regard to purchased goodwill.

4. As noted above, goodwill purchased by ASP was largely written off prior to the listing of the company. In most of the period since listing, ASP's MCS goodwill has represented a substantial portion of the market capitalization of the company (between 46 per cent and 63 per cent) and has exceeded the cost of purchased goodwill; in June 2001, a fall in the company's share price meant that, for a brief period, this was no longer true. The MCS statement clearly shows this.

5. The MCS also highlights the goodwill movements over the period; these are less extreme for ASP than for many of the dot.com companies examined. The fact that, at 30 June 2002, internally generated goodwill was reflected as negative would have highlighted the relatively negative market appraisal of ASP at that date. It would also have called into question the decision not to amortize goodwill and the valuation of IIAs. Notably, had goodwill been written off at that date, the new 'impairment' Standards would not have permitted the reversal of the write-off, despite the fact that the MCS indicates that such a reversal could be justified.

Table A1a.g UXC Ltd (UXC)

Conventionally prepared financial statements (all figures in $'000, except as noted)

Period ended	1999		2000		2001		2002
	30 Jun	31 Dec	30 Jun	31 Dec	30 Jun	31 Dec	30 Jun
Share capital and reserves	32,156	89,234	103,990	72,102	11,772	(4,430)	14,487
Goodwill per accounts							
Cost	21,142	15,666	39,854	44,085	56,085	56,085	58,512
Less:Amortized/ written off	238	947	1,733	12,838	56,085	56,085	56,095
Book value	20,904	14,719	38,121	31,247	–	–	2,417

Using Market Capitalization Statement

BALANCE SHEET

Share capital and reserves	32,394	90,181	105,723	84,104	67,857	51,655	70,582
Less: Cost of purchased goodwill	21,143	15,666	39,854	44,066	56,085	56,085	58,512
Net identifiable assets	11,251	74,515	65,869	40,038	11,772	(4,430)	12,070

MARKET CAPITALIZATION STATEMENT

Number of issued shares ('000)	436,882	442,038	464,164	485,533	529,012	539,186	550,083
Market price per share ($)	0.285	2.300	1.260	0.475	0.130	0.039	0.032
Market capitalization	124,454	1,016,917	584,847	230,628	68,772	21,028	17,603
Comprising:							
Purchased goodwill, at cost	21,142	15,666	39,854	44,085	56,085	56,085	58,512
Internally generated goodwill	92,060	926,736	479,124	146,505	915	(30,627)	(52,979)
MCS goodwill	113,202	942,402	518,978	190,590	57,000	25,458 (A)	5,533 (A)
Net identifiable assets	11,252	74,515	65,869	40,038	11,772	(4,430)	12,070
Market capitalization	124,454	1,016,917	584,847	230,628	68,772	21,028	17,603
Ratio of MCS goodwill to market capitalization (%)	91	93	89	83	83	121	37

Note: For the purpose of this statement, 'MCS goodwill' is defined and calculated as the difference between market capitalization and the book value of the company's net identifiable assets.

Comments:
1. The goodwill amortization policy of UXC reflects the changing fortunes of the company.

2000 Accounts	Amortized on a straight line basis over twenty years, being the period during which benefits are expected to arise.
2001 Accounts	Amortized...on a straight line basis over a period of ten years, which represents a change in accounting estimate as goodwill was amortized over twenty years in previous accounting reporting periods. At 30 June 2001, the directors wrote off the unamortized goodwill balance to nil. (Note: this appears contradictory, but may be designed to explain the policy in the first six months of the year – even though goodwill amortization in this period appears to be higher than 10per cent per annum.)
2002 Accounts	Goodwill...is amortized in the current year on a straight line basis over a period of ten years. (Note: in fact, goodwill had been completely written off in the previous year.)

2. The example of UXC, or Davnet as it was known up to October 2002, shows how difficult it is to establish a meaningful amortization policy, based on 'the period during which benefits are expected to arise'. The MCS provides a factual, as distinct from arbitrary, calculation of MCS goodwill at the balance dates.
3. UXC is an extreme example of market value fluctuation, from over a billion dollars at 31 December 1999 to $18 million at 30 June 2002. Conventional accounting statements fail to reflect this, while purporting to show a true and fair view of the financial position of the company.
4. Intriguingly, despite the decision to write off goodwill at 30 June 2001, the market capitalization of UXC indicates that, at that date, there was no need to do so (although the subsequent fall in the value of the company after balance date may have influenced the directors to take that decision).
5. Because UXC had written off its goodwill entirely by 31 December 2001, the negative net identifiable asset position was exposed in its interim accounts at that date, as it would have been under MCS principles. What is not disclosed is that, even at that date, MCS goodwill was material, at least in relation to the then net assets of the company. Both of these items of information are emphasized by the disclosure that, at that date, the ratio of MCS goodwill to market capitalization exceeded 100 per cent.
6. The MCS also highlights the fact that a significant portion of share capital and reserves was expended in the acquisition of goodwill, which is not emphasized under conventional accounting.
7. Even at 30 June 2002, the value of MCS goodwill, because it is positive, exceeds the value of purchased goodwill net of amortization and amounts written off. In fact, goodwill still represents 37 per cent of the market capitalization of the company. Given the fact that UXC has disposed of all the businesses in respect of which the initial goodwill was purchased, there is some intrinsic logic in the total write-off of the attendant goodwill. Nevertheless, it is clear that the market continues to attach some value to internally generated goodwill developed by this company – perhaps in relation to its battle-scarred management team.

Table A1a.h Keycorp Ltd (KYC)

Conventionally prepared financial statements (all figures in $'000, except as noted)

Period ended	1999		2000		2001		2002
	30 Jun	31 Dec	30 Jun	31 Dec	30 Jun	31 Dec	30 Jun
Share capital and reserves	28,354	45,725	27,267	459,338	422,897	403,352	109,462
Goodwill per accounts							
Cost	11,193	11,193	13,004	423,442	445,617	445,617	443,734
Less:Amortized/ written off	1,102	1,397	1,746	4,114	15,384	25,184	300,134
Book value	10,091	9,796	11,258	419,328	430,233	420,433	143,600

Using Market Capitalization Statement

BALANCE SHEET

	30 Jun	31 Dec	30 Jun	31 Dec	30 Jun	31 Dec	30 Jun
Share capital and reserves	29,456	47,122	29,013	463,452	438,271	428,536	409,596
Less: Cost of purchased goodwill	11,193	11,193	13,004	423,442	445,617	445,617	443,734
Net identifiable assets	18,263	35,929	16,009	40,010	(7,346)	(17,081)	(34,138)

MARKET CAPITALIZATION STATEMENT

	30 Jun	31 Dec	30 Jun	31 Dec	30 Jun	31 Dec	30 Jun
Number of issued shares ('000)	35,567	35,912	36,195	75,967	77,009	81,658	81,658
Market price per share ($)	3.73	8.190	9.370	9.259	2.310	1.940	0.850
Market capitalization	132,665	294,119	339,147	703,378	177,891	158,415	69,408
Comprising: Purchased goodwill, at cost	11,193	11,193	13,004	423,442	445,617	445,617	443,734
Internally generated goodwill	103,209	246,997	310,134	239,926	(260,380)	(270,121)	(340,188)
MCS goodwill	114,402	258,190	323,138	663,368	185,237 (L)	175,496 (L)	103,564 (L)
Net identifiable assets	18,263	35,929	16,009	40,010	(7,346)	(17,081)	(34,138)
Market capitalization	132,665	294,119	339,147	703,378	177,891	158,415	69,408
Ratio of MCS goodwill to market capitalization (%)	86	88	95	94	104	111	149

Note: For the purpose of this statement, 'MCS goodwill' is defined and calculated as the difference between market capitalization and the book value of the company's net identifiable assets.

Comments:

1. KYC changed its financial reporting date during the period. While it had reported at 31 December in 1999 and 2000, it only made interim reports in 2001, issuing its next Annual Report at 30 June 2002.
2. Goodwill figures at 30 June 1999 and 31 December 2001 were estimated from details available – no exact figure was furnished.
3. Like the previous company, UXC, KYC's goodwill amortization policy has varied over the period examined.

31 December 1999 Accounts	Goodwill amortized over twenty years, being the period over which benefits are expected to be received.
31 December 2000 Accounts	'Period over which benefits are expected to be received' was revised to 'between 4 and 20 years, with the major balance at 10 years'.
30 June 2002 Accounts	The period over which benefits were expected to be received was defined as 'between 10 and 20 years, with the major balance at 20 years'.

   (Note: in this period, a 'decrement in value of intangible assets of $272.4 million' was charged against profits, in addition to 'normal' amortization. This write-off is not mentioned in the note regarding accounting policies.)
4. Once again, the arbitrary nature of assessment of the period over which to amortize goodwill is emphasized. Under existing accounting principles, the effect of this variation is directly felt on reported profit, requiring adjustment to the degree (if any) which the analyst or casual reader deems appropriate. The MCS, on the other hand, presents an objective view of MCS goodwill in that it is determined by the company's market capitalization and does not impinge on reported profits.
5. KYC is an extreme case in that, over the period analysed, market capitalization consisted almost entirely of MCS goodwill. It remained virtually constant at 94–95 per cent from 31 December 1999 to 31 December 2000, when the market capitalization of the company was at its height. At the same time, KYC was amortizing goodwill (predominantly) over a ten-year period.
6. At the first four of the seven reporting dates, total MCS goodwill substantially exceeded purchased goodwill. This was maintained after the six months ended 31 December 2000, during which time purchased goodwill rose from $13 million to $423 million; the market valuation of goodwill was $663 million. After this, however, market sentiment clearly changed. At all subsequent interim and final reporting dates, the value of MCS goodwill was substantially lower, not only than purchased goodwill, but than the carrying value of goodwill in KYC's Balance Sheet. Conventional accounting provides no indication of the considerable variance between the company's view and that of the market over the period.
7. Under conventional accounting, share capital and reserves (or net assets) was reflected at $423 million, $403 million and $109 million at the last three dates illustrated. Under MCS, the corresponding figures showed a deficit of net identifiable assets of $7 million, $17 million and $34 million respectively. This is further emphasized by the ratio of MCS goodwill to total market value, which was 104 per cent, 111 per cent and 149 per cent at those dates.
8. Conversely, conventional accounting gave no indication to readers of the financial statements at the earlier balance dates of the considerable rise in the total value of MCS goodwill.
9. It has been argued earlier that, in many ways, the distinction between purchased and internally generated goodwill is a false dichotomy. It is, nevertheless, interesting

that, in the six-month period ended 31 December 2000, when additions to purchased goodwill totalled some $410 million, internally generated goodwill fell by $68 million. This may have indicated a market view that the rapid expansion of KYC ought to be treated with caution.

Table A1a.i Winepros Ltd (WPO)

Conventionally prepared financial statements (all figures in $'000, except as noted)

Period ended	1999	2000		2001		2002
	31 Dec	30 Jun	31 Dec	30 Jun	31 Dec	30 Jun
Share capital and reserves	24,059	16,180	12,334	9,881	5,823	900
Goodwill per accounts						
Cost	1,487	1,487	1,487	1,487	1,487	1,487
Less:Amortized/written off	103	207	355	504	652	1,487
Book value	1,384	1,280	1,132	983	835	–

Using Market Capitalization Statement

BALANCE SHEET

Share capital and reserves	24,162	16,387	12,689	10,385	6,475	2,387
Less: Cost of purchased goodwill	1,487	1,487	1,487	1,487	1,487	1,487
Net identifiable assets	22,675	14,900	11,202	8,898	4,988	900

MARKET CAPITALIZATION STATEMENT

Number of issued shares ('000)	50,000	50,000	50,000	50,000	50,000	50,000
Market price per share ($)	1.280	0.355	0.120	0.065	0.110	0.031
Market capitalization	64,000	17,750	6,000	3,250	5,500	1,550
Comprising:						
Purchased goodwill, at cost	1,487	1,487	1,487	1,487	1,487	1,487
Internally generated goodwill	39,838	1,363	(6,689)	(7,135)	(975)	(837)
MCS goodwill	41,325	2,850	(5,202)	(5,648)	512	650
			(N)	(N)	(L)	(A)
Net identifiable assets	22,675	14,900	11,202	8,898	4,988	900
Market capitalization	64,000	17,750	6,000	3,250	5,500	1,550
Ratio of MCS goodwill to market capitalization (%)	65	16	(87)	(174)	9	42

Note: For the purpose of this statement, 'MCS goodwill' is defined and calculated as the difference between market capitalization and the book value of the company's net identifiable assets.

Comments:

1. Of all the companies examined, this was the only one that afforded examples of all possibilities during the period analysed. In the first two periods, the company fell

into the 'normal' or 'C' category, in which the value of MCS goodwill exceeded the cost of purchased goodwill. However:

- in the next two periods, MCS goodwill was negative (Category N); the market capitalization of the company was less than the value of its net identifiable assets;
- at 31 December 2001, MCS goodwill was less than the amortized value of goodwill, per the accounts (Category L);
- at 30 June 2002, MCS goodwill was greater than the carrying value of goodwill in the financial statements, but less than cost (Category A).

2. Throughout the period, WPO's stated accounting policy was to amortize goodwill over a five-year period. It followed this policy until 30 June 2002, when the una-mortized value of goodwill was written off. In the 2000 financial year, WPO acquired the 'James Halliday' website (Halliday is a notable writer and expert on wine). The cost of this website was written off over two years, ending in the 2001 financial year.

3. The company listed in December 1999, at which stage its market capitalization was $64 million, of which MCS goodwill constituted 65 per cent. Market capitalization has steadily declined over the period to $1.5 million as at 30 June 2002, with a cor-responding fall in the value of MCS goodwill. At 31 December 2000 and 30 June 2001, MCS goodwill was negative, whereas, since then, it has returned to a small positive value while still being below the value of purchased goodwill.

4. WPO provides another example of how difficult it is for management to choose an appropriate period over which to amortize goodwill. Despite the relatively small numbers involved, the MCS gives a realistic view of MCS goodwill over the period and also identifies clearly that, at certain times, the market value of the company was well below the value of its net identifiable assets. The conventionally prepared accounts reflected those assets at their normal carrying values. As the assets in question were almost entirely cash or cash equivalents, it is unlikely that their net realizable value differed materially from carrying value. Given the information in the MCS, shareholders and other analysts may well have queried this anomaly.

5. The decision to write off goodwill completely and abandon the five-year amorti-zation principle was taken not at 30 June 2001, when MCS goodwill was sub-stantially negative, but in the 2002 financial year. Ironically, had goodwill continued to be amortized as in previous years, its amortized value at 30 June 2002 would have been almost the same as the total goodwill calculated in the MCS. The write-off decision may have been influenced by a takeover bid sub-sequent to balance date, which valued the company at little more than its net tangible asset value.

6. Unfortunately, although WPO offers examples of all possible goodwill situations involving purchased goodwill, the relatively small size of the company and the fact that, within a very short time of its listing, its market value suffered a material and permanent decline make it less interesting than some of the companies examined previously.

Table A1a.j Multimedia Ltd (MUL)

Conventionally prepared financial statements (all figures in $'000, except as noted)

Period ended	1999	2000		2001		2002
	31 Dec	30 Jun	31 Dec	30 Jun	31 Dec	30 Jun
Share capital and reserves	23,484	28,009	21,277	13,564	11,642	2,103

Goodwill per accounts

Cost	1,471	1,471	1,471	1,942	5,097	5,097
Less:Amortized/written off	37	73	110	154	271	416
Book value	1,434	1,398	1,361	1,788	4,826	4,681

Using Market Capitalization Statement

BALANCE SHEET

Share capital and reserves	23,521	28,082	21,387	13,718	11,913	2,519
Less: Cost of purchased goodwill	1,471	1,471	1,471	1,942	5,097	5,097
Net identifiable assets	22,050	26,611	19,916	11,776	6,816	(2,578)

MARKET CAPITALIZATION STATEMENT

Number of issued shares ('000)	259,363	268,112	316,178	332,688	435,843	536,446
Market price per share ($)	0.710	0.280	0.095	0.033	0.021	0.015
Market capitalization	184,148	75,071	30,037	10,979	9,153	8,047
Comprising:						
Purchased goodwill, at cost	1,471	1,471	1,471	1,942	5,097	5,097
Internally generated goodwill	160,627	46,989	8,650	(2,739)	(2,760)	5,528
MCS goodwill	162,098	48,460	10,121	(797) (N)	2,337 (L)	10,625
Net identifiable assets	22,050	26,611	19,916	11,776	6,816	(2,578)
Market capitalization	184,148	75,071	30,037	10,979	9,153	8,047
Ratio of MCS goodwill to market capitalization (%)	88	65	34	(7)	26	132

Note: For the purpose of this statement, 'MCS goodwill' is defined and calculated as the difference between market capitalization and the book value of the company's net identifiable assets.

Comments:

1. MUL has consistently followed a policy of amortizing goodwill over a period of twenty years.
2. The company's market price follows a fairly typical 'dot.com' pattern. Its market capitalization has fallen from $184 million shortly after acquiring its internet business to $8 million at 30 June 2002. The MCS tracks this significant movement, unlike conventional accounting.
3. MUL is fairly unusual in that a period in which the MCS goodwill was negative (30 June 2001) was followed by a significant improvement. At 31 December 2001, MUL was a Category L company, in that its MCS goodwill was positive, although less than the amortized value of goodwill per accounts. By 30 June 2002, MUL had reverted to being a company in which MCS goodwill exceeded the cost of purchased goodwill. (See previous comment 6 on the MCS statement of ASP.)
4. The MCS tracks this recovery in goodwill, and it is interesting to compare the MCS goodwill value so obtained with the carrying value of goodwill. Unlike a number of companies examined, MUL has maintained its amortization policy and has not written goodwill off completely, despite the contrary market view on 30 June 2001.

5. MUL made an acquisition, involving the purchase of goodwill, in the 2002 financial year. The MCS shows that, after this acquisition, net identifiable assets were negative, which is concealed by conventional accounting, as is the consequent rise in goodwill. During the 2002 financial year, the market capitalization of the company actually fell (from $11 million to $8 million); the fall in identifiable net assets outweighed the rise in MCS goodwill. None of this analysis is obvious without the MCS.

Table A1a.k Ezenet Ltd (EZE)

Conventionally prepared financial statements (all figures in $'000, except as noted)

Period ended	1999 31 Dec	2000 30 Jun	2000 31 Dec	2001 30 Jun	2001 31 Dec	2002 30 Jun
Share capital and reserves/ *net identifiable assets*	3,330	2,522	1,666	1,077	933	959

Using Market Capitalization Statement

BALANCE SHEET

No change to conventionally prepared financial statements, as above

MARKET CAPITALIZATION STATEMENT

Number of issued shares ('000)	26,000	26,000	26,000	26,000	29,900	34,900
Market price per share ($)	0.750	0.105	0.110	0.062	0.096	0.170
Market capitalization	19,500	2,730	2,860	1,612	2,870	5,933
Comprising:						
MCS goodwill	16,170	208	1,194	535	1,937	4,974
Net identifiable assets	3,330	2,522	1,666	1,077	933	959
Market capitalization	19,500	2,730	2,860	1,612	2,870	5,933
Ratio of MCS goodwill to market capitalization (%)	83	8	42	33	67	84

Note: For the purpose of this statement, 'MCS goodwill' is defined and calculated as the difference between market capitalization and the book value of the company's net identifiable assets.

Comments:
1. EZE is a small listed company. Throughout its history as a listed company, MCS goodwill has been positive, although the percentage of goodwill to total market capitalization varied sharply. Soon after listing, MCS goodwill constituted 83 per cent of market value; six months later, with the fall in the market price of the share, MCS goodwill was barely positive and made up only 8 per cent of market value.
2. By June 2002, MCS goodwill was once more the major constituent of market capitalization; ironically, it was once more at 83 per cent, although the market capitalization itself had fallen from $19.5 million to $6 million.

Table A1a.1 Easycall International Ltd (EZY)

Conventionally prepared financial statements (all figures in $'000, except as noted)

Period ended	1999		2000		2001		2002
	30 Jun	31 Dec	30 Jun	31 Dec	30 Jun	31 Dec	30 Jun
Share capital and reserves/ *net identifiable assets*	40,477	43,648	46,808	42,024	26,246	24,986	22,221

Using Market Capitalization Statement

BALANCE SHEET

No change to conventionally prepared
financial statements, as above

MARKET CAPITALIZATION STATEMENT

Number of issued shares ('000)	181,801	181,801	182,075	182,075	228,661	228,661	228,661
Market price per share ($)	0.200	0.370	0.562	0.195	0.064	0.080	0.095
Market capitalization	36,360	67,266	102,326	35,504	14,634	18,293	21,723
Comprising:							
MCS goodwill	(4,117)	23,618	55,518	(6,520)	(11,612)	(6,693)	(498)
	(N)			(N)	(N)	(N)	(N)
Net identifiable assets	40,477	43,648	46,808	42,024	26,246	24,986	22,221
Market capitalization	36,360	67,266	102,326	35,504	14,634	18,293	21,723
Ratio of MCS goodwill to market capitalization (%)	(11)	35	54	(18)	(79)	(37)	(2)

Note: For the purpose of this statement, 'MCS goodwill' is defined and calculated as the difference between market capitalization and the book value of the company's net identifiable assets.

Comments:

1. EZY carries no goodwill or IIAs in its Balance Sheet. The company has, however, written a substantial amount off plant and equipment and leasehold improvements, described as 'impairment provisions'.
2. Unlike the previous example, MCS goodwill is negative at three of the seven dates at which the analysis is carried out. Under conventional accounting, this information is not available to the reader of the financial statements, but it is extremely important if a valid assessment of the state of affairs of the company is to be made; it throws doubt on the carrying value of the assets in the Balance Sheet, even after taking into account the impairment provisions noted above. These totalled $13.7 million at 30 June 2001 and $11 million at 30 June 2002.
3. The MCS highlights the rise in MCS goodwill and market value that occurred in the 1999/2000 financial year, followed by the even sharper decline in the following year.

Table A1a.m Melbourne IT Ltd (MLB)

Conventionally prepared financial statements (all figures in $'000, except as noted)

Period ended	1999 31 Dec	2000 30 Jun	31 Dec	2001 30 Jun	31 Dec	2002 30 Jun
Share capital and reserves/ **net identifiable assets**	7,313	9,501	8,794	10,442	11,847	13,442

Using Market Capitalization Statement

BALANCE SHEET

No change to conventionally prepared
financial statements, as above

MARKET CAPITALIZATION STATEMENT

Number of issued shares ('000)	50,000	50,000	50,000	50,000	50,000	50,000
Market price per share ($)	8.529	8.387	0.650	0.630	0.660	0.410
Market capitalization	426,450	419,350	32,500	31,500	33,000	20,500
Comprising:						
MCS goodwill	419,137	409,849	23,706	21,058	21,153	7,058
Net identifiable assets, as above	7,313	9,501	8,794	10,442	11,847	13,442
Market capitalization	426,450	419,350	32,500	31,500	33,000	20,500
Ratio of MCS goodwill to market capitalization (%)	98	98	73	67	64	34

Note: For the purpose of this statement, 'MCS goodwill' is defined and calculated as the difference between market capitalization and the book value of the company's net identifiable assets.

Comments:

1. The MCS highlights the fact that, from its listing to the end of its first reporting period as a listed company, MLB's MCS goodwill constituted 98 per cent of its market capitalization; with net identifiable assets of less than $10 million, the company was capitalized at well over $400 million.
2. MLB has remained a viable company since listing; at 30 June 2002, MCS goodwill makes up only 34 per cent of its (much reduced) market capitalization. The MCS, as usual, highlights the fluctuation in the market capitalization of the company and the fluctuation in both the relative and absolute importance of the MCS goodwill portion of that valuation.
3. The company is a larger one than the two companies previously analysed in this category, and the MCS does show the advantages of being able to bring internally generated goodwill in its purest form (i.e. there is no purchased goodwill) to the attention of the reader and analyst of financial statements. It is interesting to contrast the apparent stability of the company's share capital and reserves, which is the view presented to the shareholders: it shows a rise from $7.3 million to $13.4 million over the period. The fall in MCS goodwill from $419.1 million to $7 million, which is surely crucial in understanding MLB, must currently be ascertained from sources other than the Annual Report.

Table A1a.n Fast Scout Ltd (FSL)

Conventionally prepared financial statements (all figures in $'000, except as noted)

Period ended	2000		2001		2002
	30 Jun	31 Dec	30 Jun	31 Dec	30 Jun
Share capital and reserves/					
net identifiable assets	16,389	16,173	15,970	15,240	5,196

Using Market Capitalization Statement

BALANCE SHEET

No change to conventionally prepared
financial statements, as above

MARKET CAPITALIZATION STATEMENT

Number of issued shares ('000)	85,302	85,302	85,302	85,302	81,593
Market price per share ($)	0.056	0.052	0.030	0.028	0.017
Market capitalization	4,777	4,436	2,559	2,388	1,387
Comprising:					
MCS goodwill	(11,612)	(11,737)	(13,411)	(12,852)	(3,809)
Net identifiable assets, as above	16,389	16,173	15,970	15,240	5,196
Market capitalization	4,777	4,436	2,559	2,388	1,387
Ratio of MCS goodwill to market capitalization (%)	(243)	(265)	(524)	(538)	(275)

Note: This percentage is not easy to
understand in an extreme case such
as FSL; it may be easier to replace it
by a percentage such as the ratio of
total market capitalization to net
identifiable assets in such cases (see
also WPO, MUL and EZY)

That ratio would be (%)	29	27	16	16	27

Note: For the purpose of this statement, 'MCS goodwill' is defined and calculated as
the difference between market capitalization and the book value of the company's net
identifiable assets.

Comments:

1. FSL is an extreme example of a company with 'negative MCS goodwill'. Since its
listing, the market capitalization of the company has been consistently well below
the value of its net identifiable assets. The extent of the difference is so large as to
cause considerable doubt as to whether the carrying value of the assets on FSL's
Balance Sheet is appropriate, but the difference is not shown at all in conventionally prepared accounts.

2. FSL's major asset is an intangible described as 'portal technology'. At the 2002
financial year-end, this asset (which had previously not been amortized) was written down by $8.9 million to $2 million; the write-off is reflected in the decline in
net identifiable assets.

m. Melbourne IT Ltd (MLB)

Principal activity – The administration of the internet domain '.com.au'; registration of generic domain names (.com, .net,org); registration of multilingual generic names; research and development in information technologies and telecommunications.

Listing details – The company was listed on 10 December 1999 (Table A1a.m).

n. Fast Scout Ltd (FSL)

Principal activity – The development of the Virtual Web Employee Internet Management service and the Fast Scout Internet search and navigation website portal and share investments.

Listing details – The company was listed on 7 March 2000 (Table A1a.n).

Appendix 1b

The MCS and six of Australia's leading companies

The examples illustrated in Appendix 1a were all 'dot.com' or internet related companies and, with the exception of PBL, did not fall within Australia's largest 100 companies. In order to broaden the selection and to examine the application of the MCS in relation to major, non-speculative listed companies, it was decided to apply the MCS over the same period to six of Australia's largest companies. These were chosen by reference to a list appearing in business magazine *BRW* (issue of 24–30 July 2003: 18). Companies were chosen by selecting the largest company and then the next five companies at intervals of five (i.e. the first, sixth, eleventh, sixteenth, twenty-first and twenty-sixth largest companies). Mining companies were excluded, because goodwill is not a meaningful concept in relation to such companies. Banks were also excluded, because their balance dates are 31 March (interim) and 30 September (final); all other companies examined have 30 June and 31 December balance dates.

The companies chosen on this basis were:

- The News Corporation Ltd (NCP)
- Telstra Corporation Ltd (TLS)
- Wesfarmers Ltd (WES)
- Westfield Holdings Ltd (WSF)
- Amcor Ltd (AMC)
- QBE Insurance Group Ltd (QBE)

Not surprisingly, all the results of these companies fell in the normal, or (C), category in that the total value of goodwill at every date during the period of analysis exceeded purchased goodwill. In Chapter 6.1, data have been furnished that reflect two significant conclusions derived from the analyses of their MCSs, viz.:

- on average over the period, 67 per cent of the market capitalization of the companies consisted of goodwill;

- purchased goodwill (measured at cost) was a relatively minor component of that figure of 67 per cent, averaging only 5 per cent over the period.

Averages are inherently misleading, and the number of companies examined is extremely small. However, with that rider, it is difficult to avoid the conclusion that an accounting framework that has express provisions which cause 62 per cent of the average market capitalization of companies of this size and importance to be excluded from its ambit lacks relevance in the modern business world. As noted in Chapter 6.1, after over 100 years of controversy, the accounting establishment has not found a lasting and generally accepted method of accounting for purchased goodwill, which accounts for considerably less (some 5 per cent) of their average market capitalization. This highlights the predisposition of historical cost accounting to emphasize objectivity over relevance.

The procedure and format followed in this Appendix is similar to that in Appendix 1a, except that figures are furnished in $'million, rather than $'000, because of the greater size of the companies. The examples illustrated in this Appendix show that the advantages of the MCS are applicable to large and successful companies as well as to ASX minnows and more speculative companies.

a. News Corporation Ltd (NCP)

Principal activity – Filmed entertainment, television, cable network programming, magazines and inserts, newspapers and book publishing (Table A1b.a).

b. Telstra Corporation Ltd (TLS)

Principal activity – Telecommunications services for domestic and international customers (Table A1b.b).

c. Wesfarmers Ltd (WES)

Principal activity – Retailing of home and garden products and building materials; coal mining and production; gas processing and distribution; industrial and safety products distribution; rural merchandise and services; fertilizers and chemicals manufacture; insurance; forest products and investment in rail transport (Table A1b.c).

d. Westfield Holdings Ltd (WSF)

Principal activity – Investment in, management of and the performance of development and construction services and funds management in relation to retail property (Table A1b.d).

Table A1b.a News Corporation Ltd (NCP)

Conventionally prepared financial statements (all figures in $'m, except as noted)

| Period ended | 1999 | | 2000 | | 2001 | | 2002 |
	30 Jun	31 Dec	30 Jun	31 Dec	30 Jun	31 Dec	30 Jun
Share capital and reserves	24,768	28,196	29,879	31,294	42,540	47,400	34,591
Goodwill per accounts							
Cost	934	859	905	1,081	1,221	1,221	1,143
Less:Amortized/written off	471	490	557	581	702	735	688
Book value	463	369	348	500	519	486	455

Using Market Capitalization Statement

BALANCE SHEET

Share capital and reserves	25,239	28,686	30,436	31,875	43,242	48,135	35,279
Less: Cost of purchased goodwill	934	859	905	1,081	1,221	1,221	1,143
Net identifiable assets	24,305	27,827	29,531	30,794	42,021	46,914	34,136

MARKET CAPITALIZATION STATEMENT

Number of issued shares (ord)('m)	2,020	2,022	2,037	2,045	2,092	2,093	2,094
Market price per share ($)	12.890	14.790	23.000	14.000	18.019	15.622	9.680
Number of issued shares (pref)('m)	1,750	2,131	2,141	2,147	2,661	3,081	3,209
Market price per share ($)	11.510	13.050	20.165	12.800	15.770	13.050	8.180
Market capitalization	46,178	57,717	90,031	56,107	79,653	72,911	46,521
Comprising:							
Purchased goodwill, at cost	934	859	905	1,081	1,221	1,221	1,143
Internally generated goodwill	20,939	29,031	59,595	24,232	36,411	24,776	11,242
MCS goodwill	21,873	29,890	60,500	25,313	37,632	25,997	12,385
Net identifiable assets	24,305	27,827	29,531	30,794	42,021	46,914	34,136
Market capitalization	46,178	57,717	90,031	56,107	79,653	72,911	46,521
Ratio of MCS goodwill to market capitalization (%)	47	52	67	45	47	36	27

Comments:

1. In its financial statements at 30 June 1999, NCP stated:

> *As a creator and distributor of branded information and entertainment copyrights, the Company has a significant and growing amount of intangible assets, including goodwill, free and cable television networks and stations, film and television libraries, sports franchises, entertainment franchises, and other copyright products and trademarks. In accordance with generally accepted accounting principles, the company does not record the fair value of these internally generated intangible*

assets. However, intangible assets acquired in business combinations are recorded as the difference between the cost of acquiring entities and amounts assigned to their tangible net assets. Such amounts are amortized on a straight-line basis over periods up to forty years.

This note makes it clear that NCP has a large number of intangible assets not recognized, wholly or partially, in its Statement of Financial Position; the MCS goodwill figure is consequently not a true 'goodwill' figure, but also takes into account the unrecognized intangibles.

2. NCP also followed the US standard in amortizing intangible assets over a forty-year period.

3. The opening figures for cost and amortization of goodwill at 30 June 1999 are estimated, as the financial statements only furnish a net figure. Subsequent figures for purchased goodwill have been calculated.

4. The MCS goodwill content of NCP's market capitalization has varied significantly over the period, reaching 67 per cent at 30 June 2000 and declining to 27 per cent at 30 June 2002.

5. NCP is unique among the companies analysed in that it has two major classes of listed securities, ordinary and preference shares. The MCS is able to cope easily with this variation.

Table A1b.b Telstra Corporation Ltd

Conventionally prepared financial statements (all figures in $'m, except as noted)

Period ended	1999		2000		2001		2002
	30 Jun	31 Dec	30 Jun	31 Dec	30 Jun	31 Dec	30 Jun
Share capital and reserves	10,256	11,322	11,595	13,209	13,239	13,996	14,108
Goodwill per accounts							
Cost	40	147	147	184	1,623	1,623	2,219
Less:Amortized/written off	14	24	32	42	75	117	156
Book value	26	123	115	142	1,548	1,506	2,063

Using Market Capitalization Statement

BALANCE SHEET

Share capital and reserves	10,270	11,346	11,627	13,251	13,314	14,113	14,264
Less: Cost of purchased goodwill	(40)	(147)	(147)	(184)	(1,623)	(1,623)	(2,219)
Net identifiable assets	10,230	11,199	11,480	13,067	11,691	12,490	12,045

MARKET CAPITALIZATION STATEMENT

Number of issued shares	12,867	12,867	12,867	12,867	12,867	12,867	12,867
Market price per share ($)	8.657	8.280	6.780	6.423	5.380	5.440	4.660
Market capitalization	111,386	106,535	87,236	82,642	69,222	69,994	59,958
Comprising:							
Purchased goodwill, at cost	40	147	147	184	1,623	1,623	2,219
Internally generated goodwill	101,116	95,189	75,609	69,391	55,908	55,881	45,694

MCS goodwill	101,156	95,336	75,756	69,575	57,531	57,504	47,913
Net identifiable assets	10,230	11,199	11,480	13,067	11,691	12,490	12,045
Market capitalization	111,386	106,535	87,236	82,642	69,222	69,994	59,958
Ratio of MCS goodwill to market capitalization (%)	91	89	87	84	83	82	80

Comments:

1. Goodwill was estimated as at 31 December 1999, 2000 and 2001, as no exact data were available.
2. TLS amortizes goodwill 'on a straight-line basis over the period of expected benefit, subject to a maximum of 20 years from the date of gaining control'. At 30 June 2000, the weighted average goodwill amortization period was six years, up from five years in 1999. The average period lengthened to nineteen years at 30 June 2001 and remained at that level in 2002, coinciding with a large increase in purchased goodwill during the 2001 financial year.
3. During the whole of the period analysed, MCS goodwill has been far in excess of purchased goodwill.
4. The share capital of TLS includes the 50 per cent held by the Australian government; there are some analysts who exclude these shares for some purposes in calculating the market capitalization, but their value is clearly relevant to a comparison with net identifiable assets.
5. The net identifiable assets of TLS have remained fairly constant over the period analysed, growing from $10,230 million to $12,045 million. MCS goodwill, on the other hand, has been far more volatile, and purchased goodwill is a minor component of this. Because MCS goodwill is such a high component of market capitalization, the ratio fall over the period is relatively modest (from 91 per cent to 80 per cent). On the other hand, the absolute fall in the amount of MCS goodwill (from $101,156 million to $47,913 million) has been considerable. The MCS highlights this fall.
6. In the context of TLS, where privatization plans are, to a large extent, contingent upon the amount the Australian government expects to realize from the sale of its 50 per cent shareholding, the market valuation of the company and its MCS goodwill are integral to an appreciation of the state of the company's affairs.

Table A1b.c Wesfarmers Ltd (WES)

Conventionally prepared financial statements (all figures in $'m, except as noted)

Period ended	1999		2000		2001		2002
	30 Jun	**31 Dec**	**30 Jun**	**31 Dec**	**30 Jun**	**31 Dec**	**30 Jun**
Share capital and reserves	1,206	1,223	1,225	1,272	1,594	3,307	3,400
Goodwill per accounts							
Cost	137	137	137	137	310	1,692	1,692
Less: Amortized/written off	36	40	43	47	56	93	132
Book value	101	97	94	90	254	1,599	1,560

Using Market Capitalization Statement

BALANCE SHEET

Share capital and reserves	1,242	1,263	1,268	1,319	1,650	3,400	3,532
Less: Cost of purchased goodwill	(137)	(137)	(137)	(137)	(310)	(1,692)	(1,692)
Net identifiable assets	1,105	1,126	1,131	1,182	1,340	1,708	1,840

MARKET CAPITALIZATION STATEMENT

Number of issued shares ('m)	262	267	264	268	282	370	372
Market price per share ($)	13.600	12.570	13.300	16.182	27.110	30.990	27.200
Market capitalization	3,568	3,360	3,507	4,330	7,638	11,473	10,126
Comprising: Purchased goodwill, at cost	137	137	137	137	310	1,692	1,692
Internally generated goodwill	2,326	2,097	2,239	3,011	5,988	8,073	6,594
MCS goodwill	2,463	2,234	2,376	3,148	6,298	9,765	8,286
Net identifiable assets	1,105	1,126	1,131	1,182	1,340	1,708	1,840
Market capitalization	3,568	3,360	3,507	4,330	7,638	11,473	10,126
Ratio of MCS goodwill to market capitalization (%)	69	67	68	73	82	85	82

Comments:
1. WES has consistently amortized its goodwill 'over a period not exceeding 20 years'. Material additions to purchased goodwill were made in the 2000 and, more particularly, the 2002 financial years.
2. Purchased goodwill is now some $1.7 million, and amounts charged to profits in respect of goodwill amortization will be material in the future. This will become even more important if WES follows an aggressive expansionary policy via acquisitions.
3. WES is one of the few conglomerate groups listed on the ASX, and easily the most successful. Despite the fact that its core businesses normally require a substantial investment in tangible assets, WES has consistently commanded a substantial MCS goodwill premium, moving from 69 per cent at the beginning of the period to 82 per cent at 30 June 2002. Despite the increase in purchased goodwill noted earlier, the major portion of this increase is due to internally generated goodwill.

Table A1b.d Westfield Holdings Ltd (WSF)

Conventionally prepared financial statements (all figures in $'m, except as noted)

Period ended	1999		2000		2001		2002
	30 Jun	**31 Dec**	**30 Jun**	**31 Dec**	**30 Jun**	**31 Dec**	**30 Jun**
Share capital and reserves/ net identifiable assets	492	525	640	691	746	1,402	1,459

Using Market Capitalization Statement

BALANCE SHEET

Share capital and reserves/ net identifiable assets	492	525	640	691	746	1,402	1,459

MARKET CAPITALIZATION STATEMENT

Number of issued shares ('m)	524	524	525	528	528	563	563
Market price per share ($)	9.260	9.480	11.483	13.452	14.000	16.854	14.960
Market capitalization	4,850	4,968	6,026	7,104	7,394	9,488	8,426
MCS goodwill	4,358	4,443	5,386	6,413	6,648	8,086	6,967
Net identifiable assets	492	525	640	691	746	1,402	1,459
Market capitalization	4,850	4,968	6,026	7,104	7,394	9,488	8,426
Ratio of MCS goodwill to market capitalization (%)	90	89	89	90	90	85	83

Comments:
1. WSF is the only company in this group that has never purchased goodwill. Nevertheless, it has been an extremely successful company with a very high market rating. Its MCS goodwill has consistently accounted for between 83 per cent and 90 per cent of its market capitalization.
2. The company has added $967 million in net identifiable assets to its Statement of Financial Position in the period under review; over the same period, MCS goodwill has increased by $2,609 million

Table A1b.e Amcor Ltd (AMC)

Conventionally prepared financial statements (all figures in $'m, except as noted)

Period ended	1999		2000		2001		2002
	30 Jun	31 Dec	30 Jun	31 Dec	30 Jun	31 Dec	30 Jun
Share capital and reserves	2,680	2,603	1,773	1,877	2,361	2,530	4,395
Goodwill per accounts							
Cost	801	814	866	894	1,145	1,221	1,164
Less: Amortized/written off	394	412	437	457	514	542	467
Book value	407	402	429	437	631	679	697

Using Market Capitalization Statement

BALANCE SHEET

Share capital and reserves	3,074	3,015	2,210	2,334	2,875	3,072	4,862
Less: Cost of purchased goodwill	801	814	866	894	1,145	1,221	1,164
Net identifiable assets	2,273	2,201	1,344	1,440	1,730	1,851	3,698

MARKET CAPITALIZATION STATEMENT

Number of issued shares ('m)	638	632	624	625	633	648	822
Market price per share ($)	8.398	7.134	5.841	5.245	6.620	7.150	8.240
Market capitalization	5,359	4,506	3,645	3,279	4,192	4,635	6,778
Comprising:							
Purchased goodwill, at cost	801	801	866	894	1,145	1,221	1,164
Internally generated goodwill	2,285	1,504	1,435	945	1,317	1,563	1,916
MCS goodwill	3,086	2,305	2,301	1,839	2,462	2,784	3,080
Net identifiable assets	2,273	2,201	1,344	1,440	1,730	1,851	3,698
Market capitalization	5,359	4,506	3,645	3,279	4,192	4,635	6,778
Ratio of MCS goodwill to market capitalization (%)	58	51	63	56	59	60	45

Comments:
1. AMC constantly follows the orthodox policy for goodwill amortization; it is amortized on the straight line basis over twenty years, with the proviso that the unamortized balance is reviewed annually and adjusted as necessary.
2. Of the six companies examined in this Appendix, AMC had by far the highest amount of purchased goodwill. Because of this, annual charges for goodwill amortization are significant.
3. A sharp increase in net identifiable assets in the last six-month period saw MCS goodwill fall from 60 per cent of market capitalization to 45 per cent. The MCS highlights the reason for the fall in this ratio; it occurred at the same time as MCS goodwill actually increased from $2.784 million to $3.080 million; the share price rose from $7.15 to $8.24.
4. In contrast to this, the fall in the ratio of MCS goodwill to market capitalization fell from 58 per cent to 51 per cent in the six months ended 31 December 1999. A fall in the share price accounted for most of this fall; MCS goodwill fell from $3.086 million to $2.305 million, while net identifiable assets fell marginally. Intriguingly, the MCS goodwill figures at 30 June 1999 and 30 June 2002 were almost identical.
5. The questions raised by the analyses in the last two comments exemplify matters exposed by the MCS that would not be brought to light under conventional accounting procedures.

e. Amcor Ltd (AMC)

Principal activity – Produces a broad range of plastic, fibre, PET and metal packaging products and offers packaging related services (Table A1b.e).

f. QBE Insurance Group Ltd (QBE)

Principal activity – Underwriting general insurance and reinsurance risks, management of Lloyd's syndicates, management of the consolidated entity's share of the New South Wales Workers' Compensation scheme and investment management (Table A1b.f).

Table A1b.f QBE Insurance Group Ltd (QBE)

Conventionally prepared financial statements (all figures in $'m, except as noted)

Period ended	1999		2000		2001		2002
	30 Jun	31 Dec	30 Jun	31 Dec	30 Jun	31 Dec	30 Jun
Share capital and reserves	1,074	1,135	1,346	1,709	2,072	2,620	2,720
Goodwill per accounts							
Cost	30	67	74	98	98	98	102
Less: Amortized/written off	6	6	7	8	10	12	15
Book value	24	61	67	90	88	86	87

Using Market Capitalization Statement

BALANCE SHEET

Share capital and reserves	1,080	1,141	1,353	1,717	2,082	2,632	2,735
Less: Cost of purchased goodwill	30	67	74	98	98	98	102
Net identifiable assets	1,050	1,074	1,279	1,619	1,984	2,534	2,633

MARKET CAPITALIZATION STATEMENT

Number of issued shares ('m)	388	395	422	429	459	585	600
Market price per share ($)	5.750	7.100	8.172	9.890	11.810	7.680	6.640
Market capitalization	2,230	2,805	3,447	4,239	5,416	4,495	3,987
Comprising:							
Purchased goodwill, at cost	30	67	74	98	98	98	102
Internally generated goodwill	1,150	1,664	2,094	2,522	3,334	1,863	1,252
MCS goodwill	1,180	1,731	2,168	2,620	3,432	1,961	1,354
Net identifiable assets	1,050	1,074	1,279	1,619	1,984	2,534	2,633
Market capitalization	2,230	2,805	3,447	4,239	5,416	4,495	3,987
Ratio of MCS goodwill to market capitalization (%)	53	62	63	62	63	44	34

Comments:
1. QBE also adopts the standard procedure in amortizing goodwill over twenty years. Purchased goodwill is a small, but growing, constituent of its assets.
2. The fall in MCS goodwill, and particularly the internally generated portion thereof, is largely ascribable to market reaction to the events of 11 September 2001; as an insurance company, there was concern that QBE would be particularly badly affected.
3. QBE, as an insurance company, values its investments, including listed and unlisted shares and property, at current market value, so that asset values are less distorted than is the case for companies using historical cost. This also furnishes a more consistent value for MCS goodwill. It is the closest approach, in the companies examined, to having a MCS statement similar to one prepared under Chambers' CoCoA (see Chapter 7).
4. Despite this, MCS goodwill has still continued to exceed purchased goodwill by amounts in excess of $1 billion. As with virtually all the companies discussed in this Appendix, the value of amortizing purchased goodwill, albeit over a twenty-year period, must be called into question.

Appendix 2

Data that would make a useful supplement to the MCS

Introduction

The MCS will enable goodwill to be brought to account in an Annual Report in a meaningful manner. The natural consequence is that attention will be focused on MCS goodwill and the factors that generate it. This type of pressure is by no means new, but the debate has largely been driven by proponents of two approaches (although the two are not necessarily exclusive):

i. those, such as Baruch Lev, who wish to include more financial data regarding intangibles in the conventional Balance Sheet itself; and
ii. followers of some Scandinavian companies such as the Swedish company, Skandia, who wish to supplement the financial data with additional material that helps to clarify factors, often non-financial, which drive revenue and profits.

The MCS expressly recognizes goodwill in the financial statements, albeit in a new way. The remainder of this Appendix will explore some of the significant recent contributions of those who have sought to augment the financial data in the Annual Report.

Data relevant to internet companies

Jorion and Talmor (2001), in a study regarding the relative importance of financial and non-financial information in predicting future growth in revenues and profitability, found that non-financial metrics were particularly important in the early stages of a company's development. Their study focused on internet companies, which were defined as those companies that derived most of their revenues from the internet, like most of the companies analyzed in Chapter 7.

The three fundamental net usage measures were stated as being the number of unique users, the total number of pages viewed and the total number of hours viewed. In para. 5.2 of their study, the authors concluded that the last two variables were particularly important in enabling effective prediction of revenue and profit growth; intriguingly, 'stickiness', as defined by those variables, was more important than reach.

Information regarding these variables was easily obtained by Jorion and Talmor (2001); most serious websites subscribe to monitoring services which can provide similar data, which would be of value to readers of the Annual Reports of 'internet companies'.

Non-financial data supplied by listed companies

Nasdaq listed Telco Ubiquitel included, in its March quarter earnings report for 2003 (http://biz.yahoo.com/prnews/031111/phtu033_1.html), comparative statistics regarding the following non-financial metrics, *inter alia*:

- net additions to subscribers
- churn rate
- mix of subscribers (prime and non-prime)
- minutes of use per subscriber
- total system minutes.

Global Sources, another Nasdaq listed company that earns its revenue by creating and facilitating global trade between buyers and suppliers, commented in its 2002 financial report (http://corporate.globalsources.com/IRS/ANNUAL/2002/LETSHARE 1.HTM):

> Another measure of our progress is reflected by our key non-financial metrics. ... Through Global Sources, ... the community of active import buyers ... which is certified with Ernst & Young, increased to 378,031, up 23% from 2001. Requests for information received by suppliers ... grew 17%. ...

Details of growth in these non-financial metrics were furnished for the period from 1999 to 2002.

The PricewaterhouseCoopers 'Value Reporting' concept

PricewaterhouseCoopers have developed the 'Value Reporting' concept, which it describes in its website (http://www.pwc.com/Extweb/service.nsf/docid/F7E2C942329A7DDF80256D4AD02FCD) as 'supplement[ing] traditional financial reporting by helping companies provide a more detailed, transparent picture of their performance – market opportunities, strategy, risks, intangible assets, and other important nonfinancial value drivers', with a concentration on industry-specific information. It consists of four categories of information:

- Market overview
  - industry dynamics facing the company;

- Strategy
  - the company's strategy, objectives, organizational design and governance structure
- Value Creating Activities
  - including key non-financial areas relating to customers, people, innovation, brands, the supply chain and environmental, social and ethical views
- Financial performance
  - the metrics used by management to monitor financial performance.

In 1999, PricewaterhouseCoopers carried out a study in the insurance industry (http://www.pwcglobal.com/Extweb/industry.nsf/docid/1475A92677 57D01785256839007122AE). It revealed that many of the insurance companies surveyed felt that their shares were undervalued:

> ... partly to blame are company financial reports, which by themselves cannot adequately communicate a company's true value. Company executives, sell-side analysts and institutional investors all say there is significant room for improvement in the quality of financial reporting.

The study identified a number of matters which insurance executives deemed important, but regarding which information disclosed to the market was inadequate. These included customer retention and penetration, employee satisfaction, brand equity and risk management practices, among others. Some of these items were identified, later in the survey, as being matters that company internal systems were not designed to measure reliably. The survey concluded 'management must ensure that the market has the information it needs to function properly' and that 'companies are suffering far more from too little disclosure than they are from too much disclosure'.

Pilch (2000) claims: 'In essence, minimising the reporting gap between the current financial based reporting model and the needs of investors is a major step in enabling companies to maximise returns. ...', and PricewaterhouseCoopers themselves are quoted as saying in their 'Value Reporting Forecast 2000': 'Experience has shown that companies that have experienced commercial difficulties become more transparent, normally in response to the demands of an increasingly sceptical investment community. ... Market knowledge is better than market guesswork' (Summary of 'Value Reporting' principles as per Pilch 2000: 39/40).

Logically, it would seem desirable, given the function of the Annual Report as a purveyor of information to interested and relevant readers, that it should supply data that enable those readers to assess the company's success in meeting its objectives and enabling it to generate profits and goodwill.

The 'Balanced Scorecard'

This concept, essentially a management tool, was described by Kaplan and Norton (2001). The 'Balanced Scorecard' calls for management to integrate a number of perspectives (i.e. learning and growth, internal customer value and financial) to develop strategies for enhancing company performance.

The items measured by the Balanced Scorecard differ greatly from company to company. Mobil North, for example, focused on items such as volume growth rates versus industry growth rates, percentage of volume in premium grades and customer satisfaction areas such as clean restrooms and speed of service. Store 24 identified net gross profit from concepts less than two years old as well as more obvious measures such as customers per store. The city of Charlotte, NC, measured the availability of safe, convenient transportation. Given that these items were key management objectives, information regarding success or failure in achieving them would be a useful supplement to the financial data that currently dominate Annual Reports and would assist readers in evaluating the possibility of future profit growth and hence increases in goodwill.

Knowledge assets (intellectual capital)

Goodwill has traditionally been defined as a residual value – the difference between the fair value of the total enterprise and the fair value of its identifiable assets. One attempt to reduce the residual and expand the category of identifiable assets has been the move to define and, to some extent, quantify the asset described as intellectual capital. In a comprehensive review, 'Assessing Knowledge Assets', Bontis (2001) describes a number of significant developments in this comparatively recent area. Its significance, as far as this book is concerned, is that, in isolating and quantifying the factors underlying goodwill and, in particular, internally generated goodwill, this development will supplement the MCS in enabling readers of the Annual Report to obtain a greater understanding of the factors that create goodwill in a particular enterprise. In this connection, Bontis (2001) quotes David Moore, research director for the Canadian Institute of Chartered Accountants:

> There is the growing view that financial performance measures by themselves are inadequate for strategic decision making. They need to be supplemented or even to some extent replaced by non-financial measures that cover such matters as, for example, customer satisfaction and operating efficiency.
>
> Bontis (2001)

Skandia

Skandia is considered to be the first major company to have made an integrated effort to measure intellectual capital; in 1994, it issued an intellectual capital supplement to its Annual Report. Skandia's 'Navigator' reporting model defined 'intellectual capital' as the sum of human capital and structural capital. The former was the combined skill of Skandia's employees, together with the company's value and culture; it cannot be owned by the company. The latter, often defined as 'everything the employees leave at the office when they go home', is the hardware, software, company systems, patents, etc. The Navigator system required the disclosure of up to ninety-one new metrics plus seventy-three traditional metrics. It is clearly an integrated evaluation and reporting system far more complex than most existing publicly listed companies would consider developing.

The model has set a benchmark in the area of intellectual capital accounting and, even for those who do not wish to follow it, it has highlighted important factors in company synergy and development. Bontis (2001) identifies, in particular, the importance of the role of customer capital, one of the sub-categories in the model, in creating value for an organization.

Celemi and others

The Swedish software company, Celemi, is another well known example of a company that has disclosed non-financial metrics to assist readers of its Annual Reports in evaluating its intellectual capital. It does not value intellectual capital directly but, in 1998, it included a 'value added' statement quantifying items such as value added percentage of sales, value added per employee and value added per expert, explicitly using these measures to assess its own performances.

Other companies that have made considerable non-financial information available in their Annual Reports include Shell, Camelot (the UK company that runs the National Lottery) and Novo Nordisk, a company that operates in the biotechnology and pharmaceutical industries and reports its employee practices in considerable detail.

Edvinsson and Malone (1997)

Edvinsson and Malone (1997) argued that the Skandia approach was so fundamentally different from traditional accounting that it could never be viewed as a mere adjunct to it. They simplified that approach by using only 112 measures, involving dollar amounts, direct costs, percentages and even survey results. Organizational intellectual capital is reduced to a single value (IC).

Monetary measures are combined using a pre-determined weighting system (C); percentages are combined to produce a coefficient of intellectual capacity efficiency (I). These two factors are then multiplied, so that $C \times I = IC$. This is a management tool, but movements in IC, with an appropriate commentary, could be featured in an Annual Report as an adjunct to the MCS.

A similar principle has been used by Skandia since 1997 to establish a company-specific intellectual capital index, which can be compared from year to year. Because of the need to determine weightings and the content of each index on a company-by-company basis, the development of a single generally applicable intellectual capital formula and index appears to be impractical at this stage.

The Technology Broker IC audit

This process divides intellectual capital into market assets, human-centred assets, intellectual property assets and infrastructure assets. It then requires the organization to answer a series of questions which permit quantified replies in order to evaluate intellectual capital as an aggregate dollar value. This value could be disclosed as an alternative to the IC figure derived from the Edvinsson and Malone (1997) approach.

Sveiby's intangible asset monitor

Sveiby classifies intangible assets as:

- external structure (brands, customer and supplier relationships)
- internal structure (management, systems, R&D, software)
- individual competence (education and experience of key employees)

For each of these classes of intangible asset, he has developed three measurement indicators, viz.:

- growth and renewal
- efficiency
- stability.

In a refreshing return to simplicity, Sveiby insists that the intangible assets monitor required for any company should be capable of being set out in one page, although additional comments are permitted. All Sveiby's measurement indicators are capable of quantification.

Sveiby recommends that, in any presentation to external persons, presentation of the key indicators should be accompanied by explanatory text; such a presentation could be disclosed in an Annual Report.

Ramboli

Another Nordic company, Ramboli, uses a 'holistic' company model to evaluate intellectual capital. It is similar to the other models discussed, in that it uses quantified key performance indicators on a company-specific basis to evaluate procedures and strategies that impact on customers, employees and society to produce financial results.

The Forbes value creation index

This index, created by the business magazine *Forbes*, attempted to measure the importance of various non-financial metrics in explaining the market value of companies and, hence, in enabling an assessment of factors underlying MCS goodwill. Intriguingly, a different rating was obtained when factors were ranked by managers and by analysts, as shown in Table A2.1 (the companies examined were in the durable manufacturing industry sector) (http:// www.valuebasedmanagement.net/articles_cima_understanding.pdf).

The analysts' low ranking in importance of customer satisfaction seems counterintuitive. The low ranking is, however, supported by an Ernst & Young study (cited in Bornemann et al. 1999), 'Measures that Matter', which was also based on investors' rankings and which ranked customer satisfaction eleventh out of twenty-two factors.

Table A2.1 Relative importance of non-financial factors in determining market capitalization

	Ranking	
	Managers	**Analysts**
Customer satisfaction	1	8
Ability to attract talented employees	2	2
Innovation	3	1
Brand investment	4	6
Technology	5	7
Alliances	6	3
Quality of major processes, products or services	7	4
Environmental performance	8	5

The Canadian Institute of Chartered Accountants – 'total value creation (TVC) system'

Perhaps the most ambitious of all the schemes in this area is the TVC system. The TVC system is designed specifically as a system supplementary to conventional accounting systems. Its aim is to enable measurement of and reporting on value creation as it occurs. It acknowledges the role of traditional accounting in recording the value upon its subsequent realization, but points out the inevitable (and often lengthy) gap between these two processes.

In that the MCS measures (albeit in a limited way) the stockmarket's present estimate of the value creation process, it would seem that the Canadian approach, if successful, could co-exist with it very easily; the same could be said of most of the approaches outlined in this Appendix.

Deloitte 2007 survey

In 2007, Deloitte published details of a survey entitled 'In the Dark II' (a follow-up to an earlier survey in 2004). This highlighted the need for better business understanding and reporting of non-financial metrics. Key findings of the survey were:

- 87 per cent of respondents (senior executives and board members of listed companies with more than US$1 billion in revenues) say that the market increasingly emphasizes non-financial performance measures (this figure was 83 per cent for the entire sample of respondents)
- the ability to track non-financial performance was far poorer than the ability to track financial performance, but companies are coming under greater pressure now to track those metrics
- more companies are realizing how non-financial metrics drive financial performance.

The survey indicated that respondents evaluated the following factors as being key drivers of success:

Factor cited as key success driver	% of executives citing this factor
Financial results	65
Customer satisfaction	52
Operational performance	38
Product service quality	31
Innovation	28
Employee commitment	23

Ironically, the survey showed that, if companies knew better how to measure non-financial indicators, they would focus more on them, but they would have to focus more attention on them if measurements were to improve.

The position in Australia

Sadly, a 1999 review of annual reporting practices and the internal measurement of intangibles in Australia (Guthrie et al. 1999) concluded:

i. The key components of intellectual capital are poorly understood, inadequately identified, managed inefficiently and are not reported within a consistent framework when reported at all.
ii. The main areas of intellectual capital reporting focus on human resources; technology and intellectual property rights; and organizational and workplace structure.
iii. Even in Australian enterprise thought of as 'best practice' in these regards, a comprehensive management framework for intellectual capital

is yet to be developed, especially for collecting and reporting intellectual capital formation. (Guthrie et al. (1999))

Conclusion

Goodwill, and particularly internally generated goodwill, should receive greater recognition in financial statements, given its importance in the constitution of the market capitalization of many companies. The MCS enables this to be done; logically, the disclosure will create a demand for further information regarding the major factors in creating such goodwill. This is a fertile ground for improving reporting practices, as can be seen from the fact that most of the ideas canvassed in this Appendix have surfaced comparatively recently. As far as has been ascertained, there are no accounting standards, exposure drafts or other official accounting pronouncements that currently deal with the disclosure of intellectual capital data.

Bibliography

Alfredson K. and Murray A., 'The Goodwill Game', *JASSA*, Autumn 2002.

American Institute of Accountants, 'A Tentative Statement of Accounting Principles Affecting Corporate Reports', *The Accounting Review*, 1936.

—— *Changing Concept of Business Income, Report of the Study Group on Business Income*, MacMillan, 1952.

Anderson R., 'The Usefulness of Accounting and Other Information Disclosed in Corporate Annual Reports to Institutional Investors in Australia', *Accounting and Business Research*, Autumn 1981.

Australian Accounting Research Foundation (AARF), *Measurement in Financial Accounting, an Accounting Theory Monograph*, AARF, 1998.

—— Payment of Dividends under the Corporations Act 2001, a position paper issued by the Legislation Review Board of AARF, AARF, 2002.

ASC, *Accounting and ASC Compliance*, 1993.

Australian Accounting Standards Board, Agenda Paper 10.3 for its December 2001 meeting, accessed via http://www.aasb.com.au.

Australian Accounting Standards Board Financial Reporting Council, Summary of Current Australian and Overseas Pronouncements on Intangible Assets, accessed via http://www.aasb.com.au/public_docs/annual_report-2000-01.pdf, December 2001.

Avery H. G., 'Accounting for Intangible Assets', *The Accounting Review*, October 1942.

Backer M., *Modern Accounting Theory*, Prentice-Hall Inc, 1966.

—— *Financial Reporting for Security Investment and Credit Decisions*, National Association of Accountants, New York, 1970.

Barth M., Clement M., Foster G. and Kasznik R., 'Brand Values and Capital Market Valuation', *Review of Accounting Studies* 3: 41–68, undated.

Barton A. E., *Australasian Advanced Accountancy*, Sydney and Melbourne Publishing Co. Ltd, 5th edn, 1919.

Bassett W. R., 'What is "Good Will" Worth?', *System: The Magazine of Business*, April 1918.

Bell W. H. and Powelson J. A., *Auditing*, Prentice-Hall, Inc., 1929.

Bonbright J. C., *The Valuation of Property*, The Mitchie Co., 1937.

Bontis N., Assessing Knowledge Assets, accessed via http://www.business.mcmaster.ca/mktg/nbontis/ic/publications/Bontis1JMR.pdf, 2001.

Bornemann M., Knapp A, Schneider U. and Sixl K., Holistic Measurement of Intellectual Capital, accessed via http://www.oecd.org/dataoecd/16/20/1947871.pdf, 1999.

Boswell J., *The Life of Samuel Johnson*, Routledge, 1783/1867.

Boulding K. E., *Economic Analysis*, 3rd edn, Hamish Hamilton, 1955.

Brown J. and Chrispin E., *FRS 10 'Goodwill and Intangible Assets' – a Practical Guide, with Guidance on Testing Goodwill for Impairment*, issued by Deloitte Touche, Tohmatsu, 1998.

Brown M., 'Accounting for Goodwill; Confused? Tighten the P/E Another Notch', *JASSA*, December 1988.

Canning J. B., *The Economics of Accountancy*, The Ronald Press Co., 1929.

Cata Alliance discussion paper, Variance between US and Canadian Accounting Rules Concerning Mergers and Acquisitions, accessed via http://www/.cata.ca/cata/advocacy/accounting.pdf, undated.

Catlett G. R. and Olson N. O., *Accounting for Goodwill*, AICPA Accounting Research Study No. 10, 1968.

Chambers R. J., *Accounting, Evaluation and Economic Behavior*, Scholars Book Co., 1966 (1974 reprint).

—— 'Third Thoughts', *Abacus*, December 1974.

—— 'Continuously Contemporary Accounting Misunderstandings and Misrepresentations', *Abacus*, December 1976.

—— 'Review Article: Canning's The Economics of Accountancy – After 50 Years', *The Accounting Review*, LIV(4), 1979, pp. 764–75.

—— 'The Resolutions of Some Paradoxes in Accounting', a lecture delivered at the University of Adelaide, 1961, reprinted in Chambers R. J. and Dean G. W., Vol. 5, 1986.

—— *An Accounting Thesaurus: Five Hundred Years of Accounting*, Pergamon, 1995.

—— 'The Case for Simplicity in Accounting', *Abacus*, June 1999.

Chambers R. J. and Dean G. W., *Chambers on Accounting*, Vols 1 to V, Garland Publishing Inc., 1986.

Chang J., *The Decline in Value Relevance of Earnings and Book Values Working Paper*, Harvard University, School of Business, 1998.

Choi F. and Lee C., 'Merger Premia and National Differences in Accounting for Goodwill', *Journal of International Financial Management and Accounting*, 1991.

Clarke F. L., 'Inflation Accounting and Accidents of History', *Abacus*, December 1980.

—— 'Deprival Value and Optimized Deprival Value in Australasian Public Sector Accounting: Unwarranted Drift and Contestable Serviceability', *Abacus*, March 1998.

Clarke F. L. and Dean G. W., 'Chambers and his CoCoA', accessed via Chambers. econ.usyd.edu.au/cocoa.html, 1992.

—— *Indecent Disclosure: Gilding the Corporate Lily*, Cambridge University Press, 2007.

Clarke F. L., Dean G. W. and Oliver K., *Corporate Collapse: Accounting, Regulatory and Ethical Failure*, Cambridge University Press, 2nd edn, 2003.

Cohen Committee, *Minutes of Evidence to the Company Law Amendment Committee* – 13th day (Friday 25 May 1944).

Coombs H. M. and Tayib, M. Developing a Disclosure Index for Local Authority Published Accounts – A Comparative Study of Local Authority Published Financial Reports between the UK and Malaysia, APIRA 98 Paper 22, accessed via http://www3.busosaka-au.ac.jp/apira98/archives/htmls/22.htm, 1998.

Couchman C. B., *The Balance Sheet*, AIA, 1924.

Deloitte & Touche LLP, *Implementation Guide to FASB Statements 141 and 142*, 2002.

Deloitte Touche Tohmatsu, *In the Dark II*, 2007.

Dicksee L. R. and Tillyard F., *Goodwill and its Treatment in Accounts*, Gee & Co. (Publishers) Ltd, 4th edn, 1920.

Edvinsson L. and Malone M. S., *Intellectual Capital: Realizing Your Company's True Value by Finding its Hidden Brain Power*, Harper Business, 1997, as cited in Bontis (2001).

Edwards J. R., 'The Origins and Evolution of the Double Account System: An Example of Accounting Innovation', *Abacus*, March 1985.

Eggleston Committee, *Report to the Standing Committee of Attorneys General on Accounts and Audit* – 1969–70, Parliament of New South Wales.

Ernst & Young website, accessed via http://www.ey.com/Global/content.nsf/UK/CF _._Services_._Intellectual_property.

Ernst & Young, *Goodwill Hunting*, Ernst & Young, 2001.

Esquerre P. J., 'Goodwill, Patents, Trade-Marks, Copyrights and Franchises', registered in M. Moonitz and A. C. Littleton (eds), *Significant Accounting Essays*, Prentice-Hall, Inc., 1913/1965.

Fabricant S., 'Revaluations of Fixed Assets, 1925–34' Bulletin 62 (December 1936) of the National Bureau of Economic Research, reprinted in *Asset Appreciation, Business Income and Price-Level Accounting: 1918–36*, S. A. Zeff, (ed.), Arno Press, 1976.

Financial Accounting Standards Board (FASB) *Exposure Draft, 'Fair Value Measurement'*, issued 23 June 2004, FASB.

Finney H. A., *Principles of Accounting*, Prentice-Hall Inc., 1934.

—— *Principles of Accounting*, revised edition, Prentice-Hall Inc., 1946.

Fisher I., *The Nature of Capital and Income*, 1906, reprinted by Kelley, 1965.

Goodwin J., 'Goodwill on Consolidation – an Empirical Study', *Accounting Forum*, September 1986.

—— 'Forecasting in the Prospectuses of Newly Listed Companies', *Accounting Forum*, June 1989.

Gray R. P., 'Research Note – Revisiting For Value Accounting – Measuring Commercial Banks' Liabilities', *Abacus*, 39(2), 2003.

Gu F. and Lev B., Intangible Assets; Measurement, Drivers, Usefulness, April 2001, accessed via http://www.stern.nyu.edu/nblev/.

Guthrie J., Petty R., Ferrier F. and Webb R., There is no Accounting for Intellectual Capital in Australia, accessed via http://www.oecd.org/61/40/1947783.pdf, 1999.

Guthrie J., Petty R. and Johanson V., 'Sunrise in the Knowledge Economy', *Accounting, Auditing & Accountability Journal*, 14(4), 2001.

Gynther R. S., 'Some Conceptualizing on Goodwill', reprinted in Dickenson Series, Dickenson Publishing Co. Inc., 1974.

Hall R., *The Stock Market and Capital Accumulation*, Working Paper 7180, National Bureau of Economic Research, Cambridge, MA, 1999.

—— *E-Capital: The Link between the Stock Market and the Labour Market in the 1990's*, Working Paper, Stanford University, Hoover Institution, 2000.

Hamilton R., *An Introduction to Merchandize*, Elliott, 1788, reprinted by Garland, 1982.

Harms T. W. and Gibbs A. K., Goodwill Hunting, Mercer Capital, accessed via http://www.mercercapital.com, 2001.

Harris W., 'Goodwill', *The Accountant*, March 29, 1884.

Heath J. Jr, 'Property Valuation Problems and the Accountant', *Journal of Accountancy*, January 1964.

Hendriksen E. S., *Accounting Theory*, Richard D. Irwin Inc., 3rd edn, 1977.

Hughes H. P., *Goodwill in Accounting*, Business Publishing Division, College of Business Administration, Georgia State University, 1982.

Huntleys', *Annual Stockmarket Summaries*, published by Huntleys' Investment Information Pty Ltd, accessed via http://www.aspecthuntley.com.au or, using the University of Sydney internet access, via http://www.aspectfinancial.com.au/af/dathome?xtm_licensee=dat.

Hylton D. P., 'The Treatment of Goodwill', Letters to the Editor, *Journal of Accountancy*, April 1964, p. 30.

IASC, *Framework for the Preparation and Presentation of Financial Statements*, IASC, 1989.

Johnson L. T. and Petrose K. R., 'Is Goodwill an Asset?', *Accounting Horizons*, September 1988.

Johnston T. M., Jager M. O. and Taylor R., *Company Accounting – the Law and Practice in Australia*, Butterworth, 1973.

Johnstone D. and Gaffikin M., 'Review of Asset Valuation Guidelines of the Steering Committee on National Performance Monitoring of GTEs', *Australia Accounting Review*, May 1996.

Jorion P. and Talmor E., Value Relevance of Financial and Non-Financial Information, accessed via http://www.london.edu/accounting/Research/Working_Papers/ACCT021.pdf, 2001.

Kaplan R. S. and Norton D. P., *The Strategy Focussed Organization: How Balanced Scorecard Companies Thrive in the New Business Environment*, Harvard Business School Press, 2001.

Kirkegard H., *'True Accounting – Myth or Possibility'*, Occasional Paper no. 5, Series in Accounting & Auditing, Umea University, 1994.

Knight F. H., Risk, *Uncertainty and Profit*, 1921, reprinted by the London School of Economics and Political Science, 5th impression, 1940.

Kollaritsch F. P., 'Can the Balance Sheet Reveal Financial Position?', *The Accounting Review*, July 1960.

Leake P. D., *Commercial Goodwill*, Gee & Co. (Publishers) Ltd, 3rd edn, 1930.

—— *Commercial Goodwill*, Gee & Co. (Publishers) Ltd, 4th edn, 1948.

Lee T. A., *Company Financial Reporting*, Thomas Nelson and Sons Ltd, 1976.

Leo K., Radford J. and Hoggett J., *Accounting for Identifiable Assets and Goodwill*, Australian Society of Certified Practising Accountants External Reporting Centre of Excellence, 1995.

Lev B., *Intangibles – Management, Measurement and Reporting*, Brookings Institution Press, 2001.

Littleton A. C. and Paton W., *An Introduction to Corporate Accounting Standards*, American Accounting Association, 1940.

Lonergan W., 'Where they go wrong – Traps in Share Valuation', *JASSA*, June 1988.

—— 'Goodwill and Bad Ideas; Fact and Fiction in the Amortisation Debate', *JASSA*, December 1995.

—— 'Establishing the Fair Value of Consideration Given in an Acquisition', *Australian Accounting Review*, 14(2), 2004.

Lonergan W., Stokes D. and Wells P., 'Giving Substance to Intangibles: How we can do better than IAS 38', *JASSA*, Summer 2000.

Lloyd S., 'Brand Values Surge', *BRW*, November 18–24, 2004.

Ma R. and Hopkins R., 'Goodwill – An Example of Puzzle-Solving', *Abacus*, 24(1), 1988.

McMonnies P. N., Making Corporate Reports Valuable, A Discussion Document by the Research Committee of the Institute of Chartered Accountants of Scotland, Kogan Page Ltd, 1988.

MacNeal K., *Truth in Accounting*, University of Pennsylvania Press, 1939.

Mard M. J., Hitchner J. R., Hyden S. D. and Zyla M. L., 'Valuation for Financial Reporting', John Wiley & Sons Inc., 2002, p. 20.

Mbuthia E. and Ward M., The Reliability of Pre-Listing Earnings Forecasts on the JSE, accessed via http://www.moneymax.co.za/help/max_school/journal57_part3.pdf (the article originally appeared in the *Investment Analysts Journal* No. 57, 2003).

Montgomery, R. H., *Auditing – Theory and Practice*, 4th edn, Ronald Press, 1934.

Morgenstern O., *On the Accuracy of Economic Observations*, 2nd edn, Princeton University Press, 1963.

NCSC, *Financial Reporting Requirement*, Government printer, 1983.

Nelson R. H., 'The Momentum Theory of Goodwill', *The Accounting Review*, October 1953.

Nobes C. and Parker R., *Comparative International Accounting*, 6th edn, Pearson Education Ltd, 2000.

Owen J. M., 'A Review of the Basic Concepts of Financial Accounting', *NAA Bulletin*, June 1958.

Paton W. A., 'The Significance and Treatment of Appreciation in the Accounts', Academy of Science, Twentieth Annual Report, 1918.

—— *Advanced Accounting*, MacMillan Co., 1941.

—— *Accounting Theory*, Chicago Accounting Studies Press Ltd, 1962.

—— 'The Significance and Treatment of Appreciation in the Accounts', contained in *Paton on Accounting*, The University of Michigan, 1964.

Paton W. A. and Littleton A. C., *An Introduction to Corporate Accounting Standards*, American Accounting Association, 1940.

Pilch T., *Dynamic Reporting for a Dynamic Economy*, The Smith Institute, London, 2000.

Popper K. R., *The Logic of Scientific Discovery*, NY Science Editions, 1934/1961.

Ravlic T., Impairment Testing: Ride 'im, Beancounter, accessed via http://www.fairfax.com.au, 2001.

Ross H. R., *The Elusive Art of Accounting*, Ronald Press, 1966.

Sanders T. H., Hatfield H. R. and Moore U., *A Statement of Accounting Principles*, American Institute of Accountants, 1938.

Schuetze W. P., The R.J. Chambers Research Lecture 2001, A Memo to National and International Accounting and Auditing Standard Setters and Securities Regulators, Accounting Foundation within the University of Sydney, 2001a.

—— 'What are Assets and Liabilities?', *Abacus*, February 2001b.

—— *Mark-to-Market Accounting: 'True North' in Financial Accounting*, Routledge, 2004.

Securities Institute of Australia, Edited Version of Report on Accounting for Intangibles Subcommittee, *JASSA*, September 1989.

Skinner R. M., *Accounting Standards in Evolution*, Richard Kitowski, 1987.

Spacek L., 'The Treatment of Goodwill in the Corporate Balance Sheet', Second Annual Accounting Forum, 1969.

SRI International (formerly Stanford Research Institute), *Investor Information Needs and the Annual Report*, Financial Executives Research Foundation, 1987.

Staub W. A., *Contemporary Accounting*, American Institute of Accountants, 1945.

Sterling R. R., *Theory of the Measurement of Enterprise Income*, University Press of Kansas, 1970.

—— 'Toward a Science of Accounting', *Financial Analysts Journal*, Sep–Oct 1975.

—— *Toward a Science of Accounting*, Scholars Book Co., 1979.

Tearney M. G., 'Accounting for Goodwill – A Realistic Approach', reprinted in R. Bloom and P. T. Elgers (eds), *Accounting Theory & Policy*, Harcourt, Brace, Jovanovich, Inc., 1981.

Thomas A. L., *The Allocation Problem in Financial Accounting Theory*, Studies in Accounting Research No. 3, American Accounting Association, 1969.

—— Traceability, Corrigibility, and Sterilization of Managerial Accounting: Some Tentative Conclusions – Saxe lecture given on November 10, 1975, accessed via http://www.newman.baruch.cuny.edu/digital/saxe/saxe_1975/thomas_75.htm.

—— 'Goals for Joint-Cost Allocation: An Incompatibility in the Literature', *Abacus*, December 1982.

Tobin J., 'Interview in the Region', December 1996, accessed via http://www.mafc.mq.edu.au/coursewebarea/inv/downloads/TobinInterview.pdf.

Upton W. S., *Business and Financial Reporting, Challenges from the New Economy*, Financial Accounting Series – Special Report, FASB, 2001.

Walker G. T., 'Nonpurchased Goodwill', *Accounting Review*, September 1938.

—— 'Why Purchased Goodwill should be Amortized on a Systematic Basis', originally published 1953, reprinted in S. A. Zeff and T. P. Keller (eds), *Financial Accounting Theory; Issues and Controversies*, McGraw Hill Book Co., 1964.

Walker R. G., 'Reporting Entity Concept: A Case Study of the Failure of Principles-Based Regulation', *Abacus*, 43(1), 2007.

Walker R. G., Clarke F. L. and Dean G. W., 'Options for Infrastructure Reporting', *Abacus*, 36(2), 2000.

Webber A. M., 'New Math for a New Economy', Jan/Feb 2000, accessed via http://www.fastcompany.com.

Wilson A., Davies M., Curtis M. and Wilkinson-Riddle G., *UK & International GAAP*, William Clowes Ltd, 2001.

Wyatt A., Matolcsy Z. and Stokes D., 'Capitalization of Intangibles', *Australian Accounting Review*, July 2001.

Yang J. M., *Goodwill and Other Intangibles*, Ronald Press, 1927.

Zeff S. A., *Forging Accounting Principles in Five Countries*, Stipes, Champaign, IL, 1972.

Glossary

Australia

Statements of Accounting Concepts (SAC)

SAC 1	Definition of the Reporting Entity
SAC 2	Objective of General Purpose Financial Reporting
SAC 3	Qualitative Characteristics of Financial Information
SAC 4	Definition and Recognition of the Elements of Financial Statements

Accounting Standards

AAS 18	Accounting for Goodwill (entities to which the Corporations Law did not apply)
AASB 3	Business Combinations
AASB 10	Recoverable Amount of Non-current Assets
AASB 136	Impairment of Assets
AASB 138	Intangible Assets
AASB 1001	Accounting Policies
AASB 1004	Revenue
AASB 1012	Foreign Currency Translation
AASB 1013	Accounting for Goodwill
AASB 1015	Acquisitions of Assets
AASB 1026	Statement of Cash Flows

Audit Standard

AUS 804
The Audit of Prospective Financial Information (an audit standard)

International

IAS 16	Accounting for Property, Plant and Equipment
IAS 22	Business Combinations

IAS 36	Impairment of Assets
IAS 38	Intangible Assets
IFRS 3	Business Combinations
ED 3	Business Combinations (exposure draft)

United States

Accounting Research Bulletins, etc.

ARB 1	Introduction and Rules Adopted
ARB 24	Accounting for Intangible Assets
ARB 43	Restatement and Revision of Accounting Research Bulletins
ARB 48	Business Combinations
ARS 10	Writing Goodwill off against Owners' Equity (research study)
APB 17	Intangible Assets (Opinion of the AICPA)
APB 54	Basic Concepts and Accounting Principles Underlying Financial Statements of Business Enterprises

Standards

SFAS 141	Business Combinations
SFAS 142	Goodwill and Other Intangible Assets
SFAS 157	Fair Value Measurements
FASB 115	Accounting for Certain Investments in Debt and Equity Securities

Exposure Draft

| ED 1201 | Fair Value Measurements |

United Kingdom

Standard

SSAP 22	Accounting for Goodwill
FRS 10	Goodwill and Intangible Assets
FRS 11	Impairment of Fixed Assets and Goodwill

South Africa

Standard

| AC 129 | Intangible Assets |

Hong Kong

Standard

SSAP 29   Intangible Assets

Singapore

Standard

SRS 22   Business Combinations

Index